#RhodesMustFall
Nibbling at Resilient Colonialism in South Africa

D1607574

Francis B. Nyamnjoh

Tammy Wilks,
Hope you can Chew
this

17/09/2019

Langaa Research & Publishing CIG
Mankon, Bamenda

Publisher
Langaa RPCIG
Langaa Research & Publishing Common Initiative Group
P.O. Box 902 Mankon
Bamenda
North West Region
Cameroon
Langaagrp@gmail.com
www.langaa-rpcig.net

Distributed in and outside N. America by African Books Collective
orders@africanbookscollective.com
www.africanbookcollective.com

ISBN: 9956-763-16-0

© Francis B. Nyamnjoh 2016

Acknowledgements

When Rhodes Must Fall and related student protests erupted and unfolded in 2015, I was on sabbatical and mostly away from Cape Town and South Africa. These student protests were preceded by violent 'xenophobic' (others would insist more appropriately on 'afrophobic') protests against foreign nationals mostly from African countries. The more I followed the developments from a distance, the more it dawned on me how the two forms of protest were not as disconnected as portrayed in media reports and commentary. Hence my decision to write this book showing commonalities between xenophobia and calls for the decolonisation of university education. Documenting and reading meaning into the effervescences of post-apartheid South Africa may contribute to understanding the growing impatience with and across racial, ethnic, gender and generational divides. The book delves into Cecil John Rhodes the person and as an embodiment of the dreams, aspirations and superiority syndrome of imperial Britain, as a way of accounting for Rhodes's resilience and immortality in South Africa and globally. I hope it offers a framework for situating the possibilities and limitations of current clamours for decolonisation, as well as a way forward from #WhatMustFall to #WhatMustRise, in a dynamic process of ongoing cultural creation and societal regeneration.

I would like to express my most sincere gratitude to all those who in one way or another contributed with humbling generosity their ideas, time, suggestions, and intellectual and related energies to kindle and rekindle my efforts. Of special mention are Deevia Bhana, Tinyiko Maluleke, Patience Mususa, Malizani Jimu, Sakhumzi Mfecane, Lindiswa Jan, Ayanda Manqoyi, Crystal Powell, Mohini Baijnath, Divine Fuh, Michael Rowlands, Sanya Osha, Kharnita Mohamed, Lauren Paremoer, Daniel Ogwang and participants at the British Institute in Eastern Africa (BIEA) Annual Lecture, which I delivered on 8 April 2016 in Nairobi, Kenya.

As someone who was not on the ground during these protests, I would like to acknowledge all the assistance I received from various sources in writing this book. As you will notice from my endnotes and references, the various protests have generated an enormous wealth of resources, ranging from articles in newspapers and social media, to video footage and official statements by university management and the South African government. I owe a debt of gratitude to all these sources.

My gratitude goes as well to all those who read and commented various drafts and sections of this book, pointing me as they did to sources and resources for further enrichment of my argument and its substantiation.

I am most grateful for two fellowships, one from the Stellenbosch Institute for Advanced Study (April – June 2015) and one from the Graduate School of Asian and African Area Studies of Kyoto University (June – July 2015), which fellowships enabled me to write sections of the book. I benefitted enormously from the generosity, both intellectual and social, of fellows and staff of the two institutions. I am in their debt. I am also grateful to Steve Howard and his colleagues of Ohio University, for a visiting scholarship (August – September 2015), which enabled me to write a substantial portion of the book.

Special thanks go to Mike Rowlands who generously agreed to write the Foreword, and to Moshumee Teena Dewoo and Sanya Osha who each wrote an Epilogue. I acknowledge with profound gratitude the editorial contributions of Kathryn Toure and of the Human and Social Research Council Press, which press published an earlier much shorter version of this book as a prologue to their State of the Nation for 2016. I am equally indebted to Mohini Baijnath, Patricia Johnson-Castle, Manya Van Ryneveld and Joanna Woods for assistance with proofreading.

Last but not least, I am grateful to Wandile Goozen Kasibe, Public Programmes Coordinator at Iziko Museums of Cape Town, for permission to use one of his photos of the Rhodes Must Fall campaign.

Table of Contents

Foreword

The Future Belongs to the Impure

Michael Rowlands

Emeritus Professor in Anthropology
University College London, UK
(His interests in cultural heritage encourage him
to explore issues of social rupture and repair)

"The future belongs to the impure. The future belongs to those who are ready to take in a bit of the other, as well as being what they themselves are. After all, it is because their history and ours is so deeply and profoundly and inextricably intertwined that racism exists. For otherwise how could they keep us apart" (Hall 1998: 299)

This plea from Stuart Hall was made at the end of an intervention in a conference on 'The House that Race Built' in which considerable disagreements were voiced by the participants. The focus was on the legacies of the civil rights movements in 1960s USA. Could there be any doubt, Hall asks, that as a movement, civil rights struggle had not produced new 'black subjects'? On the other hand could they be 'new' without being historically contextualised – evoking the tradition of struggle, in this case going back to the beginnings of slavery?

Traditions differ and part of the reason for disagreement was, no doubt, the fact that Hall was writing as someone who arrived at black consciousness in conjunction with a particular form of civil rights movement in Jamaica in the 1960s. In the 1970s as a migrant to Britain, he was to find the signifier 'black' being adopted as a political category of struggle both by Afro-Caribbean migrants and by migrants from the Asian continent. People who had never experienced the term 'black' as race before, adopted it since, as they said, "Since the British can't tell the difference between us, ...we, might as well call ourselves by the same name". This is no longer the case. The significance has gone. Things have moved into a new kind of ethnicised politics of difference. Paul Gilroy, in his new introduction to the 2013 edition of '*There Ain't No Black in the Union Jack*' laments the decline of race as a means of political mobilisation in Britain.

Cobbling identities may therefore be our way of preserving ourselves in new conditions of modernity. The kinds of xenophobic nationalism that are emerging in the world, are not about race or being 'black' and 'white' but about being American (are you not a Christian if you want to build walls rather than bridges to keep the 'other' out?) or English or South African. And this is the crux of the argument that Francis Nyamnjoh presents to us here. If, regardless of colour, all South Africans are *Amakwerekwere*, what kind of 'cobbling' will work to provide the flexible forms of citizenship that create conditions of harmony within some unified idea of tradition?

One might imagine that this would have to entail some flexible ideas of what it is to be African as well as South African. It is an easy step to reduce these identities to the encounter with 'blackness'. To be black is a feature of the encounter with whiteness or as Nyamnjoh says, quoting Fanon 'every Antillean, however black physically, 'expects all the others to perceive him in terms of the essence of the white man'" (Fanon 1986 [1967b]: 63). The idea that all kinds of social visibility crucially depended on fantasies of whiteness subtly or not so subtly puts being 'black' as inferior in a white dominated society.

Ironically, whilst this should be reversed in a black majority post-apartheid South Africa, the idea of being superior through the opportunities of becoming 'white', sets being 'black' in South Africa in a deadly opposition with the identifications of being black elsewhere in Africa. As a guide to understanding the demands for reform in South Africa, we might remind ourselves of Abner Cohen's classic study of the politics of elite culture in Africa, in which he showed how 'creole' cultures in Sierra Leone and Liberia were formed through the creation of dense networks of amity based on a 'civilising' ethos of their distinctiveness through historical absorption into 'whiteness' (Cohen 1981). Written before but anticipating the tensions and contradictions that led to 'civil wars, the clash between 'civilising' elites and provincialized Africans, has uncanny similarities to aspects of the political process in contemporary South Africa.

'Decolonising the mind' produces several other scenarios. One is to follow Ngugi wa Thiong'o (1986). To break the bonds of pain and suffering requires an end (cognitively) to the 'language' (sic English) that perpetrates the consciousness of its reproduction. A second seeks the end of education in Afrikaans in favour of English in traditionally Afrikaner universities such as Stellenbosch, Pretoria and the Free State. Another is to re-examine the shared values promoted by Thabo Mbeki's espousal of 'African Renaissance'. But, as we know now, his idea of 'African Civilisation' is profoundly Eurocentric, requiring that Africa has textual literacy and monumental architecture rather than its own 'Civilisation' based on orality and intangible knowledges. As Nyamnjoh has written elsewhere (Nyamnjoh 2004), African knowledges taught in universities in Africa, have been 'westernised'. Products of the Northern 'knowledge factory' return, if at all, to Africa with 'superior' credentialism to pursue the inculcation of the same knowledge as regimes of truth. 'Decolonisation should mean instead to pursue the project of an 'African archive' now dispersed on a global scale and in a multitude of moral and aesthetic forms. Also, as Mbembe[1] writes, this is not a pure archive but has, for long, been part of the Western archive, if not a co-maker of it.

Again, it is ironic that the opportunity presented to Oxford University to recognise the fact that it has been integrally involved in the creation of this hybrid archive, has been refused. This was in the face of Oxford students who demonstrated in sympathy with students of the University of Cape Town, and on 6 November 2015, protested against maintaining Rhodes's statue at Oriel College. The argument against was that this was a separate matter for the University, which could not accede to the demands of the Rhodes Must Fall in Oxford group, because it would mean indulging in a revisionist history and a devaluation of the contribution of Rhodes Scholarships. Yet this seems to give little thought to how badly this isolationist position would be received by many moderate Africans who see these protests as part of a more globalised and interconnected order.

Another again would be to ask 'when was black' and where. Black as signifier appears globally as a consequence of the Civil Rights movement in the US after the 1960s. But this is a consequence of being marginal and oppressed in a majority 'white' population. Uniquely, quite the reverse pertains in South Africa, and elsewhere in Africa, where a white influenced dominant elite had historically taken hold but has now been displaced, or just about. As Mbembe writes, it is surely part of the distinctiveness of South Africa, that a politically majority 'black' African population can change the 'language' and break the bonds of pain and suffering through renouncing self-imposed marginality and embracing better conditions of inclusion to create new forms of life. But some good thought on strategic 'cobbling' is clearly needed to achieve this.

This is where the volume presented to us provides nuanced and subtle ideas of engagement. The rage of the 'born free' is, after all, seen by all as a positive and energetic force that can be the spearhead to achieve this. But when and where? The turning back in anger on the Mandela generation is one, perhaps needed, but dispiriting consequence. As Martin Luther King saw it in his 1963 'Letter from a Birmingham jail;' – 'the stumbling block on the road to freedom is not the Klu Klux Klan... but the white moderate who is more devoted to order than to justice' (King 1986: 91). His indictment of the moderate (black or white here) anticipated the liberal retreat from race that would become the hallmark of the post-civil rights era (e.g. the ethnicising of race that Hall and Gilroy detect in the case of race politics in Britain, for instance). But in South Africa, it will be a potential condemnation of black moderates by other black South Africans/and Africans.

Is the Truth and Reconciliation Commission era in decline as a moderate force that valued order over the pursuit of equality and justice? If so, where will the anger be directed towards? There are several candidates in play. The lack of transformation and the corruption of a burgeoning new black middle class elite who benefit from the moderate control of order is one. More prevalent is the anger directed against the *makwerekwere*, in township contexts where the means to offset the rapacious behaviour of new elites is limited and other more vulnerable groups can be targeted instead. In 'civilisational' terms it is also the implicit value that Nyamnjoh indicates by naming a chapter *Not every black is black enough*. By turning anger on the presence of other Africans as inferior beings, black South Africans are distracted from understanding their presence as the mutual construction of white and black identities. We can go on, but the dangers of an anger and crisis ridden South Africa is appreciating.

What are the indicators provided to us by Francis Nyamnjoh to lessen the dangers? His 'shopping basket' critically includes all Africans in South Africa of whatever race or faith in searching for solutions. The appeal for a universal black humanism is both global and local and includes the role of whites in Africa. The right to a 'flexible citizenship' does not start with the western autonomous rights based individual but more historically situated in the 'family' or the 'homestead' as a collective right, recognising that 'individualism' in South Africa has a different history of labour migration, both apartheid and post-apartheid, and its destruction of tradition. And there is the appeal to maintain the ideals of Mandela – Tutu Truth and Reconciliation and take them forward from a therapeutic cathartic release to a massive political and economic transformation of conditions for health, education and employment for all in South Africa.

Pope Francis says that, building bridges rather walls, makes a good Christian[2]. Let's hope it also makes a good South African.

Notes

[1] Achille Mbembe, Decolonizing knowledge and the question of the archive, http://wiser.wits.ac.za/system/files/Achille%20Mbembe%20-%20Decolonizing%20Knowledge%20and%20the%20Question%20of%20the%20Archive.pdf, accessed 26 February 2016
[2] On February 18, 2016, Pope Francis said of Donald Trump, "A person who thinks only about building walls, wherever they may be, and not building bridges, is not Christian. This is not in the Gospel", see http://www.ncregister.com/daily-news/pope-person-who-thinks-only-about-building-walls-not-building-bridges-is-no/#ixzz41l6xEhfK, accessed 2 March 2016.

References

Cohen, Abner, 1981, *The Politics of Elite Culture,* Berkeley. University of California Press

Fanon, Frantz, 1986 [1967], *Black Skin, White Masks,* London: Pluto Press.

Gilroy, Paul, 2013 [1987], *There Ain't No Black in the Union Jack,* London: Routledge

Hall, Stuart, 1998, 'Subjects in History: Making Diasporic Identities', in: Wahneema Lubiano, (ed), *The House That Race Built,* New York: Vintage Books.

King, Jr, Martin Luther, 1986, 'Letter from Birmingham Jail', in: *I Have a Dream: Writings and Speeches that Changed the World,* (ed), James Melvin Washington, New York: Harper Collins.

Ngugi wa Thiong'o, 1986, *Decolonising the Mind: The Politics of Language in African Literature,* London: James Currey.

Nyamnjoh, Francis B., 2004, 'From Publish or Perish to Publish and Perish: What "Africa's 100 Best Books" Tell Us About Publishing Africa', *Journal of Asian and African Studies,* 39(5): 331-355.

Introduction

In his novel *Welcome to Our Hillbrow* (Mpe 2001), Phaswane Mpe gives us an elaborate idea of what black South Africans mean when they refer to someone as *makwerekwere¹*, a mostly derogatory term for a perceived stranger who is most likely to be mistaken for 'one of us'. But the stranger is betrayed by his or her incapable of articulating local languages that epitomise the feeling of being at home, in intimate circles and in charge. The construction of *amakwerekwere* and of boundaries between South Africans as 'deserving citizens' and *amakwerekwere* as 'undeserving outsiders' is skilfully recounted by Mpe. His novel focuses on migrants from Africa north of the Limpopo, which does not imply that only such people qualify to be termed *amakwerekwere*. South Africans sometimes mistake one another for *makwerekwere*, or use such terminology to refer to one another with an intention of difference and as an act of violence.²

In most of Africa where colonialism was non-resident, whiteness has less to do with skin pigmentation than with the privileges and opportunities that come with power and its culture of control and authority. In Cameroon for example, it is commonplace for parents to encourage their children to study hard in order to become white (not through bleaching themselves chemically or biologically – popular though this is as a currency and a passport for social visibility in its own right (Hunter 2002; Pierre 2013)³, but through a process of self-cultivation that brings power, privilege and opportunities for self-activation their way). What such parents really want is for their children to aspire to attain the perceived luxury, effortless enjoyment and boundless abundance of power and privilege which they have come to associate with the white skin or body (Nyamnjoh 2007a [1995]). The fact that whites are often conflated with whiteness (West 2009) should not blind us to the whiteness that blacks and other variants of pigmentation may aspire to enact, achieve, and eventually have in common, however hierarchized the order, with equally privileged and powerful white-pigmented others (Frankenberg 1993; Nyamnjoh and Page 2002; Pierre 2013). In this regard, even in the makings of 19ᵗʰ century

1

South Africa, for which his 'almost evangelical belief in the [British] Empire and imperialism' (Brown 2015: 19) gained him the reputation of a 'Colossus'[4], 'White Devil' and 'Grand Imperialist' with a 'missionary zeal', Cecil John Rhodes was ready to concede, however reluctantly, a little whiteness, through the right to vote (even if not to be voted for), to blacks who had proven their worth in what he termed 'civilisation' (Brown 2015: 6-10, 202). As Robin Brown recounts:

> Asked in 1899 by a representative of the coloured community to define his position on voters, Rhodes's reply was: 'My Motto is – equal rights for every civilised man south of the Zambesi' – whether white or black, as long as he was basically literate, owned some property, and was 'not a loafer' (Brown 2015: 10; see also Plomer 1984 [1933]: 132; Maurois 1953: 97).[5]

Although whites – Dutch and English alike – regarded black people as condemned by God to servitude and desperately in need of a civilising mission, Rhodes was astute enough to know that the only way the 'English-speaking citizens' of the Cape could command a parliamentary majority in the Cape Parliament where the Dutch-speaking members outnumbered the English-speaking members by two to one, was to be generous with the right to vote towards the non-white populations in their varying configurations and hierarchies, provided they did not question the superiority of the British race and civilisation (Brown 2015: 103), nor that of Rhodes.

It is worth stating that my claims on servitude and civilising mission in European encounters with Africans may be emphasising many more continuities than others would like. Some have sought to distinguish, without necessarily implying a disconnection between the slavery time justifications for the reduction of African people into property and the colonial time justifications for the dispossession and subjugation of Africans. They would argue that slavery time justifications tended to appeal to nature, the 'natural order of things', relying mainly on the distinction between humans and animals, crediting Africans with the latter, to imply that the slaves were non-human (or at the very least, subhuman). Slavery time justifications tended to use capacity for religion as an

2

important distinguisher of the human from the animal(istic). Hence the many debates then about whether slaves had souls or not, whether they were capable of religion or not and even whether they were capable of language, culture and philosophy (Chidester 1996; Hochschild 1999; Silvester and Geweld 2003; Olusoga and Enrichsen 2011).

Those who describe slavery time justifications thus, still acknowledge that these views and justifications did not cease when slavery was abolished, but insist that colonialism added a different tone and thrust to its justification for the subjugation of Africans. In a sense, colonialism was more ruthless than slavery, which was mainly about the racism of exploitation. Slavery time mentality seems to have been that, though Africans were less than human, they were needed as property and as a cheap source of labour and therefore should not be wiped off the face of the earth (Chidester 1996; Hochschild 1999; Silvester and Geweld 2003; Olusoga and Enrichsen 2011).

Colonialism incorporated the racism of exploitation and its inherited justifications but added to it, the racism of elimination. The latter relied on 'the science' of human races and various species of human beings and most significantly on social Darwinism. In terms of these, African groupings and social systems would be naturally selected for slow but eventual elimination on account of their unfitness or lesser degree of humanity and capacity for creativity and innovation. When and where the natural process of social Darwinism seemed too slow, like in Namibia, colonialists intervened to speed up the process through genocidal wars of elimination (Chidester 1996; Hochschild 1999; Silvester and Geweld 2003; Olusoga and Enrichsen 2011).

To those who make these distinctions between slavery and colonial time justifications for the subjugation of Africans, they would argue that, as well as being an imperialist and a colonialist, Rhodes was a thorough going social Darwinist. In this sense, Rhodes might have been no different in his beliefs about Africans from say, Heinrich Ernst Göring (father of Hitler's infamous Lieutenant Hermann Göring), who served as imperial commissioner of German South-West Africa between 1885 and 1890. A firm believer in social Darwinism, Göring laid the foundations for the genocidal wars of elimination which the Germans later waged against the Herero and Nama. The genocide itself was to be initiated by Göring's successors, notably, Curt von François, veteran of Leopold II's murderous army in the Belgian Congo. Placed in this context, which was the epoch in which he operated, Rhodes might be considered as one who possessed more than mere missionary zeal for the empire and the British, and more of a creature of his Social Darwinian times (Chidester 1996; Hochschild 1999; Silvester and Geweld 2003; Olusoga and Enrichsen 2011).[6]

Like many a *makwerekwere* I know, Rhodes's immediate family was large: he had five brothers and two sisters – all of whom he included in his personal success and even those of them not directly at his service as treasure hunter were frequent visitors to see him in South Africa. However, unlike most *amakwerekwere* families I have studied, Captain Ernest Rhodes was the only sibling who got married (Jourdan 1910: 204-206). Preferring celibacy to marriage (Maurois 1953: 24), Rhodes used the excuse of having too much work to do against getting married. He once told Philip Jourdan, his private secretary:

'I know everybody asks why I do not marry. I cannot get married. I have too much work on my hands. I shall always be away from home, and should not be able to do my duty as a husband towards his wife. A married man should be at home to give the attention and advice which a wife expects from a husband' (Jourdan 1910: 165).

An additional reason advanced by his intimate circles, mostly men[7], was Rhodes's shyness in the company of women. Again, in the words of his private secretary, Rhodes was 'very shy, and I have often seen him blush like a boy when conversing with ladies when there was no occasion to be bashful' (Jourdan 1910: 161). If one must talk of marriage, Jourdan describes Rhodes as 'wedded to Rhodesia with a devotion equal to that of the most ardent bridegroom', adding that the 'welfare of his bride was always uppermost in his thoughts, and he was at all times ready and willing to wait upon her and to labour for her unselfishly' (Jourdan 1910: 219).

4

That Rhodes, who started his journey into the southern African region as a *makwerekwere*, had rapidly established himself as a 'superman authority' and indeed, as 'South Africa' prior to the ill-fated Jameson Raid of the Boer Republic of the Transvaal, is described by Sir. J. Percy Fitzpatrick as follows:

> He [Rhodes] seemed to own, or to be, South Africa; and in regard to it he was as a father acting for his children. His overlordship and superman authority were accepted without question over a range and variety of peoples, classes and interests so vast that it might have seemed impossible of achievement. It is no exaggeration to say that at that time Rhodes held a position in the world which was unique. Personality and achievement had stamped him a marked man (Fitzpatrick 1924: viii).

It could be argued that Rhodes might not have lost his superman authority and grip over South Africa the way he did, had he not allowed his imperial ambitions to overly dramatize the superiority of the British while simultaneously seeking to devalue the whiteness of the Dutch. In an article 'Empire Strikes Back', excerpted from their book *Imperialism: Past and Present* (2015), Emanuele Saccarelli and Latha Varadarajan trace the origins of the term 'imperialism' to the mid-19th century, citing Cecil Rhodes as someone who proudly wore the mantle of 'imperialist'. They write:

> Although 'empire' has long historical roots, the term 'imperialism' is a relatively recent innovation, making its entrance onto the world stage well into the second half of the nineteenth century. What began as a matter of domestic policy was projected onto the international arena. Initially used to describe the policies of Napoleon III in the 1860s, 'imperialism' gradually came to be associated with the new surge of colonial acquisitions by European states. By the 1890s, both supporters and opponents of colonial expansion routinely used the term 'imperialism' in their debates over the direction of their societies and, indeed, the world. The term referred to the frenzied struggle that had broken out for a share of the rapidly shrinking pool of territories available for colonial control.
> Some observers of the day insisted that, in spite of certain superficial similarities, these were not like the vulgar empires of the past, at least in an economic sense. Men like Cecil Rhodes proudly wore the mantle of 'imperialist,' not just because of the immense wealth that was being accumulated in the enterprise but also because

imperialism promised a solution to the problem of maintaining social order at home. As Rhodes argued, the only way to deal with a burgeoning working class in England was to ensure high rates of profits that would trickle down to them, as well as to acquire new territories where they could migrate. Moreover, the benefits of imperialism would extend beyond the great unwashed at home by bringing civilization into the farthest and darkest corners of the world.[8]

John Flint, however, doubts whether Rhodes could be considered an imperialist in the true sense of the word, when in his career and policies Rhodes 'had been largely concerned with resisting the metropolitan authority of Britain, with limiting the *imperium* in British imperialism' (Flint 1974: 229). If anything, Flint argues, 'Rhodes used and exploited British imperialism for his own distinct ends and aims, which did not encompass the extension of direct British power and authority in southern Africa. To him the 'imperial factor' was remote, meddling, and dangerously color-blind on racial issues. It could be manipulated where necessary, but it must be a symbolic authority, a majesty to warn off foreigners but not to rule him or his people' (Flint 1974: 229-230; see also Baker 1934: 91; Stent 1924: 4-10; Marlowe 1972: 269-278).

Antony Thomas agrees, adding that 'Rhodes only embraced his Imperial ideal when it served his purpose' (Thomas 1996: 13). Rhodes discovered that corruption, self-deception and greed were the soft underbelly of the English establishment, and used this to his own advantage. As Thomas puts it, Rhodes 'learnt that nobody, not even Queen Victoria herself, could resist him, and that famous journalists and distinguished politicians – politicians who remain popular heroes to this day – could be bought with flattery and a few thousand pounds' He understood the power of the press and bought newspapers to serve his pursuit of power (Thomas 1996: 12-13).

It is in this sense that Geoffrey Haresnape argues that Rhodes may not have started off a pillar of the Victorian establishment, but he certainly ended up as one, having 'gained his weight and stature, not at home within the confines of the Establishment in church or army, but by founding himself upon the rights and territories of vulnerable peoples in southern Africa' (Haresnape 1984: xv). On a

6

more detailed discussion of Rhodes and the anatomy of the British Empire, see Marlowe (1972).

In South Africa the history of unequal encounters between whites and blacks has since 1652 shaped the imagination and construction of the realities of whites and whiteness as much as it has determined how blacks and blackness are imagined and realised (Crapanzano 1985; Steyn 2001, 2008; Teppo 2004; West 2009; van Wyk 2014). In her study of whiteness in the US, Ruth Frankenberg notes that 'Whiteness changes over time and space and is in no way a transhistorical essence.' She suggests we see whiteness as 'a complexly constructed product of local, regional, national, and global relations, past and present' (Frankenberg 1993: 242). Skin pigmentation may be the starting point of the journeys of power, privilege and opportunity that we undertake every now and then, but privilege, power and opportunity refuse to be confined narrowly by the diktats of pigmentation (West 2009; van Wyk 2014; Alcoff 2015). As Mary West puts it, 'Whiteness has in fact very little to do with pigmentation, but it emerges as an identification that is premised on the historical fact that white settlers of mainly European extraction colonised large tracts of the rest of the world', resulting in 'an unequal relationship between the lighter-skinned settler and the darker-skinned native, and consequently between the descendants of the settler and the native' (West 2009: 11) *Makwerekwereness*, like whiteness, far from being a birthmark, can be acquired and lost with circumstances, by whites and blacks alike, regardless of how they define or identify themselves.

It is only when a *makwerekwere* succeeds in imposing him or herself on a son or daughter of the native soil, and in insisting on his or her superiority – body, mind and soul – that the locals, initially for self-preservation and subsequently as a form of social distinction, start looking up to the *makwerekwere* as a pacesetter worthy of imitation or mimicry. Such mimicry or imitation is practiced, perfected, internalised, embodied and effortlessly reproduced and transmitted from one generation of indigenes to another, as the natural order of things.

It is this whitening up, that would explain why many a black South African insist that *makwerekwere* is strictly employed in relation to black foreigners, whom, they would also admit, are

7

generally less advanced than South African blacks, even when the latter have few material successes to show for themselves. It would thus be interesting to establish when and by what means did whites in South Africa come to lose their *makwerekwereness* to the point where, in an email reaction to an earlier version of this book, Sakhumzi Mfecane, a black South African and senior lecturer in Anthropology at the University of the Western Cape, opines:

> I wonder to what extent this labelling of Rhodes as *makwerekwere* is sustainable, given the obvious differences between Rhodes and typical *makwerekwere*. You define *makwerekwere* as 'outsider or perfect stranger'; but you said nothing about his skin colour. My understanding of *makwerekwere* is that he is specifically a black foreigner from the African continent; and the term '*makwerekwere*' is assigned primarily by his black South African host. I think that Rhodes's skin colour – whiteness – has to be accounted for because it gave him all sorts of advantages that a black *makwerekwere* would not typically get. Although Rhodes came to a predominantly black society his hosts were not black; they were fellow white '*makwerekwere*'. I think this rendered him very different to black foreigners who have to compete with local black hosts for survival. You defined him as a 'very powerful *makwerekwere*'. I think most of this power was derived from the fact that he was white and operated in a predominantly white dominated economic setup.

Those in South Africa who seek to confine the use of *makwerekwere* to denote black foreigners exclusively, only need to look at representations of whites in African fiction to understand the extent to which black Africans have employed similar negative and derogatory stereotypes vis-à-vis the whites they have encountered (Schipper 1990a, 1990b). They need as well, in comparative perspective, to appraise themselves of similar stereotypical and condescending representations of unequal encounters elsewhere in the world, when blacks are not part of the equation, including white and white encounters (e.g. between the English and the Irish). If whiteness is primarily about power and privilege and only coincidentally about having a white-pigmented body, then it is something open to being acquired and lost to whites and blacks alike. It is hardly surprising therefore, that Rhodes, in his tropical adventures, did not arrive with power and privilege in his briefcase, but acquired both through his interactions with others in

8

what today constitutes southern Africa. Like every other *makwerekwere*, Rhodes needed the opportunities of the land of his adventures to activate whatever capacity for fortune, power and privilege he may have had. Compared to some present-day *amakwerekwere*, Rhodes arrived with far less credentials in his briefcase, with the exception of '£2000 of capital loaned to him by Aunt Sophia and an allowance from his father with which to work his colonist's grant of fifty acres and the additional land he intended to buy' (Flint 1974: 13). He arrived without a university degree (something many a *makwerekwere* flowing into South Africa have to their credit), and as a sickly seventeen year old whom few believed would live long enough to threaten or be threatened by those he encountered (Roberts 1987: 1-14). As John Flint puts it, 'physically weak and prone to sickness', Rhodes was a most 'unlikely vehicle for greatness'. Indeed, Rhodes may have been 'shrewd' and 'calculating', but he was far from 'highly intelligent' and 'his mind lacked power, thrust and originality'. If anything, he 'remained locked in the fantasies of a schoolboy', often 'suspicious, lonely, [and] isolated' (Flint 1974: xiv-xv).

In this book, I draw inspiration from Mpe's novel and related studies to argue that Sir Cecil John Rhodes is best understood as more than the 'stripling *Uitlander*' that the Boers considered him to be during their scramble for the riches of southern Africa (Brown 2015: 39) – accusing him and his fellow British of 'having effectively stolen their rich diamond fields' from the newly established republic of the Transvaal (Brown 2015: 72). The term *Uitlander* was used by the Boers 'to denote any settler in the Transvaal not Dutch by birth and not naturalised, and it was especially applied to British settlers'.[9] This term was applied regardless of the fact that the 'numerous and active' *Uitlanders* 'had turned a poverty-stricken backveld state into a country with an important income' following the discovery of gold. 'Instead of trying to turn them into contented citizens, he [Paul Kruger, president of the Transvaal] denied them all political and municipal rights, and treated them not simply as outsiders but almost as enemies', as Paul Kruger was said to be of the view that these *Uitlanders* 'who had thrust themselves upon his country were mostly of the scum of the earth; that they had shown no signs of loyalty

9

towards the Transvaal; and that, although they had enriched his treasury, they had enriched themselves much more' (Plomer 1984 [1933]: 88-89). While the leaders of the Transvaal wanted the *Uitlanders* to recognise that 'they owed allegiance to, and had a duty to respect the institutions and traditions of, the foreign state in which they had chosen to come and live and under whose protection they were, most of them, making more money than they had ever made elsewhere', the *Uitlanders* on their part complained, among other things, 'of the compulsory use of the Dutch language in government offices, in schools, and in the law courts' (Marlowe 1972: 188).

In addition to being an *Uitlander,* Rhodes should also be understood as a *makwerekwere,* with much in common with the black African migrants of yesteryear who joined him and his fellow Europeans to dig for diamonds in Kimberley where:

> diamonds were the most ordinary things in the world. It was not unusual to find small, one carat, diamonds which had fallen off the carts, in the roadways. They were to be found in the sand on the top of the ground, where the tents were pitched, and in the gizzards of hens, who liked pecking at these stones. Even cooks were getting rich. Not everyone was making his fortune, but, in spite of disappointments, everyone lived in hope and dug feverishly (Maurois 1953: 34)?

Rhodes should equally be seen as having a lot in common with present-day *amakwerekwere,* who are targeted by xenophobic violence (Adam and Moodley 2015; Alhaji 2015; Crush et al. 2015; Landau 2011; Mangezvo 2014; Mano 2015; Neocosmos 2010; Nyamnjoh and Shoro 2014; Steinberg 2015; Owen 2015; Powell 2014) caused by the narrow nationalism fostered by Rhodes in the name of empire-building for Britain and the British as God's chosen country and race. We may not know what exactly southern Africans experienced during their encounters with Rhodes and his fellow white treasure-hunting adventurers, because the history of such encounters is preponderantly recounted by the whites and those they have schooled to reproduce their ways and art of storytelling. But if the current scapegoating of Rhodes and his descendants by the post-apartheid 'liberated' sons and daughters of the native soil is anything to go by, it is very likely that their forefathers and mothers cursed, lamented and scapegoated whites for all the ills that befell them following their encounters. The following words by Rhodes after the failed Jameson Raid of the Transvaal, for which he [Rhodes] was blamed by the *makwerekwere* of yesteryear – some of whom (the Boers for example), feeling themselves more entitled to the soil and its riches than Rhodes was, could have been spoken by any *makwerekwere* from north of the Limpopo in present-day South Africa, those who are too readily scapegoated for South Africa's ills. Addressing an electoral crowd in Griquatown following the Jameson Raid, Rhodes said:

'I have been painted very black, and have been represented to you as the embodiment of everything that is bad. The worst acts and the most evil designs have been imputed to me; but, gentlemen, I can assure you, although I have many faults, I am incapable of such things' (Jourdan 1910: 60).

Without pretending to be a present-day Cecil Rhodes, both Johnny Steinberg's Asad Abdullah of Somalia (Steinberg 2015) and James Jibraeel Alhaji of Cameroon (Alhaji 2015), *amakwerekwere* in today's South Africa, would identify with the above sentiment of Rhodes. It is the ever diminishing circles of inclusion or narrow nationalism, which post-apartheid South Africa inherited (ironically from Rhodes and those whom he was criticising in his speech) and perpetuates, and about which James Jibraeel Alhaji, a *makwerekwere* from Cameroon, complains in the following terms in his biography, *Sweet Footed African*:

I am a Cameroonian immigrant. I live in Cape Town. I have been in South Africa for almost 20 years. When some years ago there were outbreaks of violence here and there in South Africa against black immigrants from other African countries – those usually referred in most unflattering terms as *makwerekwere* –, many journalists, along with academics and students came knocking to interview me. The questions they asked, however deep they tried to be, always left me thirsty and hungry, wishing they had gone this way or that way, explored this or that theme, dug deep, or followed a particular line of enquiry to a crescendo that did not always serve the purpose of overly simplifying the issues or my situation. They would stop only when I

11

was warming up to a serious conversation, warming up with surging questions of my own. I detested the tendency to see us, a priori, as a problem and the resistance, even by those who should know better, to see the extent to which we were more of a solution than an encumbrance.

Sometimes I followed the accounts of their interviews with me and other immigrants on radio or as articles in newspapers and on blogs. Although I have never read the more scholarly accounts in theses and dissertations written by students, or in books and journal articles by interested academics posing as migration experts, I have often wondered why very few of them have ever treated me as if I had a life prior to my arrival in South Africa. Few want to know how I came to be here. They imagine and impose a reason on me for coming to this country, often in contradiction to what I tell them if they bother to ask. And, even as they are interested in my life in South Africa, their questions often leave me perplexed as to why they frame things in such terms as not to do justice to the fullness of my life and experiences as an immigrant in their beloved country. Many suppose that I am here to stay, that I would do everything to remain in South Africa, and that the country I come from is not worthy of modern human life, which is why – they suppose rather than ask me – I am running away, and have taken refuge – illegally, they love to insist – in South Africa, in my desperate quest for greener pastures. Nothing I say, or wish I could say in the interest of nuance, seems to matter in the face of such arrogant and admittedly, it must be said, ignorant accounts.

My frustrations with what I read and hear have pushed me to the conclusion that South Africans would perhaps understand and relate with much more accommodation if they were to get to know us, *amakwerekwere*, in our wholeness as human beings – as people composed of flesh and blood, people shaped and humbled by the highs and lows, whims and caprices of human existence – and not simply as statistics of inconvenience or as odd strings of phrases, often quoted out of context, to illustrate news stories by journalists in a hurry to meet deadlines. Sometimes the impression is strong in me, very strong indeed, that some are reluctant to allow such a thing as reality to stand in the way of a good story. Sensationalism craved to the detriment of the complex messiness and intricate interconnections of the everyday lives of South Africans and *amakwerekwere* in urban South Africa (Alhaji 2015: 1-2).

This extract emphasises the importance of putting identity claims and counter claims in historical perspective, and instructing ourselves and our scholarship on social formations on how such processes play out in terms of power, privilege and opportunities. It is significant to see the role played by a very British narrow-nationalism in justifying or legitimating Rhodes's treasure-hunting exploits and ruthlessness vis-à-vis the indigenous and endogenous populations of southern Africa as well as their parallel histories and processes of interconnections equally shaped by and productive of power, privilege and opportunities.

Even among European outsiders with different degrees of claim to insiderness in southern Africa, Rhodes's fundamentalist assertion of British supremacy was a source of continued tension and conflict. His jingoism left little room for compromise. The Boers, already considering themselves as more insiders than the British by virtue of having preceded the latter to these 'free-for-all' fields of abundant diamond deposits (Brown 2015: 68), must have been furious that Rhodes – who described and proved himself as 'an amalgamationist' (Roberts 1987: 62; see also Maurois 1953: 46-47, 63-71; Plomer 1984 [1933]: 50--57) – and his band of British *amakwerekwere* or *Uitlanders* did not content themselves with stealing their land, instead proceeding to rename the land (just as the Boers had renamed it before them – renaming being the prerogative of the victor in unequal encounters (Crapanzano 1985; Terreblanche 2002; Nyamnjoh 2013a), in the zero-sum manner of a veritably powerful aggressor:

> The secretary of state for the colonies, Lord Kimberley, decided that the farm Vooruitzicht, where the first diamonds were found, was unpronounceable, and so the place was called Kimberley (Brown 2015: 26).

> The Boers had no idea that a stripling *Uitlander*, Cecil John Rhodes, had already begun to dream of an Africa in which they would play no part whatsoever – unless, of course, they agreed to play a passive role. In Rhodes's scheme of things, if the republics remained in Boer hands they would be nothing but roadblocks on the British highway he was planning from the Cape to Cairo (Brown 2015: 39).

Whether afflicted by *amakwerekwere,* or by *Uitlanders* or both, Frantz Fanon perceptively predicted in the nascent years of postcolonial nationalisms in Africa that citizenship: 'instead of being the all-embracing crystallization of the innermost hopes of the whole people, instead of being the immediate and most obvious

13

result of the mobilization of the people', turn out, under narrow nationalism, to be 'only an empty shell, a crude and fragile travesty of what it might have been' with a greater sense of inclusiveness (Fanon 1967a: 119-126).

The making of contemporary South Africa is the story, per excellence, of visible and invisible mobilities (Peberdy 2009, Klaaren 2011). As elsewhere, unregulated and even regulated human mobility in South Africa are presented as a threat to the economic and physical well-being and achievements of insiders. To be visible for citizenship, nationality or belonging, bounded notions of geography and culture are deployed. Official and popular discourses are infused with a deep suspicion of those who move, particularly those moving to urban areas and between countries and continents. Freedom of movement, especially by people deemed to be less endowed economically, is perceived by those who consider themselves more economically gifted as potentially disastrous and thus needing to be contained at all costs and against all odds. There is clamour for policies to contain foreigners, mostly those from the rest of Africa, who continue to be seen as the source of backwardness, diseases and crime, and a threat to South African jobs and cultural values or of stealing South African women by corrupting them with money and consumer gifts in the name of love (Landau 2011; Neocosmos 2010; Sichone 2008).

Capitalism thrives the most among those who have invested the least in taming basic instincts. If accounts of Rhodes as someone trapped in childhood all his life are anything to go by, he firmly belonged with this category. William Plomer maintains that throughout his life, 'It was not Rhodes that grew, but his bank balance, his activities, and his power, and in many respects he always remained what one of his chief intimates considered him – 'a great baby." (Plomer 1984 [1933]: 161). Plomer argues that in many ways, Rhodes, who liked referring to 'the natives' as children,

> was in many ways like a child, and he treated the natives with that mixture of harshness and generosity which is more characteristic of the child or the tyrant than of the thoughtful, responsible adult man (Plomer 1984 [1933]: 126-127).

14

Vere Stent shares this telling quote of Rhodes, speaking of 'the natives' in Rhodesia:

'These are children; they are cruel; so are children, sometimes. Have you never seen a child pull off a fly's wing in wanton cruelty? They are children, and we must treat them as children. The first thing you need in treating children, is sympathy' (Stent 1924: 26).

As someone who himself is considered by some to have stayed trapped in his childhood fantasies and wanton cruelties, could this declaration be seen as Rhodes the child asking to be treated more with sympathy than judged harshly as the adult that he was not? Typically like a child who 'left little room for argument', Rhodes 'could not see both sides of a question: being certain that anyone who even criticized his methods was doing harm'. Anyone who opposed him was 'not only wrong but malignant and mischievous' (Stent 1924: 50). Perhaps because of his childlike instincts, Rhodes was most qualified, instinctively, to force 'Capital to admit and acknowledge its obligations as well as its claims, its duties as well as its rights, its responsibilities as well as its power' (Stent 1924: 63).

Like the global consumer capitalism, which it serves and services, the South African state, which exhibits many Rhodes-like characteristics, requires mobility and immobility simultaneously to function, but both seem to want this exclusively on their own terms. The very idea of South African citizenship has historically been shaped by preoccupations with mobility and its regulation with yardsticks such as *official status*, *lawfulness* and *residence*. Klaaren (2011) traces the current inclusive and simultaneously structurally unequal legal-cultural concept of citizenship based on official residence to the regulation of the mobility of three populations (Asian, African and European) in South Africa between 1897 and 1937. He argues that the interests of economic actors in restricting the mobility of labour and the interest of political elites in establishing and safeguarding their status and identity within their communities together motivate and influence the regulation of mobility and, by extension, the South African concept of citizenship (Klaaren 2011). The situation is compounded by elites motivated to distinguish between 'our' poor and 'other' poor (Sharp 2008), and by the fact of unequal citizenship in terms of material possibilities and service delivery between urban-based and rural-based South Africans (Vigneswaran 2011).

This book focuses, additionally, on the momentum generated by the Rhodes Must Fall (RMF) student protest movement at the University of Cape Town (UCT) to ask critical questions about belonging and citizenship in Africa where, like everywhere else, aspirations for and claims of purity, authenticity, and primary and often parochial identities coexist with notions of the nation state and its logic of large-scale, exclusive communities. This would suggest that citizenship is necessarily bringing the parochial and the cosmopolitan into conversation aimed at providing for and encouraging a citizenry that negotiate and navigate conviviality from the intersection of myriad identity margins. Yet, everywhere in the world, we are all familiar with the question: 'Where do you come from, originally?' which seems ready for no answer short of the land of one's birth, or the birth of one's father, and only occasionally on one's mother, especially in view of the patriarchal order of things. Here is an exchange which reportedly took place between an English woman and a black British girl:

> English woman: Where were you born?
> Black girl: Manchester
> English woman: I mean before that.

Similarly, when people I meet for the first time seem to think they know where I come from, as revealed by questions such as: 'Are you from X?' – X standing for the village, town, city or country of their guesswork – I usually leave them perplexed when I answer: 'Not yet.'

Within the framework of hierarchies among nationals as insiders and between nationals and non-nationals in Africa, even where citizenship is granted to mobile outsiders, the emphasis in official documentation on 'original country of birth' means that naturalised citizens are always haunted by the potential inferiority of 'legal citizenship' to 'citizenship by birth.' After all, claims of authentic belonging as 'sons and daughters' of the 'native' soil – autochthons – can always be invoked to exclude those who belong only by force of the law. We have seen manifestations of this almost everywhere in Africa – ranging from 'Ghana Must Go' in

16

Nigeria and '*Cam No Go*' in Cameroon, to '*Makwerekwere*' in Botswana and South Africa, through '*Nyak*' in Senegal and '*Ivoirité*' in Côte d'Ivoire. In this sense, the law facilitates violence against those seen not to be lawful or official rights-bearers. To make a case about who belongs, states do not hesitate to explore and embrace the distinction between 'hand-held' and 'heartfelt' citizenship and indicators of belonging, even when the hearts which feel might be transplants from donors beyond the confines of national borders. It is not enough to carry official documentations of belonging and wave the national flag of a given country; one must be seen to belong by hard-core or bona fide blood-and-umbilical-cord insiders who arrogate to themselves the prerogative of ultimate legitimisers of belonging. This is the framework within which I examine Rhodes's credentials as *makwerekwere* and seek to understand the RMF movement.

Notes

[1] Please note: *makwerekwere* (singular); *amakwerekwere* (plural)
[2] As Desmond Tutu puts it, 'We are a deeply wounded people. We carry the recent scars of apartheid and the ingrained hurt of centuries of colonialism before that. Some of us feel superior to others, and some feel inferior. For generations, instead of following the universal golden rule of reciprocity, to love one another as ourselves, we have been trained to be mistrustful, to dislike – even to hate.' Each one of us must help the miracle happen, *Timeslive*, 29 April 2012, http://www.timeslive.co.za/local/2012/04/29/each-one-of-us-must-help-the-miracle-happen, accessed 29 April 2012.
[3] According to Margaret Hunter (1993: 190), European colonisation and slavery have contributed to 'skin color hierarchies that continue to privilege light skin over dark skin', especially among black and Hispanic women in the US seeking access to resources.
Reporting for the BBC in January 2013, Pumza Fihlani cites a UCT study that 'suggests that one woman in three in South Africa bleaches her skin', with most women claiming to 'use skin-lighteners because they want "white skin"'. Ms Nomasonto Mnisi, who bleaches to feel and look beautiful, and to enhance her social standing says:

17

Yes, part of it is a self-esteem issue and I have addressed that and I am happy now. I'm not white inside, I'm not really fluent in English, I have black kids. I'm a township girl, I've just changed the way I look on the outside.

In the same report, Fihlani quotes Jackson Marcelle, a Congolese hair stylist who 'has been using special injections to bleach his skin' for 10 year:

'I pray every day and I ask God, "God why did you make me black?" I don't like being black. I don't like black skin... I like white people. Black people are seen as dangerous; that's why I don't like being black. People treat me better now because I look like I'm white.'

See Pumza Fihlani, 'Africa: Where black is not really beautiful', http://www.bbc.com/news/world-africa-20444798, accessed 9 April 2016.
Conscious of the health risks of skin lightening, Lester M. Davids, Professor of Cell Biology at UCT, calls on African governments to put in place mechanisms to check the use of dangerous chemicals for skin lightening. See 'Why it's time all African countries took a stand on skin lightening creams', http://theconversation.com/why-its-time-all-african-countries-took-a-stand-on-skin-lightening-creams-49780?, accessed 11 December 2015.
[4] Some label him a 'Flawed Colossus'. Brian Roberts, for example, titles his book *Cecil Rhodes: Flawed Colossus*, and argues that 'for all his failings', Rhodes 'was not a monster and account should be taken of his human frailties' by those keen to portray him as 'an enigma', 'an egocentric impostor', and as 'a megalomaniac' (Roberts 1987: 205).
[5] Ironically, this declaration, a reluctant concession though it was, 'earned Rhodes the dubious soubriquet of 'nigger-lover', which stuck with him for the rest of his life'. Almost 5,000 working class black people reportedly marched to his Groote Schuur home to pledge their loyalty to Rhodes, in recognition of his magnanimity (Brown 2015: 202). Baker quotes McDonald, one of Rhodes's acolytes, who affirms that Rhodes 'was the best friend the natives ever had', and Jameson saying that Rhodes liked to be with the natives and that 'he trusted them and they fairly worshipped him' (Baker 1934: 93; see also Plomer 1984 [1933]: 128; Maurois 1953: 97). His nigger loving notwithstanding, Rhodes is also credited with saying: "I prefer land to niggers" (Plomer 1984 [1933]: 13; Thomas 1996: 14), and with voting for 'the so-called 'Strop' Bill, which was to give white people the right to flog their native servants' (Plomer 1984 [1933]: 120). Could these contradictions have accounted for 'the natives' giving Rhodes

18

a nickname that signified "The Bull that separates the Fighting Bulls" (Stent 1924: 45; Plomer 1984 [1933]: 9)?

[6] I am grateful to Tinyiko Maluleke, Professor of Theology, University of Pretoria, for drawing my attention to the need for nuance in my claim of continuities in European perceptions and relations to Africans during the periods of the transatlantic slave trade and colonialism.

[7] One of them was Johnny Grimmer, whom Rhodes liked to have near him, because of Grimmer's 'quiet demeanour' which 'had a restful and soothing effect on him', and because Grimmer 'always managed to rouse and excite him' (Jourdan 1910: 242).

[8] See Emanuele Saccarelli and Latha Varadarajan, https://www.foreignaffairs.com/articles/2015-12-17/empire-strikes-back accessed 27 December 2015. See also Jourdan 1910: 213.

[9] Paul Kruger, the President of the Transvaal, blamed Rhodes, 'a bare-faced financier and the Devil incarnate', for using 'his gold and diamonds' to attract 'so many greedy foreigners to the country' to the point of outnumbering the Boers in 'their own' land (Maurois 1953: 105). By denying the foreigners or 'Uitlanders' 'political rights, the right to naturalisation as well as the right to vote', Kruger hoped to contain them (Maurois 1953: 106). Kruger and Rhodes were singing from the same hymnal of narrow nationalism, a European model of life as a zero sum game of 'everyone for himself and God for us all'.

Chapter 1

Sir Cecil John Rhodes:
The *Makwerekwere* with a Missionary Zeal

If whiteness and blackness are afflictions, burdens or blessings, they are the permanence of no particular pigmentation in a dynamic world of ever unfolding permutations of human agency and socialisation. The Nigerian writer Amos Tutuola (1952, 1954) teaches us that there is more and less to bodies than meets the eye, just as there is much more and much less to what strikes us in things or facets of things. When copies or shadows mimic or parody in convincing ways, what reason is there to argue against a thing and its double being two sides of the same coin or cowry? While surfaces are obviously important and often suffice for many ends and purposes, delving beneath appearances and digging deep into the roots of things is critical for understanding eternally nuanced and ever-shifting complexities of being and becoming, and in acknowledging the necessity to supersede the often frozen or static gazes at our beck and call. Delving deep makes impossibilities possible, just as it makes the possible impossible. Being and becoming as works in progress require borrowings and enhancements to render them beautiful and acceptable. It is this capacity to enable and disable simultaneously that makes absence present and presence absent in certain places and spaces, private and public alike. Particular contexts challenge us in particular ways to elevate or lower the bar and threshold of acceptability and tolerability.

Our bodies as humans are envelopes or containers for forms of consciousness that have been shaped by the external world, which in turn is shaped by our consciousness (Bourdieu 1990; Butler 1990, 1993; Foucault 1988; Mauss 1973; Martin et al. 1988; Salpeteur and Warnier 2013; Sanders 2008; Warnier 2006, 2007, 2009). As vehicles, containers or envelopes, bodies are malleable, amenable to being compressed, contorted and extended, dissected, dismembered and remembered, and branded. Auras and essences are as much attributes of the parts as they are of the whole, just as the part is in the whole and the whole in the part. What seems more important than the forms bodies take is the consciousness which inhabits bodies and body parts. Even when a body is seemingly palpably the same and contiguous, the consciousness that inhabits it may be fluid and flexible, pointing to a reality that impoverishes fixations with permanence and stability. The human body can assume the consciousness of an ordinary human just as it can that of a god or a spirit, as well as it can project its own consciousness onto a plant, an animal, or whatever other element of nature is available and handy. Bodies and forms are never complete; they are open-ended malleable vessels to be appropriated by consciousness in its multiplicity. Bodies provide for hearts and minds to intermingle, accommodating the dreams and hopes of both, and mitigating the propensity of the one to outrace the other. As melting pots and mosaics of possibilities, bodies are amenable to being melted and mosaicked by possibilities.

If we take the underlying idea of *makwerekwere* as a mechanism for detecting strangers, outsiders or those who do not belong, then there is no reason why we should confine the idea of an outsider or a stranger to a particular skin colour. The borders or intimacies we seek to protect can be violated by anyone with a capacity to cross borders. Seen more in terms of consciousness than container, *makwerekwere* is any outsider or a perfect stranger who crosses borders nimble-footedly. A *makwerekwere* often comes uninvited and without seeking consent from those who regard themselves as bona fide sons and daughters of the native soil or homeland. He or she has little mastery of local cultures, tends to stutter in local languages or to speak in foreign tongues, has an unmistakeable nose for a quick fortune at all costs, and is usually perceived to be ruthless and greedy in his or her pursuit of self-interest.

Seen in these terms, Sir Rhodes, the nimble-footed 19th century adventurer-treasure-hunter from England, was an exemplary *makwerekwere*. As one would expect of a *makwerekwere,* Rhodes sought to penetrate and harness opportunities in distant unfamiliar lands, with the assistance of maps. As Jordan puts it, 'Maps had a fascination for him and he was always studying them' (Jourdan 2010: 163). 'I want to see all that red', he once declared, pointing to a vast area on a map, 'between the Orange river and the great lakes of Central Africa' which he coveted for the British Empire (Maurois 1953: 55).

Rhodes had a lot in common with all other sweet-footed *amakwerekwere*, be they Europeans, Asians, Americans or Africans. He was 'not afraid of risks and… did not believe in chance' (Maurois 1953: 31). Writing about Rhodes's last voyage to Africa, William Plomer notes that 'Many weeks of his life had been spent on voyages' (Plomer 1984 [1933]: 155). Only a *makwerekwere* who had taken seventy days to voyage from England to Durban by ship (Plomer 1984 [1933]: 14; Maurois 1953: 26), and who believed in flexible mobility of people, things and information could have distinguished himself the way Rhodes did with the reputation of 'the greatest builder of railways and telegraphs that Africa has known' (Lunderstedt [undated]: 4).[1] His single-minded devotion to his quest in a foreign land, even at the risk of jeopardising personal comfort and health, was characteristic of the *amakwerekwere* of his day and still resonates with many *amakwerekwere* today, be they foreign or internal migrants. The arrivals of fortune-hunters in Kimberley in Rhodes's day is hardly dissimilar from the influx of *amakwerekwere* to various centres of accumulation in today's South Africa. As William Plomer puts it, Kimberley in those days was characterised by feverish activity:

> Fortune-hunters of all kinds arrived in a steady stream, many from the slums of Europe. It was not unusual for as many as thirty wagon-loads of newcomers to arrive in one day, and at New Rush there was soon a collection of forty thousand people, all living under tents or corrugated iron, amid heaps of gravel, clouds of dust, and a variety of smells. 'The dust of the dry diggings,' said an eye-witness, 'is to be classed with plague, pestilence and famine, and if there is anything worse, with that also.' The price of necessaries was very high, and water cost threepence a bucket. In Rhodes's own words, the place looked 'like an immense number of ant-heaps covered with black ants, as thick as can be, the latter represented by human beings.' (Plomer 1984 [1933]: 16-17).

Rhodes may have had a heart condition upon arrival, but 'there was profitable business to be done' in Kimberley, and this made his heart 'throb with eagerness' (Plomer 1984 [1933]: 19). Rhodes apparently 'loved property … for the power that it brings' (Plomer

23

1984 [1933]: 106-107), and had 'few wants'. 'His servants found it difficult to get him to wear decent clothes, to eat proper meals or even to dress for and attend theatrical performances' (Brown 2015: 22). This *makwerekwere* attribute of Rhodes's and others is very well depicted in the following passage about life in Kimberley during the 19th century diamond rush:

> When one considers how Rhodes lived – in an unsanitary tin shack without running water – and with whom he lived – a mixture of ruffians, Jewish diamond buyers and money lenders, poets, sons of the world's aristocracy, black peasants from remote tribes – in an environment of murder, mayhem and drunkenness, there is every possibility that there was a touch of madness in this nineteen-year-old son of the manse. Yet it was here, on the edge of the Big Hole, and clutching Marcus Aurelius as his bible, that Rhodes refined his plan for a secret society, led by himself, that would eventually control the world (Brown 2015: 28).

Be that as it may, Rhodes was very conscious of the need for distinction in taste and status between whites and blacks, and among whites of different categories and backgrounds. His recognition that both the Dutch and English were dominant races, and that 'There is always trouble when two dominant races have to live side by side' (Stent 1924: 22), meant that he had to explore ways of legitimising himself and his Britishness as superior to being Dutch and the whiteness that came with Dutch identity in general, and in South Africa specifically. As soon as the wealth of diamonds started materialising, Rhodes and his fellow white *amakwerekwere* used their membership of the Kimberley Club to distinguish themselves. Vere Stent describes the Kimberley Club as 'the last South African word' in 'comfort and in elegance'. It was at the Kimberley Club that 'the best of the Diamond Fields people' 'sought refreshments after their day's work' and where they went to dine and talk, and to display their satisfaction with their outlook on world affairs, and their contentment with their prospects and happiness (Stent 1924: 1). This improvisation of using the Kimberley Club to activate ideas of social distinction among *amakwerekwere* from Europe constitutes a key moment in and building block of the historical construction of whiteness with a South African flavour.

In other regards, Rhodes was unlike most *amakwerekwere* from Africa north of the Limpopo whose mobility seems reduced to push and pull factors and tends to be confined effortlessly when it ventures across borders. Rhodes was white, unlikely to be physically mistaken by black Africans as 'one of us', irrespective of whatever intimacies and interests they shared digging for diamonds in Kimberley. The fact that Rhodes lived among 'black peasants from remote tribes... in an environment of murder, mayhem and drunkenness', and 'in an unsanitary tin shack without running water' (Brown 2015: 28), did not undo the fact that he was white and in charge. Unlike the *amakwerekwere* of today who are black (thus likely to be mistaken by black South Africans as 'one of us'), and who also share the same underserved townships with mostly black South African labour migrants, Rhodes was a very powerful *makwerekwere* and a missionary for the ways and values of his people, to which he clung with evangelical zeal.

Of course, Rhodes did not arrive in South Africa an all-powerful individual; he earned his power and activated himself to higher levels of potency through his interactions with others on the ground and back home in Britain. His attitude, drive and vision set him apart. Unlike many other *amakwerekwere* of his day, white and black alike, he thought himself on a divine mission to change the world. He felt himself divinely ordained to ensure that 'the English people ... fulfil their divine mission of ruling the world to the exclusion of war and for the greater happiness of mankind' (Maurois 1953: 52).

Other *amakwerekwere* of his day, including his business associate Charles Dunnell Ruud, a Scot, wanted to accumulate a personal fortune. Rhodes wanted wealth that would facilitate his game of empire building (Brown 2015: 30). As a man with political ambition, Rhodes 'wanted money – a great deal of it – not for what it would buy, but for the power it conferred' (Maurois 1953: 40-41). His prime objective for accumulating wealth was 'the defence and the extension of the British Empire' (Brown 2015: 40). Armed with a dream to conquer and impregnate the world with the superior values of the British in God's name, Rhodes arrived in what in those days was a 'free-for-all of Southern Africa' in 1870 (Brown 2015: 9), as a poor, unknown seventeen year old, and within a short time, 'he had been blessed with the gift of the Kimberley diamonds' (Brown 2015: 21), where he dug his 'way to enormous, untold, inconceivable wealth', just what 'he needed to finance his dream' (Brown 2015: 9).[2] According to Brown, Rhodes:

> had arrived in South Africa penniless and unknown, and within five years he was a millionaire with a fortune growing exponentially, with no end in sight. Within another five years he was prime minister of the Cape, and English privy councillor – and about to acquire a fiefdom a quarter the size of Europe.
>
> As his fortune and political influence grew, as the arid earth and the high savannah produced a cornucopia of diamonds and gold beyond imagining, Rhodes began to feel he had been put on this earth for some greater purpose. He would expand the English-speaking sphere of influence until it was so powerful that no nation would dare oppose it, and war would be a thing of the past... (Brown 2015: 18).

Like all other treasure hunters, Rhodes came uninvited, indulged unauthorised and conquered unprovoked. Brown describes Kimberley of the late 19th century as a place where 'Every conceivable cast and colour of the human race' – 'a smattering of people from every nation of the face of the earth' was represented, 'digging, sifting and sorting from morning until night, day after day, month after month until they ... [had] obtained a sufficiency' (Brown 2015: 26). In tune with his missionary fervour 'Rhodes had come to believe that, unlike lesser mortals, he had the benefit of divine guidance' (Brown 2015: 32), even if he 'feared death, and had no hope for an existence after death except the one that history could make for him on earth' (Flint 1974: 173). Thus driven by 'a concern for a heroic and immortal place in history' (Flint 1974: 212), Rhodes 'believed that his good fortune was nothing more than destiny justifying his messianic beliefs and ambitions' to facilitate the governance of the world by Britain (Brown 2015: 86). He saw himself as 'a messiah, the prophet of Anglo-Saxon dominion' (Maurois 1953: 106; see also Marlowe 1972: 105).

Instead of being defined and confined by the locals of the host communities of his encounters (the way most *amakwerekwere* are nowadays), Rhodes defined and confined those he encountered in his hunter-gatherer endeavours. It was on a quest as much for greener pastures as for fresher pleasures. Given that the driving force for empire-building was less about the export of surplus capital and more about the export of surplus emotional and sexual energy, 'The enjoyment and exploitation of black flesh was as powerful an attraction as any desire to develop economic resources' (Hyam 1976: 135). Armed with the powerful technologies of dominance (writing, books, maps, guns, ships, trains, telegraphs, cars, telephones, etc.) inherited from his forebears and perfected in the course of his own adventures (Ferguson 2011), Rhodes was able to penetrate, conquer, possess and tame at will and at first contact the powerful – mind, body and soul – of the strange and distant lands of the Heart of Darkness that Africa represented to the civilised savagery of his native England (Samkange 1966; Rodney, 2012 [1972]; Vambe 1972; Chinweizu 1975; p'Bitek 1989 [1966]).

A good case in point of the devastating magic and terror of Rhodes's imperial power and its technologies in southern Africa is provided by Ronald Hyam thus:

> The Mpondo did not fight the British. They simply accepted the facts of life as presented to them by Rhodes. He mowed down a field of mealies with machine guns before the eyes of the paramount chief and his councillors, and told them that their fate would be similar if they did not submit (Hyam 1976: 162).[3]

In other instances, those for whom Rhodes had created a home in Rhodesia through his ruthless transgressions, conversion and renaming, while accusing African villagers of stealing everything in sight, did not think twice when the very same Africans gave away their goods below the perceived monetary or market value of the goods in British terms. Robin Brown reminisces driving through African villages as a ten-year-old with his parents thus:

> We drove through savannah filled with stupendous herds of game in vast, soon-to-be-promulgated national parks like the Serengeti and Tsavo. In every little thatched settlement – most of which looked as if they would blow away in the next wind, and often did – smiling Africans came out to stare and giggle, ready to wait on us hand and foot. We quickly realised that the people had no idea of the value of money, or indeed the market value of some of their goods. One group offered us a large lump of fresh bush meat (furry tail and all), an ostrich egg, and an eagle's quill filled with at least two ounces of alluvial gold. For these we gave a yard or two of

27

'Amerikani' cloth (denim), and their gleeful faces told us they felt they had got the better part of the bargain. They were much more interested in the durable, tightly woven cloth (Brown 54-55).

Aided and abetted by his repertoire of perfected technologies of the self and power (Brown 2015), Rhodes took over, ruled, developed and exploited for his personal profit and that of Britain the lands and bodies of those he conquered, turning them into *amakwerekwere* on their own native soil, their homeland.[4] Among these excesses, Brown mentions 'the outlandish decision to invade and occupy a vast chunk of southern Africa which he then named after himself' and 'his key involvement in the attempt to take over the Boer republics by armed force, in the incident that came to be known as the Jameson Raid' (Brown 2015: 32). Indeed, Rhodes was so thrilled with 'Rhodesia'[5] as a symbol of his personal power and achievements, that he is reported to have responded to Lord Selborne, the bearer of the news that the British authorities had confirmed to name the new territory after him: 'Has anyone else had a country called after their name? Now I don't care a damn what they do with me!' (Flint 1974: 156; see also Plomer 1984 [1933]: 64).

To Herbert Baker, at the pinnacle of his achievements in empire-building, Rhodes 'used to eat and drink… with absent-minded carelessness, swallowing food as he "swallowed continents"' (Baker 1934: 82; see also Brown 2015: 164). Lobengula, King of the Matabele, had anticipated Rhodes's ferocious appetite for the land and things of others when he complained to Queen Victoria about Rhodes: 'He wants to eat up my country!' (Brown 2015: 46). In Episode 5 of the 8 part *Rhodes, The Life and Legend of Cecil Rhodes* documentary film produced by Anthony Thomas, Michael Wearing and Rebecca Eaton, Lobengula compares himself to a fly being eaten up by Rhodes the chameleon.[6] Convinced that a man who came rampaging around his kingdom uninvited could mean no good, King Lobengula was worried that the days of the Matabele were over. He expressed his concerns to Leander Jameson, medical doctor and 'the flag-bearer of Rhodes's dreams' (Brown 2015: 179), who pretended to cure Lobengula of the pain in his legs, inflicted by gout, apparently, while planning to turn him into an addict who would have to depend on

28

tranquillisers of morphine which only Jameson could administer by injection (Brown 2015: 117):

> Have you ever watched the chameleon when she hunts the fly? How she changes her colour to be like the grass, the rocks or the earth... So the fly cannot see the danger. How she comes forward, very slowly. Then back a little. Then forward a little more ... till the fly is close... and out darts the tongue, and the fly is eaten up? Doctor, England is the chameleon and I am that fly.[7]

Others 'have suffered undue neglect' as a result of 'white intrusion' such as Rhodes's, according to historian Christopher Saunders's portraits of nine 'well-known' key nineteenth-century black leaders in southern Africa (Saunders 1979). Anthropologist Monica Hunter [Wilson], the daughter of a clergyman with evangelical commitments of her own (Bank and Bank 2013), provides a rich and comprehensive ethnographic survey of the changing relations and dynamics of power that came with European conquest and imposition of Western value systems and hierarchies of civilisations among the Pondo of South Africa (Hunter 1961).

Like his fellow adventurers-*amakwerekwere* of the same background and origins who had harnessed and exported their hosts as slaves and freak-show entertainers to Europe and the Americas, Rhodes, was said to 'look on men in the abstract as instruments of the work to be done, and had little use for those human tools, which he could not sharpen for his purpose' (Baker 1934: 88). Thus,

> Desperate for labor as the mines grew deeper, he used blacks ruthlessly, penning them up in compounds, destroying their family and tribal life, and giving them wages that made them little better than slaves, so creating the economic base of apartheid (Flint 1974: xv).

Rhodes was able to discipline and punish the locals he met by transforming them into labour zombies – mostly through use of colonial taxes (including the 1884 Glen Grey Act which he personally sponsored in his capacity as Premier of the Cape Colony). In his words, these taxes were a 'gentle stimulus' to blacks to work and 'remove them from that life of sloth and laziness...

29

teach them the dignity of labour ... and make them give some return for our wise and good government' (Lipton 1986: 119; see also Beinart 2001: 21)[8] – for his accumulation and self-aggrandisement projects. If anything, the stimulus was far from gentle, as Hyam recounts:

> Rhodes, as the leading mining magnate of his day, played an especially dominant role in the evolution of a harsh racially-determined labour system. He imposed a poll tax which forced all families to some extent out of subsistence and into the cash economy; he pioneered the break up of communal landholding systems with his Glen Grey enactment, ensuring individual tenure in certain areas, and did so with the full intention of creating a supply of landless labourers. The result, it is said, was a degree of exploitation never achieved by a plantation system of slavery (Hyam 1976: 298).

It is little wonder that when Rhodes boasted that diamond rich Kimberley was the 'richest community in the world for its size', this was perhaps true of everyone but Kimberley's black migrant workers (Beinart 2001: 28) from all over the vast territory that was yet to pass for South Africa as we know it today. The precarious economic and social conditions of black labour, migrant and indigenous alike, has failed to improve in any significant way since the diamond and gold rushes of yesteryear (Thomas 1974; Webster 1978; Wilson 1972), even with the end of apartheid, as the violent suppression and massacre of striking Marikana mineworkers in August 2012 revealed (Alexander et al. 2012). Ironically, black labour remains confined to the margins in townships or seething slums of hurriedly erected shacks, desperately seeking to get by, despite the 'enormous, untold, inconceivable wealth' (Brown 2015: 9) that they have helped to dig out of their native soils to fill the insatiable imperial pockets of Rhodes and his band of *Uitlanders* or *amakwerekwere* from Europe since the Kimberley days. Meanwhile, middle class whites, from the protective distance and comfort of their securitised secluded suburbs, continue to delude themselves that their economic and social positions can be safeguarded irrespective of the social and economic misery of the bulk of their black compatriots. Paradoxically, poor working class whites, increasingly finding it difficult to live up to the illusion that there is a certain class of work which is beneath the dignity of whites to do, are perceived to bring shame on the white race and to pose a threat to white dominance (Bottomley 2012; Teppo 2004). Put differently, they are fast losing the whiteness which was propped up by the deliberate, systematic and collective suppression of blacks and often taken for granted under apartheid (van Wyk 2014). The idea that whites are fast losing out in the competition for whiteness is an increasing preoccupation beyond South Africa (Acolff 2015), as the rise and proliferation of right wing political and cultural fundamentalism in Europe, North America and their global satellites attest. In this regard, Donald Trump's campaign message of making America great again by making it white again through exclusion, intolerance, and vitriol is particularly telling about the resurgence of white supremacy in a context of the globalisation of whiteness.[9]

To feed his rise to prominence and material superabundance, Rhodes tracked down and domesticated everything and everyone he saw, purely on his own terms. He 'believed that his actions were predestined' or 'written in his stars' (Brown 2015: 159). Like his missionary contemporaries who assaulted difference with the Holy Bible (Comaroff and Comaroff 1991, 1997; Viswanathan 1998; Walker 1911), Rhodes privileged conversion over conversation with a bible of his own, *The Meditations of Marcus Aurelius* (Brown 2015: 13-14). Like the imperialist that he was, 'Rhodes believed … that anyone who could stand their ground was entitled to keep it', and that 'Englishmen had a divine right and mission to control Africa, and indeed the world' (Brown 2015: 20). In the words of Jameson, one of Rhodes's acolytes, Rhodes 'dwelt repeatedly on the fact that their great want was new territory fit for the [English] overflow population to settle in permanently, and thus provide markets for the wares of the old country – the workshop of the world' (cited in Brown 2015: 102). Although ambivalently 'stressing his English domicile in his wills', Rhodes 'became South African and made his home there', and 'increasingly his commitment was in South Africa, and he struck down roots there' (Flint 1974: 171). He once said of Rhodesia (Zimbabwe): 'To be in this country is surely a happier thing than the deadly monotony of an English country town.' (Plomer 1984 [1933]: 56). Indeed, as John Flint reports,

In recruiting senior employees, though he [Rhodes] favoured Englishmen and Oxford graduates, he looked for the man who would settle permanently, and lost interest in those who merely wished to work for the day they would return to England (Flint 1974: 171).

And Philip Jourdan, who served as Rhodes's private secretary adds:

> He was very anxious to populate the country, and whenever he heard that any of the settlers contemplated marriage, or that a child was born in the country [Rhodesia], he used to say, 'That is good, it will help to populate the country,' or 'So-and-so is a good citizen' (Jourdan 1910: 46).

Rhodes was indeed determined to populate the lands of his conquests as if these lands had no populations of their own prior to conquest. Jourdan reports that as Prime Minister Rhodes 'received on an average from twenty to twenty-five applications for employment every day', the majority of which were from 'total strangers' often recommended by prominent men in England. And as the 'great reader of character' that Rhodes was, he 'almost invariably went by first impression', insisting on meeting the promising applicants face-to-face before making up his mind (Jourdan 1910: 24-25). According to Stent, when the going was tough for British immigrants in Rhodesia, the request which hurt Rhodes the most, 'but to which he too often acceded, was for assistance to get out of the country' by those, 'deserving and undeserving alike', whom he had incentivised with 'many thousands of pounds of his private fortune... to make Rhodesia their home' (Stent 1924: 9-10).

In this regard, Rhodes stands tall as an example to all *amakwerekwere* the world over who are victims of the exclusionary violence of zero-sum games of belonging played by powerful states and those they co-opt in the name of bona fide nationhood and citizenship. Rhodes's lesson to all those defined and confined as *makwerekwere* is clear: the only way to outgrow the status of *makwerekwere* within the logic of zero-sum games of ever-diminishing circles of inclusion is to rise and challenge – with violence and superior technology – the status of social, political, cultural and economic invisibility which others readily confer on their real or imagined 'outsiders'/'foreigners' or *'Uitlanders'* and 'strangers.' As someone with a hobby for 'dreaming "cosmic dreams"' (Hyam 1976: 152), the first of Rhodes's many wills was an unequivocal roadmap for all *amakwerekwere* with similar imperial ambitions. An excerpt of it reads:

> I leave all my worldly goods in trust … for the establishment, promotion and development of a Secret Society, the true aim and object thereof shall be the extension of British rule throughout the world, the perfecting of a system of immigration from the United Kingdom, and of the colonisation by British subjects of all lands where the means of livelihood are attainable by energy, labour and enterprise, and especially the occupation by British settlers of the entire Continent of Africa, the Holy Land, the Valley of the Euphrates, the islands of Cyprus and Candia, the whole of South America, the Islands of the Pacific not heretofore possessed by Great Britain, the whole of the Malay Archipelago, the seaboard of China and Japan, the ultimate recovery of the United States of America as an integral part of the British Empire… (Brown 2015: 42; see also Hyam 1976: 152; Plomer 1984 [1933]: 25).

Committed to 'the crude colonial belief that the welfare of a country can be permanently based on fear felt by the majority for a powerful ruling minority' (Plomer 1984 [1933]: 131), Rhodes proved that a powerful settler equipped with 'a good supply of maxims and field-guns', including 'a gun called "Long Cecil,"' of which the shells were inscribed *With compts. C. J. R.*' (Plomer 1984 [1933]: 78, 150; see also Jourdan 1910: 120-122) and with ruthless indifference to the humanity of others can become a native and the native a settler (Roberts 1987: 226-241; Plomer 1984 [1933]: 74-82). Simply by defining and imposing himself and his own as superior, Rhodes was able to deny the native sons and daughters he encountered any claim to civilisation, and then to limit aspirations for equality only to those certified to be civilised by the imperial gendarmes of value and taste for Britain, the place where, in his own words, 'the finest race in the world' was to be found (van der Westhuizen 2007: 15, 58). At one of his peace-seeking indabas in Matabele following a rebellion by his 'conquered natives', a 'sulky and dangerous' young chief asked: 'Where are we to live, when it [the fighting] is over?'; Rhodes replied, 'We [he and his settler whites] will give you settlements. We will set apart locations for you; we will give you land'; and the chief retorted in anger, 'You will give us land in our own country! That's good of you!' When Rhodes suggested that the young chief should follow the example of Somabulane the 'great chief' and put down his rifle before talking, the young chief told Rhodes: 'You will have to talk to me with my rifle in my hand' adding, 'I find if I talk with my rifle in my hand the white man pays more attention to what I say. Once I put my rifle down I am nothing. I am just a dog to be kicked' (Stent 1924: 59-60). How ironic! Rhodes had turned the tables: the settler turned native, and the native turned settler! Being a son or daughter of the soil ceases to be merely a matter of who settled first, but rather of who is powerful enough to dispossess the other with impunity. This is not dissimilar to what happened when the Dutch first landed in the Cape in 1652. They named the local populations they met as 'hottentots', to denote 'stutterers', thereby denying the locals an intelligible language, and thus earning themselves the right to impose their vision of the world and their social system on the locals. However generous and magnanimous they were ready to be at first contact, if all the Dutch could hear was gibberish and a 'barbaric' form of 'stuttering', then how could they, in good conscience, qualify those they encountered as human, let alone as equals (February 1991)?

Not only did Rhodes dispossess the native sons and daughters (or those whose own migration had preceded his) of their land and the resources it exudes, he also set about reconfiguring the land and its native occupants in his image, dictating taste, beauty and decency (Comaroff and Comaroff 1991, 1997; Erasmus 1997; Magubane 1971; Salo 2003, 2004; Magubane 2004; Nuttall 2006; Jansen 2008; Ross 2010; Nyamnjoh and Fuh 2014) – in the manner of a priest who symbolically sprinkles water on a convert and renames him or her in the miraculous act of baptism. To Rhodes, Africa or any part thereof belonged to those who had the energy, the will and the ambition to make it fruitful. Africa was fair game for the treasure hunters of his day. Put differently, Africa belonged to whites (preferable of the one and only superior race and country – the British and Britain) who could enslave or make labour zombies of

34

the local populations they encountered or attracted in their treasure-hunting expeditions.

To consolidate his grip on the land, bodies, minds and souls of his new-found lands, Rhodes and his progeny erected statues and monuments in his honour (and in honour of some of his acolytes and fellow *amakwerekwere* like Jameson), and named places, things and people after him, to ensure that he, like Dracula with a drop of blood, would continue to reactivate himself into life eternally, even when physically he was no more.[10] With dreams of building a British African empire that would stretch from the Cape to Cairo, Rhodes had an unquenchable thirst to humble every native encountered, an appetite that only grew with every new conquest, including having present-day Zimbabwe and Zambia named after him as Northern and Southern Rhodesia respectively in 1895, and recognised by Britain as Crown colonies. Since 1902, Rhodes's grave lies in the Matopos Hills – 'Where four great boulders kept eternal guard upon the summit of the World's View' (Stent 1924: 77)[11] – of Matabeleland in Zimbabwe, with the inscriptions: 'Here Lie the Remains of Cecil John Rhodes'. His last words were reportedly: 'So little done, so much to do' (Brown 2015: 22; see also Baker 1934: 123-125). Rhodes is said to have 'decided against a stone slab at Westminster Abbey alongside the likes of his imperial architect Herbert Baker' (Brown 2015: 235). It is reported that the people of Matabeleland defeated by Rhodes and his acolytes, orchestrated or not, 'gathered in numbers at his Matopos funeral' under the leadership of indunas, and 'roared the royal salute *"Bayethe!"* as Rhodes was lowered into his tomb on the remote Matabeleland hillside' (Brown 2015: 19). Of the royal salute, Roberts (1987: 295) adds, 'It was the first time that such an honour had been accorded to a white man'. Stent adds that the greeting was an acknowledgement that Rhodes's spirit was sitting 'in Council with the manes of Umzilligaze and of Lobengula' (Stent 1924: 76). And to Williams (1921: 3), 'to him [Rhodes] alone among white men they gave the royal salute of their tribes', for 'By the natives he was trusted blindly for his just dealings and the respect he showed them'. Williams quotes Faku, one of the chiefs, saying:

'I am an old man and am on the brink of the grave. I was content to die knowing that my children and my people would be safe in the hands of Mr. Rhodes; who was at once my father and my mother. That hope has been taken from me and I feel that the sun has indeed set for me.' (Williams 1921: 326; see also Maurois 1953: 138).

Whatever the world may think of President Robert Mugabe and human rights in Zimbabwe (Morreira 2016), Mugabe has decided to allow this 'strange and mischievous man', who had the habit of crossing borders without passports and disturbing the social systems of those he encountered, to have his final resting place in the country that was once named after him. Responding to journalists during a state visit in Pretoria, amid the RMF protests by UCT students, Mugabe declared: 'We have his corpse and you have his statue', adding, 'We cannot tell you what to do with the statue but we and my people feel we need to leave him down there.'[12] Given the importance of where one is buried as a crucial criterion of where one belongs in Africa, and in view of the fact that many Africans insist on being buried and reburied in their home villages (Geschiere and Nyamnjoh 2000)[13], could Mugabe's declaration be read as an olive branch and acknowledgement of Rhodes as a bona fide citizen of Zimbabwe? Could this be a gesture of accommodation of the *amakwerekwere* of yesteryear on Mugabe's part? If we are to believe Vere Stent, Rhodesia quickly became to Rhodes 'as her first-born to a woman, and the love of that country, which led him eventually to elect to lie amid the granite chaos of the Matopos, was already burning in his great heart' (Stent 1924: 10). Or was it simply to reinforce Mugabe's determination to contain and police the consciousness around a *makwerekwere* that had devastated the land of his birth, so Rhodes must never be allowed to rise again to wreak havoc? A case could be made to see it as an olive branch, if Mugabe's speech as Prime Minister elect to the nation of Zimbabwe on 4 March 1980 is anything to go by. In the speech he made the following conciliatory gesture:

> I urge you, whether you are black or white, to join me in a new pledge to forget our grim past, forgive others and forget, join hands in a new amity, and together, as Zimbabweans, trample upon racialism, tribalism and regionalism, and work hard to reconstruct and rehabilitate our society as we reinvigorate our economic machinery.[14]

36

Mugabe's 'strange and mischievous man' died on Wednesday 26 March 1902 before he could see the entire continent of Africa lie silenced under his giant conquering feet, flattened by his *makwerekwere* imperial ambitions of dominance. Yet, for many, he had earned himself, the reputation of 'a philanthropist, military strategist of the empire, diplomat, and successful businessman'[15]. To some, 'South Africa would have been little less than a paradise' 'if Rhodes had not been born' (Williams 1921: 3). According to Brown, 'from the time he died the myth of Rhodes the Colossus, the Founder, the Immense and Brooding Spirit, began to rise from his lonely grave' (2015: 236). Although a man who 'was not really happy in the land of his birth', rarely staying 'in England longer than was necessary and not until the end of his life', Rhodes became 'the embodiment of the imperial ideal; a personification of all the glories of the British Empire' (Roberts 1987: 2-3). The journalist Bruce Whitfield describes Rhodes as 'a rabid colonialist who instigated the Anglo-Boer War and whose ambition to have the Union Jack fly from the Cape to Cairo was thwarted only by ill-health and his death at 49.'[16] While Flint, writing in the early 1970s, notes that 'Rhodes ... has become a symbol of all that the black South African hates – exploitation combined with rabid racism' (Flint 1974: xiv). Others, like Brian Roberts, argue, that whatever his excesses or flaws, Rhodes 'was wholly in tune with the spirit of his times' – which was 'the age of world powers, of land-hungry visionaries, of aggressive nationalism, of the spread of European civilization' –, adding that 'Rhodes was not alone in expounding high-flown theories of racial superiority' (Roberts 1987: 2).

To borrow a proverb from Chinua Achebe, those who argue thus would say, in joining the scramble for Africa, Rhodes was merely dancing the dance prevalent in his time[17], which was to use the ideal of racial supremacy as justification for the aggressive pursuit of material wealth and national glory with ruthless and reckless abandon, and with callous disregard for the humanity of perceived lesser others (Plomer 1984 [1933]: 72). This was a sentiment or justification Rhodes shared, when, in a speech acknowledging a doctorate honoris causa awarded him by Oriel College in 1899, he said:

'Sometimes, in pursuing my object, the enlargement of the British Empire and with it the cause of peace, industry and freedom, I have adopted means in removing opposition which were the rough and ready way and not the highest way to attain that object. *But you must remember that in South Africa where my work has lain, the laws of right and equity are not so fixed and established as in this country. ... It is among those men that my own life must be weighted and measured.*' (Maurois 1953: 125, emphasis mine).

However, as Antony Thomas observes, such an argument 'ignores the tensions and ideological crosscurrents in Rhodes's day' and 'is deaf to those clear contemporary voices that were raised in protest against him and his methods' (Thomas 1996: 12). These debates suggest that, despite the proliferation of books on Rhodes, not enough has been written about him as a human being, consisting of flesh and blood, mind and body, emotion and reason, with everyday highs and lows, and the frailties of being human – if for no other reason but the fact that Rhodes reportedly 'seemed to think it a weakness in a man to be overcome by his feelings' (Jourdan 1910: 26). Accounts of Rhodes like Vere Stent's (1924), Philip Jourdan's (1910), William Plomer's (1984 [1933]) and Robin Brown's (2015) are rare in their insights to Rhodes the person beyond his public deeds and image. Because Rhodes the individual human being is as scarce as a rare diamond (e.g. 'the South African Star'), Rhodes the stereotype, the caricature and the figment of the imagination lends himself easily to prototyping and rationalising, and as an excuse or a scapegoat. I may not be alone in yearning for more representations of Rhodes along these lines: 'Rhodes dropped the tangle meekly and with no more than a grunt; but his face was a study. The look of deep amusement and affection in his eyes and the softened expression on his face spoke volumes!' (Fitzpatrick 1924: xii).

In honour of his public image, many spaces and places have been named (whitened) after Rhodes in South Africa, including Rhodes University (RU) in Grahamstown, which will not rename itself in a hurry because, in the words of Vice-Chancellor (VC) Sizwe Mabizela, 'The name of Rhodes has now become synonymous with advancement of education. You think of the Mandela-Rhodes scholarship and you can think of Rhodes

University. It's about excellence in academics'[18]. As a crowning glory of his achievements, and in recognition of his generous donation of some of 'his' land – the Groote Schuur estate[19] – and 'his' wealth to UCT (Phillips 1993: 2, 136, 145-148, 220-221; Baker 1934: 37-55), where several places, spaces, buildings and things are named after him and his fellow *amakwerekwere* disciples (old and new, dead and alive), a most provocatively imposing blot-on-the-landscape statue was erected in Rhodes's honour at the very heart of the campus. There sits his bronzed likeness, overlooking the city and seemingly yearning for the lands beyond – lands which his nimble-footed *makwerekwereness* was certain to bring him with time and raw greed. I can well imagine some comparing Rhodes and his creed of 'the survival of the fittest nations' (Baker 1934: 140) to the Nile Perch of Lake Victoria, 'a voracious predator' introduced in the 1960s 'as a little scientific experiment', but which has turned out to be a veritable 'Darwin's Nightmare'[20] to the local human and non-human populations.

Njabulo Ndebele, former VC of UCT, describes Rhodes's godlike presence, symbolised by the statue sculpted by Marion Walgate and unveiled in 1934[21], as follows:

There is a nineteenth-century figure who significantly shaped the southern African sub-continent. His compulsive and daring ambitions for the entire continent of Africa evoke strong emotions. He is either praised or denounced, admired or mocked. Enduring controversy around him has assured him an indelible place in history. Whichever way you turn, you will encounter him, whether on campus, or elsewhere in South Africa; or beyond, in Zimbabwe. His name, Cecil John Rhodes, echoes from Cape to Cairo, the span of continental distance by which he expressed the extent of his vision.

You may not see him clearly in the iconic wide-angle view of UCT. Yet he is decidedly there. Perhaps it is just as well that his visual presence is not more prominent. He is part of campus history, not the whole of it.

Rhodes is memorialised on campus by a bronze statue of him, now weathered green by time. On a closer look you will make him out, the hippo on the surface of UCT's river of time, defying casual embarrassment and willed inclinations to have it submerge, perhaps forever. Its broad back defiantly in view, it is never to be recalled without thoughts and feelings that take away peace of mind.

Indeed, Rhodes, the donor of the land on which the University of Cape Town was built, exerts a presence on campus which often prompts a desire for his absence. But, like Moby Dick the whale, he will blow.[22]

Journalist Alexander Parker regards Rhodes's ambition and arrogance as boundless. He knew no law, treating Africa as a hunting ground for gold and diamond deposits and Africans as devalued humanity (reduced to a commodity) to be exploited with impunity. Through his British South Africa Company, 'to which Britain outsourced the messy and unpleasant business of empire, he stole more than a million square miles of Africa from its inhabitants, dominating life from the beaches of Muizenberg to the shores of Tanganyika.' Parker shares various quotes by Rhodes that show just how disparaging and condescending his attitude to Africa and Africans was: 'Africa is lying ready for us. It is our duty to take it'; 'The native is to be treated as a child and denied the franchise. We must adopt a system of despotism in our relations with the barbarians of SA'; 'I contend that we are the first race in the world, and that the more of the world we inhabit the better it is for the human race…'; 'We must find new lands from which we can easily obtain raw materials and at the same time exploit the cheap slave labour that is available in the colonies. The colonies would also provide a dumping ground for the surplus goods produced in our factories'; 'I would annex the planets, if I could. I often think of that.' These excesses, deep imperfections, catastrophic flaws and brutal tyranny of Rhodes notwithstanding, Parker believed that he 'was at the heart of a history that created the idea of SA.'[23] (See also Brown 2015: 44; Marlowe 1972: 64). This demonstrates the attitude of conquest and of assuming that there are bountiful resources there for the taking.

Tokelo Nhlapo, deputy president of the Student Representative Council (SRC) at the University of the Witwatersrand (Wits) adds that Rhodes:

is today associated more with Oxford scholarships than with the black mass killings he committed. It was Rhodes who originated the land grabs to which Zimbabwe's current miseries can ultimately be traced. It was Rhodes who told the House of Assemblies in 1887 in Cape Town that 'the native is to be treated as a child and denied the [Cape] franchise. We must adopt a system of despotism in our ['whites'] relations with the barbarians of South Africa'. Rhodes' attitude towards Africa and its people was bluntly racist; in his own words he 'prefer[red] land to niggers.' Moreover, Rhodes is linked with the Jameson Raid, an illegal attempt to annex Transvaal territory then held by the Boers, a primary cause of the South African War in 1899-1902. He is clearly an enemy of black people.[24]

Nhlapo's point about Rhodes having orchestrated the land grabs that account to the current misery in Zimbabwe echoes a similar sentiment by Brian Roberts who recounts how 'the coming of the white man had brought nothing but disaster' for the Ndebele, who had lost their country through 'a sudden, brutal and devastating take-over' (Roberts 1987: 226), and many of whom had been rendered homeless as their villages were destroyed and their cattle and land confiscated (Plomer 1984 [1933]: 102-109; Roberts 1987: 226-235). In Roberts's words:

> The volunteers in Jameson's army had lost no time in claiming the farms that had been promised them. Not all these farms were occupied immediately – gold prospecting prevented that – but ownership was very quickly established. No sooner were the troops demobilized than they began swarming over Matabeleland, pegging out their ill-gotten properties. …. The disposed Ndebele had no right of redress. If they tried to reoccupy their former homes, or were bold enough to complain, they were simply told that they were now living on white men's land and must obey the orders of their overlords. Most of them were allowed to stay, not as home owners but as tenant labourers. Needing a workforce, the new settlers and absentee landlords were prepared to accept the Ndebele as 'native residents' only if they earned their keep. Almost overnight a once proud nation was reduced to serfdom (Roberts 1987: 226).

Indeed, such were the brutish, violent and savage imperial and colonial beginnings of the Zimbabwean land problem (Ranger 1999; Fontein 2015), which historian Stanlake Samkange masterfully reconstructed, popularised and lamented in a historical novel *On Trial for My Country* (1966), and the socio-political, economic and cultural ramifications of which sociologist Sam Moyo documented abundantly until his passing in 2015 at a conference in Delhi, where he was making a presentation on the matter (Moyo 2000, 2008; Moyo and Yero 2005; Moyo and Chambati 2013; Moyo et al. 2015).

41

A powerful *makwerekwere* can be difficult to dislodge, especially when he has reproduced himself abundantly – as did Rhodes through an internationally influential imperial secret society[25] and a trust fund which have both continued to influence and shape Southern Africa and the world after his death (Brown 2015) – and has penetrated and humbled purported sons and daughters of the native soil with feelings of inferiority and aspirations of achievement in his very own image (Fanon 1967a: 169, 1986 [1967b]). The following observation by Fanon in *Black Skin, White Masks*, is most telling in the interiorised feelings of inadequacy that are the result of a blind subscription to the hierarchy of humanity enshrined by whiteness and its civilizational order. In the Antilles, Fanon remarks:

> It is in white terms that one perceives one's fellows. People will say of someone, for instance, that he is 'very black'; there is nothing surprising, within a family, in hearing a mother remark that 'X is the blackest of my children' – it means that X is the least white. [....] Let me point out once more that every Antillean expects all the others to perceive him in terms of the essence of the white man. (Fanon 1986 [1967b]: 63).

This is why the term 'independence' when used to label the lived reality of those once directly defined and confined by an omnipotent *makwerekwere* is often a misnomer – an extravagant illusion, just as is the term 'postcolony'. When one has been configured and reconfigured by the violence of conversion (Viswanathan 1998) – mind, body and soul – it is not that easy for one to deactivate oneself from the violations and falsehoods to imagine and seek fantasy spaces and creative regeneration. The violence of conversion is like gangrene – it penetrates and humbles one's entire being, loosening screws and messing up one's anatomy, sense of self and sense of being. It is an affliction I would hesitate to describe as curable, even in my most optimistic disposition. This is what I understand philosopher, political scientist and public intellectual Achille Mbembe[26] to be saying when he argues that no critique of whiteness is credible that does not start from the assumption of our very own entanglement (however accursed) with the very same whiteness that so threatens our very own existence,

42

and calls for a proper engineering of the death of whiteness through its demythologisation:

If we fail to properly demythologize whiteness, whiteness – as the machine in which a huge portion of the humanity has become entangled in spite of itself – will end up claiming us.

As a result of whiteness having claimed us; as a result of having let ourselves be possessed by it in the manner of an evil spirit, we will inflict upon ourselves injuries of which whiteness, at its most ferocious, would scarcely have been capable.

Indeed for whiteness to properly operate as the destructive force it is in the material sphere, it needs to capture its victim's imagination and turn it into a poison well of hatred.

For victims of white racism to hold on to the things that truly matter, they must incessantly fight against the kind of hatred which never fails to destroy, in the first instance, the man or woman who hates while leaving the structure of whiteness itself intact.

As a poisonous fiction that passes for a fact, whiteness seeks to institutionalize itself as an event by any means necessary. This it does by colonizing the entire realms of desire and of the imagination.

To demythologize whiteness, it will not be enough to force 'bad whites' into silence or into confessing guilt and/or complicity. This is too cheap.

To puncture and deflate the fictions of whiteness will require an entirely different regime of desire, new approaches in the constitution of material, aesthetic and symbolic capital, another discourse on value, on what matters and why.[27]

There is much evidence in the thinking and practices of black staff and students at UCT, as I have argued elsewhere (Nyamnjoh 2012a), and in the business-as-usual manner in which white staff at UCT go about researching and teaching Africa (Mamdani 1998a, 1998b[28]; Morreira 2015; Nhlapo and Garuba 2012[29]; Ntsebeza 2014; Nyamnjoh 2012b), to suggest that decolonising the mind *à la Ngugi wa Thiong'o* (1986) or demythologising whiteness is far more challenging than previously imagined. South Africa has an estimated population of 50.5 million, of which, according to Statistics South Africa, 'Africans' are in the majority at 40.2 million (79.5 per cent of the total population). 'Whites' and 'coloureds' are estimated at 4.5 million (9 per cent) each, and 'Indians/Asians' at 1.3 million (2.5 per cent)[30]. Despite the fact that not every white South African has direct ties with Europe or the West, and in spite of the country's long association with whiteness, in social anthropology for example, the discipline with which I am currently associated, very few studies of whiteness by local and visiting anthropologists exist. Yet, as I have argued elsewhere, South Africa has not only attracted some of the most renowned anthropologists from Europe and North America, it has also produced and exported its own anthropologists to some of the most prestigious institutions in North America and Europe (Nyamnjoh 2012b). I drew attention to this peculiarity in 2012 when I wrote:

There is very little published research by white anthropologists in South African universities on white South Africans. There are very few ethnographies to substantiate or contest what sociologist Melissa Steyn and psychologist Don Foster (2008) – both South African academics – argue are white discursive practices circulated in the mainstream press that aim to enact, establish, entrench and promote 'the dominant white ideology' in post-Apartheid South Africa. What little anthropological research does exist is largely unpublished and mostly on non–English-speaking whites (cf. van der Waal and Robins 2011) or on 'poor whites' (cf. Teppo 2004). Neighbouring Zimbabwe – where 'the political disenfranchising of whites has failed to render them symbolically unthreatening' (Fox 2012) – boasts more published anthropological studies of whites than does South Africa. Such ethnographies of whites – their limitations notwithstanding (Hartnack 2012) – argues author of Whiteness in Zimbabwe (2010), David McDermott Hughes[31],address a significant gap in scholarship' given that 'we study 'down' to marginal and disempowered people but rarely study 'up' to the privileged'. The overwhelming tendency in South Africa is to study down, but hardly ever horizontally or upwards. If the dearth of studies on white South Africans is anything to go by, it would appear that to most South African anthropologists knowledge of the country they inhabit must be confined to knowledge of blacks (indiscriminately considered) or of whites who have failed to live up to the comforts of being white (Crapanzano 1985; Thornton 1990; du Toit 2001, Steyn 2001; Magubane 2004; Kalaora 2011; Fox 2012).

The relatively little anthropological curiosity regarding whites in South Africa might suggest that South African whites are – regardless of their internal hierarchies of purity – beyond ethnographic contemplation or that because they have the same genealogy as the majority of anthropologists who have arrogated to themselves the business of mapping out and documenting the cultural diversity of their country, their essence defies taming by geography and by the social (Morris 2012). This leads to some white South African anthropologists claiming explicitly or implicitly that objectivity is not only a possibility, but a reality made possible by their physical or social distance from the people, things and places studied, even when one is amongst and participates in them. Far from being determined by race, place, class, gender and/or age, whites in Africa determine race, place, class, gender and age for themselves and for others. Yet, as Graham Fox (2012) argues, '[to] understand whiteness is to better understand the lived experiences of contemporary Africa', where, 'though colours of skin no longer differentiate people according to value or virtue, the colonial histories embedded in that skin are visible, powerful and indelible' (Nyamnjoh 2012b: 70-71; see also Nyamnjoh 2013b).

In post-apartheid South Africa, 'whiteness ... continues to exude a powerful sense of normativity' (West 2009: 11) as a currency and an arbiter of taste, art, decency, culture and beauty. It has remained firmly in charge, suggesting normativity even as it is undermined, and often exuding 'residual assumptions of entitlement that are at odds with emergent reconciliatory gestures' (West 2009: 4). Even among the so-called born-frees of South Africa – those referred to as the 'freedom generation' (Newman and De Lannoy 2014), the standards of beauty at UCT continue to be determined by whiteness, if a survey by Qamran Tabo, published in the university's official student newspaper Varsity, is anything to go by. Conducted in 2013, the survey asked students 'who had spent the majority of their lives living in SA, most of them born in the early 1990s ... about their thoughts on interracial dating.' In total, 60 students were surveyed, 'ten from each of the following racial groups: white, coloured (culturally), Indian, East Asian, biracial and African.' All respondents stated that they would date someone of a different race, but with certain preferences:

> Quite unsurprisingly, Caucasians were chosen as the most attractive by most non-whites. White respondents also expressed the highest percentage of intra-racial attraction, meaning that they considered their own race as one of the most attractive. African and Indian respondents are the only groups that found members of their own racial groups unattractive. They, and East Asians, were also ranked the lowest by other races.
>
> Apart from colonialism, media has had a major effect on who we consider beautiful and worthy of attention and who not. There is still an overwhelming amount of white faces on TV, in movies and

45

magazines. As a quick experiment, ask some of your friends what their favourite TV show is; chances are its cast will be predominantly Caucasian.

Dating a white person is perceived as being the ultimate status symbol for many people of colour. I have heard many male students of colour stating that nothing says 'I have arrived' quite like having an Aryan nymph on your arm.

Stereotyped as having high standards, white partners are supposedly more difficult to attract. Hence, bagging one is an achievement. With white South Africans being statistically the most educated, literate and wealthy population group in the country, more 'value' is added to having them as romantic partners. You could think of it as romantic Darwinism.[32]

Although the survey was rightly criticised abundantly in mainstream and social media because of the smallness of the sample size and because some people felt it perpetuates the already existing stereotypes about beauty, the fact of the resilience of such racialized Eurocentric indexes of beauty in Africa, and especially among youth, is very significant (See also Nyamnjoh and Page 2002; Nyamnjoh and Fuh 2014). Also resilient and indeed celebrated among South African youth is consumerism[33], which can be traced back to Rhodes and his imperial ambition to conquer the world culturally. The reality of unequal access for the world's cultures which Rhodes championed in his imperial ambitions, combined with the aggressive targeting of budding, young and often innocent consumers by the neoliberal global corporations inspired by his empire building and penchant for amalgamation since his Kimberley days, poses a real threat to the marginalised cultures of Africa in the global arena. Seduced by mass advertising by the global machines of desire, the youth of South Africa are united in their consumerism, flooded as they are with first and second-hand cultural goods, to which they succumb to varying degrees. With youth caught in the web of such localised monolithic global consumerism, how can clamours for cultural equality or representation be taken beyond lip service? How can Rhodes truly fall in the face of such homogenisation and standardisation of consumer palates that emphasises passive internalisation and regurgitation of Western menus, in lieu of global buffets, critical ingestion, digestion and engagement? In this context, should we be

46

surprised that 'the global culture game' succeeds in making of difference an 'obsession' and 'an essence that neither reality nor the imagination seems able to dislodge' (Oguibe 2004: xiv)? To join or maintain one's spot on the consumer bandwagon, people resort to making a business of difference.

It is unfortunate, though understandable in the light of difference as business, commodity and resource, that twenty two years after apartheid, the atmosphere in South Africa is still rife with accusations and counter accusations of racism. Despite the efforts at truth and reconciliation and nation-building of the Mandela presidency, race relations seem to be degenerating instead, with increasingly little evidence of social cohesion. Even the usual lip service to non-racialism induced by political correctness is fast evaporating under the burning heat of rising economic hardships and social tensions. It is worrying that despite the RMF protests of 2015 when social media bled racism among warring black and white students and academics, 2016 has been greeted by a slew of incidents involving individuals who have publicly made racist remarks. This is a disturbing indication of lessons unlearnt, and begs the question of the extent to which the South African rainbow nation is indeed ready to turn a new page by shedding individual and collective delusions of completeness and embracing a future of interdependent, inclusive and flexible personal and collective identities (Lategan 2015).

In an apparent reaction to litter being left behind on Durban beach after the 2016 New Year's Day celebrations, white South African state agent, Penny Sparrow made racist comments about black people using Durban's beach.[34] In a Facebook posting that went viral, she explicitly referred to black beachgoers in Durban as 'monkeys' without education of any kind, who must not be allowed loose to spread 'huge dirt and troubles and discomfort to others'.[35] Reminiscent of the apartheid days when blacks were not allowed to occupy certain spaces, Sparrow implied that 'black people do not know how to behave when they are given permission to occupy public spaces'[36], and that access to such spaces should be limited to them in the interest of the good taste and social distinction of whites in South Africa. Her assertions, similar to other postings about which black students complained during the RMF protests at

UCT[37], attracted much criticism, and complaints about her comments were lodged with the South African Human Rights Commission. South Africans offended by her posts reportedly sent her angry voice and text messages. She also lost her job and was rumoured to have gone into hiding.[38]

Despite the backlash caused by her comments, Sparrow remained unrepentant, claiming that she was just 'stating the facts', and was within her right of freedom of speech. How could it be a fact that black South Africans are monkeys? To Sparrow the answer is simple: 'I see the cute little wild monkeys do the same pick drop and litter'[39] She stated: 'I wasn't being nasty or rude or horrible, but it's just that they [black people] make a mess. It is just how they are.'[40] In this she was defended by Gareth Cliff, radio DJ and Idols judge, in the name of 'freedom of speech'.[41] Ex-Talent Bloom employee, Nicole de Klerk, a white South African, also justified her use of racist name-calling towards blacks by saying, 'that's what they are'. In January 2016, de Klerk was fired after reportedly calling a group of black party-goers *kaffirs*.[42] This is as much as saying that, to Penny Sparrow and Nicole de Klerk, dirt and being messy are essential indicators of being black in South Africa – something no amount of whitening up can ever undo, much more like another common insults: you can take a black person out of the bush, but you can never take the bush out of a black person.

Little wonder the so-called 'coconuts' (Matlwa 2007) – such as Panashe Chigumadzi and Kharnita Mohamed, cited later below – find themselves caught betwixt and between in post-apartheid South Africa where they are deluded into thinking that they can be whatever they want to be on their own terms, and without strings attached. Many a white South African who cannot think past race are not in a position to condone the possibility of whiteness without whites. They are determined to keep shifting the goalposts of indicators of whiteness ad nauseam (Steyn 2001, 2008; West 2009; van Wyk 2014).

Another incident also involving a white South African, Chris Hart, who was an economist and strategist at Standard Bank, resulted in his being summarily suspended[43] – others reports say he was fired[44]– after tweeting a message stating: 'More than 25 years after Apartheid ended, the victims are increasing along with a sense

48

of entitlement and hatred towards minorities...' In response to the backlash resulting from this comment, Hart later tweeted, 'This tweet has caused offense – never intended for which I apologise wholeheartedly. Meant to be read in context of slow growth.'[45] Business academic and consultant, Dr. Bheki Shongwe, a black South African, came out in his defence, stating that Hart was a well-meaning South African who wants to make a difference in the country.[46] To Shongwe, South Africans should be cautious with their interpretations of social media content, as social media platforms offer little context, enabling viewers to make their own interpretations of postings and comments.

If visible or effective racism is an attribute of power and privilege, and if power and privilege can be achieved and lost, then it is problematic, a priori, to seek to confine racism to a particular skin colour or pigmentation – whites – especially in a South context where political, social, cultural and economic power are not a categorical or absolute monopoly of whites. It is hardly surprising that the racist statements found on social media go both ways, as no racial or social category has the monopoly of stereotypes and prejudices, even if not every race or social category is always in a position to have their prejudices and stereotypes protected and given added visibility by power and privilege. Black South African, Velaphi Khumalo of the Gauteng Department of Sports, Arts, Culture and Recreation was reportedly fired[47] – another report says he was suspended with full pay[48]– after posting on Facebook that black South Africans should do to white people what 'Hitler did to the Jews'. He stated that he wanted the country 'cleaned' of all white people, because, to him, whites are 'all a bunch of racists'[49] An internal disciplinary hearing process was instituted against Khumalo by his employer.[50] Chastising Khumalo, MEC Faith Mazibuko regretted the detrimental effects of such racist pronouncements to nation-building and social cohesion in South Africa. 'His [Khumalo's] sentiments take our country backwards'[51], said Mazibuko. At UCT, a person wearing a T-shirt with the words: 'Kill all whites' inscribed reportedly entered and sat in a UCT dining hall. The behaviour was roundly condemned by UCT management as 'a direct incitement to violence', as 'hateful and vindictive', and as a beach of 'all limits of free speech'.[52]

Of significance in the recent incidents of racial bigotry is the use of social media. Penny Sparrow and Chris Hart – descendants of *amakwerekwere* of yesteryear – and Velaphi Khumalo all spread their undesirable views through Facebook and Twitter. Social media as a platform for engaging in free (and largely uncensored) speech is increasingly becoming problematic in this regard. In response to the aforementioned incidents, the ANC noted that,

> given the reach of social media; (Facebook has approximately 1.55 billion and Twitter has 307 million monthly active users respectively) the circulation of such bigoted comments have the potential for causing irreparable harm to the dignity and reputations of individuals and social groups.[53]

In a country still heavily inflicted by racial inequality and where the tentacles of racialized poverty run deep, what becomes of free speech – or 'a passion for freedom' (Ramphele 2013) – when it merely serves to reinforce racism, power and privilege? How can one transcend a past that is in no hurry to bury its nightmares?

These incidents of racism were sufficiently worrying to preoccupy President Jacob Zuma in his state of the nation address for 2016. He made a plea in Parliament for everyone to unite against racism. As a follow up on Zuma's call to action, on 18 February 2016 the ANC organized an anti-racism march in Pretoria.[54] Donning ANC party colours, members and supporters marched from Burgers Park in the City Centre to the Union Buildings, chanting struggle songs, to present a memorandum on 'unity, non-racialism and democracy' to the Presidency.[55] During the march, one ANC member stated, 'Today we are marching for unity and non-racism. We want the people of South Africa to stand together against racism, especially [with] what is happening at our universities'.[56] Njabulo Nzuza, the ANC Youth League Secretary General, blamed members of the DA for perpetuating racism. Nzuza commented: 'We must find a way to make racism to be criminal; there must be a consequences for it.'[57] ANC Secretary General Gwede Mantashe emphasised the need to 'build a non-racist and prosperous nation'. He called for a united country adding that: 'If we were not united we would not have defeated apartheid.

We must build a non-racist society where we see people as people'.[58]

Building a non-racist society is contingent on changing negative, individual and collective thoughts, and verbal expressions around issues of race. These negative verbal opinions are often most damaging as they often result in the perpetuation of stereotypes. Stereotypes are constant and consistent and are rooted in historical imagining. 'They are relentless and are too often left undisturbed in people's circles of intimacy and public representation'.[59] The wrath of such narrow-minded and stereotypical thinking in South Africa's current racial turmoil has surfaced several times this year in response to racial statements made in public.

Perhaps less in South Africa than elsewhere, whitening up and blackening down are never ending desires. One only needs to see the lengths to which blacks would go to acquire whiteness and its correlations, and how much whites who can afford to would bend over backwards to suntan and sunbathe in the tropics. If one sees a touch of class and relative advantage in a tanned white skin body for example, one is saying that one has been rich enough to afford a holiday in the tropics or pay to have chemicals sprayed onto their body to look as though they were there, where there is more sunshine than in the temperate zones of Europe, for example. Whites would not risk their health sunbathing, if they were not convinced that a tanned skin is superior to a pink skin, and that it makes them more socially visible in their circles. What bleaching and tanning say is that however we seek to rationalise it away, neither whites nor blacks feel quite complete without the other. They are like complementary aspects of reality that acquire creative energy and potency only when they blend together with productive intent. Seen in abstraction, they exude little but sterile destructiveness (Nyamnjoh 2007a [1995]: 77-83). This would suggest that purity of nature and culture seem to appeal to few, unless when abstracted into an ideological and political weapon, as was the case in South Africa under apartheid.

In a context still infused with hierarchies of humanity such as present-day rainbow South Africa, a country profoundly penetrated and gangrened by the rhizomic Rhodes and his tentacles of insatiable violence of desire, to disentangle and extricate identities

51

to a real or imagined state of purity and authenticity is to dream the impossible dream of dismembered dead bodies mangled by the ghastly car accidents of history (Lategan 2015). Co-production and co-implication are the order of the day in the violence of encounters between aggressive self-aggrandising *amakwerekwere* like Rhodes and his progeny, and the multiple gradations of sons and daughters of the native soil humbled by and complicit in their pursuit of dominance.

Notes

[1] Apart from sending and receiving telegrams, riding horses and trains, Rhodes, reportedly, 'was not very partial to letter-writing, and only wrote when it was absolutely necessary' (Jourdan 1910: 55). He was a word-of-mouth sort of person, who, as a *makwerekwere*, would have thrived very much in the 21st century of the internet, cell phone and social media.

[2] Robin Brown describes the big hole created by diamond mining in Kimberley thus:

> This pit would soon become the largest hole ever to be dug on the surface of the earth. Mined for almost half a century, the Kimberley 'Big Hole' finally closed in 1914, after an estimated 50,000 miners had dug a crater some forty-two acres across. Wielding mainly picks and shovels, the men eventually excavated to a depth of 1,097 metres (Brown 2015: 25).

> Today, the hole is a popular local attraction which tourists may visit by train along the track built by Rhodes as the first part of his route from Cape to Cairo. It seems inconceivable that this was once a mine teeming with a diverse mob, all hand-digging for diamonds, and that the water-filled hole had produced such extraordinary wealth (Brown 2015: 29).

[3] Plomer (1984 [1933]: 73) quotes Rhodes telling the Pondo chief: 'And that is what will happen to you and your tribe… if you give us any further trouble'.

[4] The drama, violence and hypocrisy of first contact in unequal relations between British colonialists and indigenous populations in South Africa and elsewhere are eloquently captured by the South African comedian Trevor Noah, in his clip on colonisation as the most arrogant form of patriotism, presented on the UK's *John Bishop Show*, 30 May 2015. https://vimeo.com/130619176, accessed 15 September 2015.

5 According to Plomer 1984 [1933]: 65] 'Rhodesland' and 'Cecilia' were other names suggested for the new country.

6See https://www.youtube.com/watch?v=kzOeXpQsglg, accessed 9 December 2015.

7 See 'The Chameleon and the Fly, Episode 5', https://www.youtube.com/watch?v=kzOeXpQsglg, accessed 9 December 2015. See also Plomer (1984 [1933]: 66).

8 This was an imposition that has carried through into present-day perceptions of 'White saviour complex'.

9 See Kelly J. Baker, 'Make America White Again? Donald Trump's language is eerily similar to the 1920s Ku Klux Klan—hypernationalistic and anti-immigrant', http://www.theatlantic.com/politics/archive/2016/03/donald-trump-kkk/473190/, accessed 13 March 2016.

10 In addition to monuments, memorials and related symbols of recognition in South Africa and Zimbabwe, such as the Rhodes Trust and Rhodes Scholarships housed by Rhodes House at Oxford University demonstrate, this is exactly what has come to pass. See http://www.rhodeshouse.ox.ac.uk/rhodes-house, accessed 9 December 2015.

11 The Matopos Hills are 'forty-five miles from Bulawayo, a mound of rock standing up in the middle of a prodigiously wide stretch of green and wild country'. Rhodes reportedly fell in love with the Matopos in 1896, while settling the Matabele revolt, and decided to call it 'one of the world's views'. In a tomb nearby is King Mozelikatze, 'who has asked to be buried in a sitting position at this, the highest point, point in his kingdom, so that even in death he could look at the magnificent vista before him'. Upon hearing the story, Rhodes had exclaimed, 'What a poet', and given instructions to be buried there as well (Maurois 1953: 137).

12 See http://www.bdlive.co.za/national/2015/04/09/zimbabwe-will-let-rhodes-lie-says-mugabe, accessed 17 September 2015.

13 Although he died in Cape Town, Rhodes, just like many a *makwerekwere* I know, had left instructions to be buried at home, by which he meant, not at Bishop's Stortford in Hertfordshire, England, where he was born on 5 July 1853 to Reverend F.W. Rhodes and Mrs. Louisa Peacock Rhodes (Maurois 1953: 22-23) – a 'very ordinary upper middle-class Victorian family' (Brown 2015: 5), but rather, in Matabeleland, which he had conquered and renamed after himself, where he had chosen a final resting place in the Matopos hills (Stent 1924: 66).

14 See Robert Mugabe, https://adamwelz.wordpress.com/2009/06/04/robert-mugabes-first-speech-in-the-parliament-of-zimbabwe-4-march-1980/, accessed 2 March 2016.

[15] Max Price, Response to Sunday Independent article: 'Adebajo distorts Price's view on Rhodes', http://www.uct.ac.za/dailynews/?id=9068, accessed 6 October 2015.

[16] See http://www.bdlive.co.za/opinion/2015/04/12/rants-and-sense-toppling-statues-wont-change-students-future, accessed 17 September 2015.

[17] See Chinua Achebe's *Arrow of God* 1964, for the proverb which reads: 'a man must dance the dance prevalent in his time' (p.233-34).

[18] See http://www.bdlive.co.za/national/education/2015/03/23/uct-open-to-further-engagement-with-protesting-students, accessed 2 October 2015.

[19] Groote Schuur, translated as 'Great Barn', was 'an old warehouse at the foot of Table Mountain, which had belonged to the Netherlands East India Company', and which Rhodes bought in 1893 (Maurois 1953: 99). Of the Groote Schuur estate, Herbert Bake, Rhodes's architect, notes that Rhodes's dislike of the Boers did not match his love of their art, and that he had 'a deeper feeling of sympathy for the history of the early settlers and of respect for their achievements in civilization' than he did for 'the Victorian art and industrial materialism of his age' (Baker 1934: 25-26). Commenting on Rhodes's decision to maintain the Dutch name and style, Maurois observes, 'It is a strange thing to see how this great English adventurer wanted to link himself to the Dutch, or even pre-historic, origins of the country he had recreated' (Maurois 1953: 99).

[20] This is the name of documentary film by Hubert Sauper, about the Nile perch, which has devastated the lake's other marine life, and is known to eat up its own young ones. However, the Nile perch is as useful as it is harmful; it also happens to be the region's most profitable export. Understandably, everyone with a stake in the market tends to turn a blind eye on the ecological disaster associated with the perch. For more see http://www.darwinsnightmare.com/darwin/html/startset.htm, accessed 13 February 2016. I am grateful to Professor Edward Kirumira of the College of Humanities and Social Sciences, Makerere University, Kampala, Uganda, for inspiring this thought.

[21] See http://allafrica.com/stories/201503230163.html, accessed 1 October 2015.

[22] Njabulo Ndebele, 'Reflections on Rhodes: A story of time', http://www.uct.ac.za/dailynews/?id=9038, accessed 6 October 2015.

[23] See http://www.bdlive.co.za/opinion/columnists/2015/03/24/vrroom-with-a-view-hard-to-explain-away-the-racist-rhodes-was, accessed 30 September 2015.

[24] See http://www.dailymaverick.co.za/opinionista/2015-03-11-ucts-poo-protest-violence-is-a-perfect-reaction/#.VfXL4Jce4TZ, accessed 4 October 2015.

[25] According to John Flint,

Rhodes conceived of a secret elite of white Anglo-Saxons dedicated, like Plato's philosophers, to bringing authority and order to the whole world, ruling other peoples for their own good. These dedicated young men were to be drawn from Britain, North America and Germany, for Rhodes regarded these countries as being not only truly white, but also destined for world rule. This dream he embodied in wills that he wrote and rewrote throughout his life (Flint 1974: xvi).

[26] For an address to the RMF students at UCT by Achille Mbembe, see 'RMF in conversation with Achille Mbembe Part 1', filmed by Wandile Kasibe, https://www.youtube.com/watch?v=g-lU4BCsL8w, accessed 8 October 2015; and 'RMF in conversation with Achille Mbembe Part 2', filmed by Wandile Kasibe, https://www.youtube.com/watch?v=mc4RSN_05ow, accessed 8 October 2015. Mbembe emphasises the need for black South Africans to rise beyond a position of victimhood to a position of strength as the foundation of rising above a society configured around white and whiteness as supreme, to a more inclusive equalitarian dispensation.

[27] See http://africasacountry.com/2015/09/achille-mbembe-on-the-state-of-south-african-politics/, accessed 1 October 2015.

[28] See also slightly different versions of the same paper published in *CODESRIA Bulletin*, No.2, pp.11-15; and at http://ccs.ukzn.ac.za/files/mamdani.pdf, accessed 26 October 2015.

[29] See also http://www.africanstudies.uct.ac.za/sites/default/files/Celebrating%20Africa%202012.pdf, accessed 26 October 2015.

[30] See 'SouthAfrica.info, South Africa's Population', online: http://southafrica.info/about/people/population.htm#introduction, accessed 15 August 2012.

[31] David McDermott Hughes' 'Response to Bram Büscher's Review of Whiteness in Zimbabwe: Race, Landscape, and the Problem of Belonging', in: *Conservation and Society*, 9(3): 259-260, online: www.conservationandsociety.org/text.asp?2011/9/3/259/86997, accessed 30 September 2012.

[32] See Qamran Tabo, Is Love Colour-Blind, http://varsitynewspaper.co.za/opinions/1468-is-love-colour-blind, accessed 12 October 2015. For a related discussion of Eurocentric indicators of beauty in South Africa and elsewhere on the continent, see Nyamnjoh and Fuh (2014).

[33] For some interesting surveys of student consumer practices and spending habits in South Africa, See: http://www.sabc.co.za/news/a/30cb1100485ef7d98081fe5b1218e3e0/Survey-reveals-lavish-student-spending-habits;

http://www.news24.com/SouthAfrica/News/Students-spending-on-booze-bling-and-clothes-20150513;
http://www.moneyweb.co.za/mymoney/moneyweb-personal-finance/students-arent-saving-want-learn-report-shows/;
http://www.702.co.za/articles/3013/students-are-in-debt-and-spending-like-there-s-no-tomorrow;
http://www.studentmarketing.co.za/;
http://www.financialmail.co.za/mediaadvertising/2015/05/21/student-spending-cool-brands-and-trends; accessed 16 March 2016.
[34] Sisonka Msimang, http://www.theguardian.com/commentisfree/2016/jan/07/south-africa-penny-sparrow-apartheid-nostalgia-racist, accessed 2 March 2016.
[35] Shana Genever, http://www.sabreakingnews.co.za/2016/01/04/penny-sparrow-black-people-are-monkeys-tweet-goes-viral/, accessed 2 March 2016.
[36] Sisonka Msimang, http://www.theguardian.com/commentisfree/2016/jan/07/south-africa-penny-sparrow-apartheid-nostalgia-racist, accessed 2 March 2016.
[37] See University assembly: the Rhodes statue and transformation, https://www.youtube.com/watch?v=eWVJnBVnyPc, accessed 7 October 2015. The students who read out these posts requested management to disengage itself through positive action to demonstrate that they were not complicit in perpetuating such racist innuendos.
[38] Sisonka Msimang, http://www.theguardian.com/commentisfree/2016/jan/07/south-africa-penny-sparrow-apartheid-nostalgia-racist, accessed 2 March 2016.
[39] See http://connect.citizen.co.za/39388/sa-reacts-to-gareth-cliff-being-voted-off-as-idols-judge/, accessed 5 March 2016.
[40] Jeff Wicks, http://www.news24.com/SouthAfrica/News/its-just-the-facts-penny-sparrow-breaks-her-silence-20160104, accessed 2 March 2016.
[41] See http://connect.citizen.co.za/39388/sa-reacts-to-gareth-cliff-being-voted-off-as-idols-judge/, accessed 5 March 2016.
[42] Robin Henney, http://www.iol.co.za/news/south-africa/western-cape/your-racism-will-cost-you-your-job-1968851, accessed 2 March 2016.
[43] Deshnee Subramany, http://mg.co.za/article/2016-01-06-questions-about-chris-harts-qualifications-answered-by-wits, accessed 2 March 2016.
[44] See Eusebius McKaiser, http://www.iol.co.za/the-star/why-chris-hart-got-an-easy-ride-1968112 and http://www.fin24.com/Tech/News/black-entrepreneur-editors-defend-chris-hart-20160106, accessed 2 March 2016.
[45] Deshnee Subramany, http://mg.co.za/article/2016-01-06-questions-about-chris-harts-qualifications-answered-by-wits, accessed 2 March 2016.
[46] http://www.fin24.com/Tech/News/black-academic-backs-chris-hart-calls-for-race-dialogue-20160111, accessed 2 March 2016.

[47] Thulani Gqirana, http://www.biznews.com/undictated/2016/01/07/if-this-is-the-revolution-chris-hart-started-hes-given-sa-a-lasting-gift/, accessed 2 March 2016.
[48] See Naledi Shange, http://www.sowetanlive.co.za/news/2016/01/08/velaphi-khumalo-suspended-with-full-pay, accessed 2 March 2016.
[49] Thulani Gqirana, http://www.biznews.com/undictated/2016/01/07/if-this-is-the-revolution-chris-hart-started-hes-given-sa-a-lasting-gift/, accessed 2 March 2016.
[50] See also Thulani Gqirana, http://mg.co.za/article/2016-01-07-hateful-facebook-post-lands-khumalo-in-hot-water, accessed 2 March 2016.
[51] Thulani Gqirana, http://www.news24.com/SouthAfrica/News/khumalo-in-hot-water-over-racist-facebook-post-20160107, accessed 2 March 2016.
[52] See https://www.uct.ac.za/usr/press/2016/2016-02-11_UCTCondemnsHateSpeech.pdf, accessed 16 March 2016. See also http://www.law.uct.ac.za/news/law-faculty-comments-protest, accessed 16 March 2016.
[53] Staff writer, http://businesstech.co.za/news/government/108103/anc-defends-white-south-africans-in-racism-row/, accessed 2 March 2016.
[54] Rapula Moatshe, http://w ww.iol.co.za/news/politics/anti-racism-march-anc-leaders-slam-jz-critics-1987457, accessed 2 March 2016.
[55] Rapula Moatshe, http://w ww.iol.co.za/news/politics/anti-racism-march-anc-leaders-slam-jz-critics-1987457, accessed 2 March 2016.
[56] See http://www.news24.com/Live/SouthAfrica/News/da-is-the-party-of-racists-anc-anti-racism-march-20160219, accessed 4 March 2016.
[57] Rapula Moatshe, http://w ww.iol.co.za/news/politics/anti-racism-march-anc-leaders-slam-jz-critics-1987457, accessed 2 March 2016.
[58] Rapula Moatshe, http://w ww.iol.co.za/news/politics/anti-racism-march-anc-leaders-slam-jz-critics-1987457, accessed 2 March 2016.
[59] Danielle Bowler, http://ewn.co.za/2016/02/01/OPINION-Danielle-Bowler-Coloured-people-are-constantly-reduced-to-tired-stereotypes, accessed 2 March 2016.

Chapter 2

Black Pain Matters:
Down with Rhodes

As mentioned in the general introduction to this book, skin pigmentation may be the starting point of the journeys of power, privilege and opportunity that we undertake every now and then, but privilege, power and opportunity refuse to be confined too narrowly by the diktats of pigmentation. We only need to see the lengths to which the wealthy, white and black alike, are ready to go to put pigmentation in its place (by whitening up or blackening down physically or culturally), to understand our ambivalence and discomfort with letting our nature (as epitomised by appearances) be the final or dominant arbiter of whom we really are. *Makwerekwereness*, like whiteness and blackness, far from being a birthmark, can be acquired and lost with circumstances, by whites and blacks alike, regardless of how they define and identify themselves or are defined and identified by others. As consumers, it would be risky for us to instinctively go shopping for whiteness and blackness respectively among whites and blacks, as every now and again, we are likely to be confronted with the truism that there is a lot more or a lot less to things than meets the eye. If whiteness and blackness were afflictions, burdens or blessings, they are the permanence of no particular pigmentation in a dynamic and interconnected world of ever unfolding permutations of human agency.

This, in my estimation, is what Frantz Fanon draws attention to in the passage quoted earlier from *Black Skin, White Masks*, on how in the Antilles, people define themselves and relate to one another mostly in terms of whiteness, not because they are necessarily white physically, but in terms of how much of the values of social visibility enshrined by and through their encounters with whites, they have acquired or aspire to achieve through self-cultivation and self-activation. This is not limited simply to acquiring, internalising, embodying and reproducing indicators of success and/or the good life prescribed by or associated with whites and whiteness. It is also

59

about imagining and imposing on whites one encounters, one's fantasies of whiteness. As Fanon puts it, every Antillean, however black physically, 'expects all the others to perceive him in terms of the essence of the white man' (Fanon 1986 [1967b]: 63) and in tune with a hierarchy of visibility and credibility championed by real or imagined civilising missions that stretches out across the Atlantic into the legitimators of social visibility at the very heart of the French aristocratic and subsequently bourgeois establishments of which both Norbert Elias (2000) and Pierre Bourdieu (1984, 1996) have written so eloquently. What was frustrating beyond pardon for Fanon, was to have invested sumptuously in whitening up as a young Antillean, only to be made to feel, upon arrival in France from Martinique, that he was nothing but a black skin with a white mask, bearing French citizenship and carrying a French passport, and therefore only marginally different from the absolutely and scandalously depersonalised 'wretched of the earth' (Fanon 1967a) bearing the brunt of French colonialism in Africa. Hence his resolve to harken to the desperate cries of the oppressed and dispossessed over and above the lip service and equivocations on liberation of white French intellectuals, left, right and centre. Freedom for Fanon is freedom from a humanity predicated a priori upon determinants such as race, class, gender, generation and cultural geographies as essences or fixities (Zeilig 2014).

To VS Naipaul, who has chronicled mobility, both social and physical, among Trinidadians of all shades and colours, whitening up is a lifelong aspiration and pilgrimage to the apex of the world as configured and perfected by the imperialism and colonialism of Europeans. At the apex of such racialized imperial and colonial hierarchies are, as Cecil Rhodes makes abundantly clear, the British, tall and proud in divine commitments and achievements – a people and penultimate set of values to be followed unquestioningly by colonial subjects such as Naipaul, even to the point of eternal mimicry and beating the English at the game of being English, as *The Enigma of Arrival* (Naipaul 1987) amply illustrates. To various degrees and gradations, whitening up is a permanent core theme of many of Naipaul's other novels, from *A House for Mr Biswas* to *Half a Life*, through *A Bend in the River*.

However, whitening up, a process and commodity in which many a black man and woman has invested with great distinction (Comaroff and Comaroff 1991, 1997; Erasmus 1997; Magubane 1971; Magubane 2004; Nuttall 2006; Nyamnjoh and Fuh 2014; Ross 2010; Salo 2004), can be a very frustrating pursuit, especially when investors and their desires of whiteness are stubbornly confronted and ignored by white gatekeepers, some of whom have little whiteness to show for themselves despite purporting to be salesmen and women of this prized commodity, but who insist nonetheless on skin pigmentation as the overriding basis of their choices, decisions and discriminations. As Naipaul repeatedly demonstrates in his novels, blacks or non-whites seeking whiteness as do many of his protagonists – entrapped in the web of ever diminishing circles of inclusion in a bizarre bazaar to which many are called but few are chosen or left with clear cut choices – are caught betwixt and between their aspirations for a purportedly universal civilisation that is stiffly oppressive and exploitative, and the pursuit of more inclusive and accommodating ways of being human championed by the very societies and age-old beliefs, traditions and practices they are urged to abandon in a hurry.

Thus, in *A Bend in the River*, Africans are represented as condemned to be 'nothing', unless they 'trample' and 'crush' the past – which 'doesn't exist in real life' but in the 'mind alone' (Naipaul, 1979: 120), by breaking 'free from primitive ties to a doomed continent' with little more than 'bush' to offer civilization (Achebe, 2000: 89–90). If Africa is presented as a hunting ground for treasure hunters, and Europe as the place to aspire to return to with the hunt, Africans who subscribe to such dichotomies between the civilised and the primitive, the sacred and the profane, but feel really let down when they are turned back, or made to feel that however much they seek and invest in whitening up, they can never really qualify to be counted among the truly great races of the world. Try as they may, acquire as much whiteness as they can, dignified inclusion shall mostly elude them, because, in essence, they are not white, pregnant with fantasies of whiteness as they may be. Those blacks or non-whites who aspire to break free through physical, psychological and cultural emigration to the purportedly cosmopolitan metropolitan centres of culture, power and desire of

61

the former colonisers are immediately greeted with ambivalence and ridicule if not outright rejection. This is what happens to Mr Biswas, the protagonist in *A House for Mr Biswas*, who is led to believe that owning a house he can call his own would bring him the personal fulfilment and freedom from the haunting feeling of failure 'to lay claim to one's portion of the earth' by living and dying as he 'had been born, unnecessary and unaccommodated' (1969 [1961]: 14). No amount of flaws was enough to dampen his feeling of ownership, even if he died deeply indebted soon after occupying the house he could indeed call his own, in whatever transient a manner. His is a lesson on the illusions of completeness peddled by a universalism narrowly configured around the worldviews and interests of whites. The idea that whites and the West are at the apex of human civilisation, and that it is only appropriate for them to serve as the one and only model for others to follow, is what makes whites and the West feel they have little to learn from anyone else or from any other part of the world. In this logic, Africa is seen and related to as the scum of the earth, and as desperately in need of an infusion of the capacity to aspire, in order, hopefully, to rise and shine and transform its circumstances in tune with prescriptions from whites and the West as embodiments and centres of the one and only truly universal civilisation.

In terms of physical presence in the metropolis, even when a black person has made it to the centre, such as Marcus from West Africa, who has made it to London in Naipaul's *Half a Life*, the joy of being a white man in black skin is not there for long, because 'The Negro gene is a recessive one' (Naipaul 2001: 95). We are told that in 'the eighteenth century there were about half a million black people in England' who 'all vanished' or 'disappeared in the local population' because 'They were bred out' (2001: 94-95). This does not deter Marcus, a 'very charming, very urbane' man, who is 'dedicated to inter-racial sex and is quite insatiable', from whitening up (Naipaul 2001: 89). This is how Marcus Naipaul captures Marcus's ambitions:

> He is now training to be a diplomat for when his country becomes independent, and to him London is paradise. He has two ambitions. The first is to have a grandchild who will be pure white in appearance. He is half-way there. He has five mulatto children, by five white

women, and he feels that all he has to do now is to keep an eye on the children and make sure they don't let him down. He wants when he is old to walk down the King's Road with this white grandchild. People will stare and the child will say, loudly, 'What are they staring at, Grandfather?' His second ambition is to be the first black man to have an account at Coutts. That's the Queen's bank.' (Naipaul 2001: 89-90).

Colonial encounters and education have played a major role in igniting and keeping alight such ambitions of whitening up through consumption of everything directly or remotely suggestive of whiteness, from white bodies to white minds and the ideas, desires, practices and things they make possible. In his novel *Wizard of the Crow*, Ngugi wa Thiong'o (2007) reminds us just how topical are ambitions and the pursuit of whiteness in contemporary Africa. Ngugi recounts, inter alia, the story of Tajirika, who, upon landing himself three big bags of money in bribe, becomes afflicted by desires of whiteness. He starts 'aching to be white', an affliction so overwhelming that he loses his capacity to voice his thoughts in words. All he can do is repeat the words 'If! If only!' (Ngugi wa Thiong'o 2007: 174) Unblocked by his visit to the Wizard of the Crow, Tajirika is finally able to say the words: 'If ... my ... skin ... were ... not... black! Oh, if only my skin were white!' (Ngugi wa Thiong'o 2007: 179). The wizard diagnosed Tajirika's 'white-ache' thus:

As he [Tajirika] looked into the future, he suddenly realised that at the rate that the money was coming in he would end up the richest man in Africa, and the only thing missing to distinguish him from other black rich was white skin. He saw his skin as standing between him and the heaven of his desire. When he scratched his face, daemons within were urging him to break ranks with blackness and enter into union with whiteness. In short, he suffers from a severe case of white-ache (Ngugi wa Thiong'o 2007: 179-180).

The cure to Tajirika's 'white-ache', according to the wizard, was in Tajirika assuming 'his white destiny', the opportunities and privileges of which he, Tajirika, was not in doubt. Becoming white would entail, among other things, giving up his African name and language, which Tajirika readily did by adopting the name 'Clement Clarence Whitehead' and committing to perfecting his English – the

English of the United Kingdom, and not its inauthentic Americanisation. He also agreed to marry up by marrying white, and to abandon 'black emotion' for 'white logic' in his thoughts and deeds (Ngugi wa Thiong'o 2007: 180-184). When he suggested he would divorce his black wife to marry a white one, the wife, who was listening in, caught the same affliction. 'If my skin were not black would my husband have thought of leaving me? If only I could become white!' (Ngugi wa Thiong'o 2007: 185). At that point, both husband and wife declare: 'We want to be English …. We want a pure English Skin'. (Ngugi wa Thiong'o 2007: 185). They yearn to be real English whites – 'The colonial type, like the ones who used to lord over us', the 'pure white, with their special clubs and attack dogs', 'Lords. Aristocrats. Blue blood' (Ngugi wa Thiong'o 2007: 186). The wizard conjured up an image of them as an English couple, which he described thus:

> I see a silver-haired couple, Sir Clement Clarence Whitehead and Lady Virgin Beatrice Whitehead, holding hands, crossing a road near palace gardens in London, talking about their life in the old colonial days. A pair of authentic colonial aristocracy. They talk of how he was nearly made the governor of Aburira… (Ngugi wa Thiong'o 2007: 187).

The wizard continues with his futuristic diagnosis, which includes the couple heading for 'an old people's home', but still praying for 'the recolonization of Africa', and 'dreaming about the possible return of their good old days of power and glory in Africa' (p.188). Tajirika is tortured by his 'white-ache' until science catches up with his fantasy:

> And then one day at a New York street corner somebody handed him a leaflet, and when he later looked at it he saw that it was an advertisement for a clinic specializing in genetic engineering, cloning, transplants, and plastic surgery. The ad claimed that the company, Genetica Inc., grew all the body parts in its own laboratory and that its very highly trained staff could change anybody into any identity of their desire, quickly and efficiently, without any side effects (Ngugi wa Thiong'o 2007: 741)

Tajirika pounced on the opportunity and before his return to Africa, 'he was the recipient of a white right arm as the first stage in his transformation'. At his next visit to New York, he 'added a white left leg to his one-white-armed body', and, 'Half white, half black, he always wore pants and long-sleeved shirts, and of course a glove on the right hand.' (Ngugi wa Thiong'o 2007: 742). His excitement did not last. His white destiny was not consummated as 'tragedy struck'. He was:

> making preparations to return to America for the other body parts to complete his transformation when he read in a newspaper that the clinic had been closed because it was not licensed. He also read, to his dismay, that the company, Genetica Inc., was bankrupt and under police investigation (Ngugi wa Thiong'o 2007: 742).

Ngugi wa Thiong'o through his writing and storytelling shows that to dream, as Tajirika does, of becoming white is a dangerous and 'unattainable desire, and to yearn for the unattainable to the point of paralysis was indeed an illness that might plague him [Tajirika] for the rest of his life' (Ngugi wa Thiong'o 2007: 180). It could also be argued that what Tajirika really wanted was the power, privilege and social visibility that being white had come to represent. The fact that Tajirika and his wife were ready to contemplate transformation into only a particular type of white – those who had lorded over them in colonial times (the lords, aristocrats and blue blood) – and were determinedly averse to the idea of ending up 'a poor white' (Ngugi wa Thiong'o 2007: 178-188), is indicative that it is more the opportunities, privileges and power made possible by inhabiting a white skin, than the white skin in itself that Tajirika and his wife craved.

It is against this background of various degrees of 'white-ache' or 'longing to be white' (Ngugi wa Thiong'o 2007: 338) by 'a black man celebrating the negation of himself' (Ngugi wa Thiong'o 2007: 208), that no decolonisation would be radical enough without the decolonisation of the bodies and minds of those seeking decolonisation (Ngugi wa Thiong'o 1986). What manner of decolonisation is appropriate for a black person whose self-esteem has been crushed by an obsessive and excruciating desire to whiten-up as the ultimate indicator of achievement and social visibility – an ambition which is masked ad infinitum by a rich repertoire of diversions and rationalisations clothed in the language of freedoms?

As a self-critical struggle for meaning (Hountondji 2002), decolonisation can hardly be a cosmetic gesture, given all the whiteness that Africans have internalised and embody – body, mind and soul – for centuries of unequal encounters with whites, and in view of much of the invention of traditions identified as indigenous, orchestrated in the name of indirect rule through native authorities with little legitimacy vis-à-vis the cultural communities over whom they presided (Mamdani 1996). Indeed, it could be argued, that given the zealousness and fervour with which Africans greet their encounters with difference, tending to accommodate such difference almost with reckless abandon, Africans have probably accumulated and display more whiteness than most whites that they encounter in their lives. I can well imagine many an African totally perplexed by some of the whites they meet, who look and behave in a manner that amounts to bringing whiteness into disrepute: 'What is your business being white, when you have very little whiteness to show?'

In a recent article (Nyamnjoh 2012a) I argued that education is one of the core areas where whitening up takes place in Africa. Rhodes was well aware of this when he provided for the setting up of a Rhodes Scholarship programme in his will, one that would bring students from across the British Empire and the English-speaking world to Oxford University, which in his eyes was the epitome of the superior civilisation of the English race (Brown 2015: 251; Flint 1974: 244-247; Marlowe 1972: 287-294; Baker 1934: 135; Williams 1921: 321). It is hardly an accident that education as an institution has maintained its colonial roots, as most African elites have embraced a Eurocentric index of social visibility and social mobility at the heart of which are Western symbols of achievement and the good life (Fonlon 1965; Magubane 1971; p'Bitek 1989 [1966]). This is captured brilliantly by Lawino, the 'traditional' wife of the 'Western educated' Ocol, in Okot p'Bitek's *Song of Lawino* (p'Bitek 1989 [1966]). To Lawino, 'My husband's master is my husband's husband. My husband runs from place to place like a small boy, he rushes without dignity', doing the bidding of the white man. Rendered blind by the libraries of white men, Ocol has lost his dignity and authority by behaving 'like a dog of the white man', lying by the door to 'keep guard while waiting for

66

leftovers' from the master's table. He has lost his 'fire' and bull-like prowess and has succumbed to living on borrowed food, wearing borrowed clothes, and using his ideas, actions and behaviour 'to please somebody else'. He may have read extensively and deeply and can challenge the white men in his knowledge of their books and their ancestors of the intellect, but to Lawino, this has come at a great price: 'the reading has killed my man, in the ways of his people. He has become a stump. He abuses all things Acoli; he says the ways of black people are black' (p'Bitek 1989 [1966]: 91–96). And if Ocol has chosen the path of passive and sterile subservience, let him not, in frustration, 'shout at me because I know the customs of our people', customs that make him feel so desperately inferior to the white man (p'Bitek 1989 [1966]: 46). I argued that, whatever its justifications in terms of whitening up credentials, the resilience of colonial education in Africa sacrifices local relevance for international recognition. Education allows for the inculcation of facts as knowledge. Through its formalisation of teaching and learning, it produces sets of values used to appraise the knowledge in question. As I indicated:

> When the values are not appropriate or broadly shared, the knowledge acquired is rendered irrelevant and becomes merely cosmetic or even violent. In Africa, the colonial conquest of Africans – body, mind and soul – has led to real or attempted epistemicide – the decimation or near complete killing and replacement of endogenous epistemologies with the epistemological paradigm of the conqueror. The result has been education through schools and other formal institutions of learning in Africa largely as a process of making infinite concessions to the outside – mainly the Western world. Such education has tended to emphasize mimicry over creativity, and the idea that little worth learning about, even by Africans, can come from Africa. It champions static dichotomies and boundedness of cultural worlds and knowledge systems. It privileges teleology and analogy over creative negotiation by Africans of the multiple encounters, influences and perspectives evident throughout their continent. It thus impoverishes the complex realities of those it attracts or represses as students (Nyamnjoh 2012a: 129-130).

The insistence of zero sum games of whitening up means that only through despising their very own ancestral customs and worldviews, in favour of foreign customs little understood, admired or desired locally, do African elites seeking the contrived modernity of colonial education hope to attain visibility in the eyes of their white superiors. In this regard, colonial education did not discriminate between those of noble birth and the commoners of the different cultures it encountered. It made 'dead fruit' even of the sons of chiefs, who behaved 'like foolish… little children' towards their past and the ways of their land (p'Bitek 1989 [1966]: 12) – including rejecting meaningful local names and adopting 'the names of white men' that all sounded like 'empty tins, old rusty tins thrown down from the roof-top' (p'Bitek 1989 [1966]: 62), attracting songs of laughter instead of songs of praise. It was an education to cultivate a 'bitter tongue' – 'fierce like the arrow of a scorpion', 'deadly like the spear of the buffalo-hornet', 'ferocious like the poison of a barren woman', and 'corrosive like the juice of the gourd' – vis-à-vis one's past, one's traditions, one's people, one's relations (p'Bitek 1989 [1966]: 12–14). Those emasculated and neutralised by colonial education in turn seek to neutralise and emasculate all those and everything around them. They fancy and favour imported thinking and things in their European greenhouses under African skies.

This zero sum game of whitening up, to Lawino (p'Bitek 1989 [1966]: 25–41), was unacceptable: 'My husband, I do not complain that you eat white men's foods. If you enjoy them go ahead! Shall we just agree to have freedom to eat what one likes?' Lawino commented how Clementine, her husband Ocol's girlfriend, wore 'the hair … of some white woman who died long ago'. Little wonder that Ocol and Clementine in p'Bitek's (1989 [1966]) *Song of Lawino* – the 'modern' educated man and woman à la Cecil Rhodes and his Scholarship scheme for an Oxford education – are incapable of producing or reproducing anything of substance, preoccupied as they are with ostentatious consumption (ballroom dances, white people's foods, dressing and speaking like whites, naming themselves after and following the religion of whites) to demonstrate the value of so-called 'modern education'. The 'thirst for ease', 'craving for luxury', and 'itch to get rich quick' are still 'running riot everywhere' (Fonlon 1965: 23–26), despite herculean needs for social transformation. Few cases of radical nationalism have survived neutralization after independence (Fanon 1967a:

118–165), as colonialism has always succeeded in staying on despite its formal ending. In South Africa, the achievements of Steve Biko and his 'Black Consciousness' movement in using the popular creativity of everyday life (music, song, poetry, etc.) in classrooms, churches, neighbourhoods and townships as effective resources in anti-apartheid struggles, in the promotion of knowledge of protest history, and in affirming the integrity and humanity of marginalised black masses and their cultures (2004 [1978]; Pityana et al. 1991; Malusi and Mphumlwana 1996; Mngxitama et al. 2008a), seem to have suffered a major reversal under the new, negotiated post-apartheid dispensation (Ramose, 2003, 2004, 2010; Mngxitama et al. 2008a, 2008b; Gumede and Dikeni 2009). This is a fate not dissimilar to that of other anti-colonial and resistance movements in Africa and beyond, where aspirations for liberation and self-determination have almost invariably been watered down to accommodate continuity for the value system and interests of the dominator, who champions divide and rule to compound the predicaments of the marginalised masses (Nyamnjoh 2012a: 132 - 133).

Education in Africa is still the victim of a resilient colonial and colonising epistemology, which takes the form of science as ideology and hegemony. It is an education which is impatient with conviviality. By conviviality I understand involving 'different or competing agentive forces which need a negotiated understanding' that privileges 'the spirit of togetherness, interpenetration, interdependence and intersubjectivity' (Nyamnjoh 2002: 111-112). Just as Arthur Schopenhauer's porcupines are compelled to keep their quills in check in the interest of huddling together for warmth in winter (Farmer 1998: 422), conviviality makes interdependence possible amongst humans, whose tendency is to seek autonomy even at the risk of dependencies. Of course, members of the postcolonial African elite often justify the resilience of the unconvivial colonial epistemology and the education it inspires with rhetoric on the need to be competitive internationally and relevant to the needs and expectations of their captive humanity, institutions and ways of life. As I argued:

Despite some encouraging examples, calls to rethink education in Africa are yet to be translated into action in any significant way. Education in Africa and for Africans continues to be like a pilgrimage to the Kilimanjaro of metropolitan intellectual ideals, but also the tortuous route to Calvary for alternative ways of life (Mazrui, 1986, 2001; Ngugi wa Thiong'o, 1986; Copans, 1990; Mamdani, 1990, 1993; Rwomire, 1992; van Rinsum, 2001; Ramose, 2003, 2004). The value of education in postcolonial Africa can be understood in comparison with the soft currencies of the continent. Just as even the most stable of these currencies is pegged and used to taking nosedives in relation to the hard currencies of Europe and North America, so has the value of education on the continent. And just as African presidents prefer to beg and bank in foreign currencies – ignoring even banknotes that bear their own faces and stamp of omnipotence – so is their preference for the foreign intellectual and expert over homegrown expertise. With rhetoric on the need to be competitive internationally, the practice since independence has been to model education in Africa after educational institutions elsewhere, with each country drawing from the institutions of the immediate past colonizer, and from the United States of America (USA) and Canada (Crossman and Devisch, 1999: 20–23; Mazrui, 2001: 39–45). Universities are internationally rated using criteria which few universities in Africa have contributed to establishing, but to which they subject themselves. African universities push lecturers to publish in international journals yet do little to promote journals of the continent. In selecting a university, students consider the universities where their lecturers obtained PhD degrees, and (in South Africa) may consider criteria like catering and parking services, but hardly the relevance of curricula to local needs (Jansen, 2011: 10–153).

The elite have, just as in colonial times, 'often in unabashed imitativeness' and with little attempt at domestication, sought to reproduce, even without the finances to sustain their efforts, the Oxfords, Cambridges, Harvards, Stanfords and Sorbonnes of England, the USA and France (Mazrui, 2001: 39–38). Some, like the late Presidents Banda of Malawi, and Houphouet-Boigny of Côte d'Ivoire, sometimes carried this craving to ridiculous proportions, seeking to be identified by europhilia in education and consumption. Education in Africa has been and mostly remains a journey fuelled by an exogenously induced and internalized sense of inadequacy in Africans, and one endowed with the mission of devaluation or annihilation of African creativity, agency and value systems. Such 'cultural estrangement' in the place of cultural engagement has served to reinforce in Africans self-devaluation and self-hatred and a profound sense of inferiority that in turn compels them to 'lighten their darkness' both physically and metaphorically for the gratification of their colonial and postcolonial overlords (Fanon, 1967a: 169, 1986

70

[1967b]). Nyang has described this predicament as 'a pathological case of xenophilia', whereby Africans are brought to value things foreign 'not for their efficacy but simply because of their foreignness' (Nyang, 1994: 434) and persuaded to consume to death their creativity and dignity, their very own humanity (Soyinka, 1994). This is carried through by students privileged to be part of exchange programmes involving African and European or North American universities. In these programmes, African students are only too ready to downplay their home institutions and professors, as they shop up for recognition by their European counterparts. The inverse experience of European and North American students is equally telling.

This cultural uprooting of Africans has been achieved literally by uprooting children of the well-off from their communities and nurturing them in boarding schools, 'almost like potted plants in greenhouses' (Mamdani, 1990: 3), while relegating the children of the poor to what in South Africa has come to be known as 'bantu education' (Ramose, 2003, 2004, 2010; Jansen, 2011: 31–153). In the long run, neither the children of the lowly and poor, who in effect cannot afford the same chance to excel in this type of xenophilia, nor the children of the well-off schooled in such appetites, are in a position to contribute towards reflecting the complexity, dynamism and creativity in being African (Nyamnjoh 2012a: 37-38).

The outcome is often a devaluation of African creativity, agency and value systems, an internalised sense of inadequacy and a perpetuation of the oppressive system through a culture of dependency championed by whitening up as an eternal pursuit. The problem is only compounded by the fact that Africans have placed and continue to place a very high premium on getting educated in the West or in local variants and franchises of European and North American institutions. This is the case with South Africa, where:

despite numerous local universities and a relatively long history of university education, a doctorate from Britain or the USA is still valued higher than anything obtained locally. Like other Africans, South Africans instinctively ask one another or others: 'Where did you do your degree?' Depending on the university you name, you could be treated as a superior, an equal or an inferior by a fellow academic. Some Africans would rather graduate from Oxford, Harvard or the Sorbonne, even if this means changing their specializations to accommodate the limited academic menu offered in these heavyweight Western universities. Africans continue to flood Europe and North America to research aspects of their own countries, mostly for the prestige and status that studying abroad

71

brings, only to end up as 'disillusioned' (Nyamnjoh, 2007) and 'incomplete' Africans. Parents continue to send their children to Europe, North America and elsewhere for education, with the conviction that a degree even from a commercialized and second-rate Western university is worth a lot more opportunities than one from a purportedly top university in Africa, unless such African universities are those generally perceived to be Western universities in Africa, such as some in South Africa. Could this extraversion and xenophilia in matters educational explain the inability to radically transform curricula even when their irrelevance is widely recognized? Could this also explain the often ludicrous obsession with maintaining without problematizing inherited 'standards'? (Nyamnjoh 2012a: 143).

It is against this perpetual and consistently perpetuated sense of inferiority and inadequacy that black students in South African universities decided to protest, twenty one years into the post-apartheid dispensation that was meant to have redressed the situation.

The demand for Rhodes's statue to be removed from the UCT campus may have taken many by surprise, but the statue's inconvenience as a blot on the intellectual landscape of the university had been noted and expressed in the past, since at least the years of the Archie Mafeje Affair – when the university of Cape Town rescinded his appointment as senior lecturer in social anthropology in 1968, claiming pressure from the apartheid state, a decision that was roundly criticised (Hendricks 2008; Ntsebeza 2008) – in the late 1960s, even if its removal had never before been formally requested. The RMF protest began on 9 March 2015 on UCT's Upper Campus[1], while the VC, Dr Max Price, was away in Dakar, Senegal, attending the African Higher Education Summit.[2] In her capacity as the acting VC, Deputy Vice-Chancellor (DVC) Sandra Klopper issued a statement on the protest action. She condemned in the strongest terms as 'unacceptable' and 'reprehensible' the actions of 'An individual among the protesters [who] threw excrement at the statue of Cecil John Rhodes.' She concluded her statement with the reiteration that 'UCT endorses freedom of expression. We encourage open debate, as all universities should do, and urge our students and staff to participate in discussions that contribute to responsible action.'[3]

The 'individual' who threw a bucket of human excrement at Cecil John Rhodes's statue was not quite acting as an individual. Apart from the fact that some students reportedly followed his example by throwing urine and pig manure at the statue, while others covered it with a white cloth, 'as if to hide the imperial stain',[4] Chumani Maxwele, the 'individual' referred to by the acting VC, viewed himself as acting on behalf of a group of students who saw themselves as products of a history and sociology of collective debasement, violation and victimisation by outsiders – powerful, 'influential people ... to be feared' – who came flying aeroplanes and claiming the status of superior beings and bearers of superior values.[5] He argued that black students would not want to study in a university suffocating with relics of colonial plunder, including having to graduate in a hall named after the imperialist, Leander Jameson, more than two decades into a democratisation process that should already have proven itself by darkening some of the landscape with images and representations (of ideas and ideals, heroes and heroines – dead or alive, individual or collective) that black students could relate to.[6] The students had had enough of repeated claims that transformation cannot happen overnight, as if the institution were some sort of science-fiction setting where a night is longer than 21 years.

Maxwele was that 'individual' who refused to be treated simply as *an individual*. There was little provision in his upbringing for frivolous claims of individuality. As the son of a poor miner from the Eastern Cape, he was a stranger to power, 'something Maxwele had only glimpsed at a distance, wielded by South Africa's apartheid state'.[7] It did not come naturally for someone who could neither find employment in Delft nor in next door Khayelitsha as a young man reduced to sharing intimacies with excrement, to see himself as self-made, and as schooled in rational choices with predictable outcomes. From Maxwele's subsequent pronouncements, to smear Rhodes with excrement was a sort of balancing of equations, an invitation to experience, however momentarily, how those in Khayelitsha lived in communion with excrement and often reduced to excrement themselves – the Khayelitsha that supplied maids and cleaners to Rhodes's descendants who proliferate the suburbs of Rondebosch and Claremont, the neighbourhood of UCT.[8] This is a neighbourhood much preoccupied with keeping 'bin miners' and 'garbage mining' at bay. An article – 'Don't invite bin miners' – warns residents of Rondebosch against enticing garbage miners by putting their wheelie bins outside the night before refuse collection day. According to the article, 'Garbage mining by people who come into the area in large numbers searching for recyclable materials … makes the place untidy and puts properties at risk'.[9] Shirley Aldum of the Rondebosch Community Improvement District adds:

> Garbage miners scrape through the bins, removing everything. Papers are left flying and they are messing up the street. As long as garbage bins provide a source of income to miners, it complicates efforts to deal with homeless people and theft out of cars. Petty thieving, like stealing outside lights, brass numbers and post boxes, will continue, often leading to more serious criminal activity in the area…
> [….]
> It's not safe to leave your bin outside for long. It can be used as a ladder and the miners jump to people's properties and steal. We should all act responsibly and not invite people to the area. This is something that we can avoid, so we have to work together to make the area clean and to avoid petty stealing…[10]

In a context where and to people for whom excrement is a permanent blot on the landscape, it becomes pretentious to cultivate a sense of decency or *ordentlikheid* (Salo 2003, 2004; Jansen 2008; Ross 2010) that ignores the ubiquity of excrement as part and parcel of what it means to live the life of a devalued and debased humanity. The gentility, respectability, responsibility, cleanliness and neatness needed for the decency of being human in the manner of the white-dominated suburbs of sumptuous superabundance are not to be found in the 'impoverished and improvisational conditions of daily life' (Ross 2010: 36, 2013) in violent, peripheries such as Khayelitsha and Delft, where Maxwele and the majority of black South Africans learn to cope daily with unfulfilled dreams of whitening up to give mean to their status of bona fide South African citizens, and of sons and daughters of the native soil.

As Eve Fairbanks notes, in Khayelitsha, 'a black-only settlement, built on sand', Maxwele discovered that people loitered on the streets because there was hardly room to stand up in their dark, claustrophobic shacks. Families defecated in plastic boxes collected once a week by the municipality. While the boxes sat by the kerb, children played around them. In the winter, a bluster of whipping wind and sideways-slanting rain, Khayelitsha flooded, and sometimes the makeshift shacks dissolved wholesale, their tarp roofs and cardboard-box sidings disintegrating like sandcastles in a heavy wave.[11]

The precarious sanitation of Khayelitsha is by no means unique more than two decades into post-apartheid South Africa. Indeed, some would argue that Khayelitsha is much better off with its boxes than other parts of the country. The continued existence of informal settlements without basic facilities, such as running water or decent public toilets, electricity, or decent sanitation, and with mass unemployment and millions still living below the R422 per month poverty line, means the majority of South Africans have yet to experience in real terms the comforts of freedom, human rights, democracy, citizenship and dignity promised by their unique Constitution. Basic facilities, such as running water and decent toilets, complementary to the comforts of freedom, for example, are luxuries that some informal settlement residents rarely experience. Many of these residents find alternative means of 'comfort' in this regard, using buckets to both harness water from (functional) communal taps and to relieve themselves (Pillay et al. 2013).

Crystal Powell, who did ethnographic fieldwork for her doctoral research in Langa township from 2011 to 2014, describes her experience of using a bucket in this way for the first time:

> While standing in the middle of the shack I realized that I had to use the bathroom… There was no bathroom. This was not a house. It was a shack. The bed, kitchen and sitting room were all one in the same. Where did I expect a bathroom to be? There were several women in the house and one of them motioned to another to get the bucket…There was a light yellow liquid already in the bucket. It did not look like urine though. My guess was that it was a cleaning detergent diluted with water. She placed the bucket on the floor in the middle of the shack. There was too short a window between the time the bucket was placed on the floor and when the other women began turning their backs to

give me privacy before I could object. I was uncomfortable... It seemed to be a natural experience for them and I did not want to draw any more attention to myself. The women talked as I urinated. The sound of my urine entering the bucket seemed excruciatingly loud amongst the talking voices and I was embarrassed though no one else seemed to be. When I was done I asked...can I have some toilet paper? At this question, the same girl who got the bucket frowned. I could not tell if it was a 'now I have to go find some toilet paper' frown or an 'oh no, we don't have any toilet paper' frown. Regardless of what she was thinking I was huddled over the bucket with my pants down and my knees bent and I wanted someone to give me something to clean myself so I could get out of the situation. She left the shack and came back quickly enough... I cleaned myself and happily pulled my pants up.[12]

As anthropologist Harri Englund reminds us, 'contemplating human rights in the abstract is a luxury that only the most isolated occupants of the ivory tower can afford' (2006: 47). Such abstraction, he argues, 'serves elite privileges rather than the democratic expectations of rights talk' (Englund 2006: 49). Claiming rights in abstraction often entails denying rights (what, for example, are the implications of claiming a middle class existence in a post-apartheid South African context where most cannot begin to aspire even to belonging to the rudimentary stages of the working class, because of indifference to desperate calls for a measure of redistribution?). Experiences like Powell's are commonplace in post-apartheid South Africa, arguably the most unequal society in the world (Pillay et al. 2013). Writing in the *Cape Times* in 2011, anthropologist Steve Robins argues that toilets were used as 'political dynamite' during election campaigns in townships such as Khayelitsha, where residents who 'had to relieve themselves in buckets and plastic bags, and threw these bags, 'flying toilets', into the wetlands where it was not possible to build houses', were determined to 'render Cape Town ungovernable until service delivery needs in informal settlements were satisfied.'[13] Even those of them upgraded through provision of portable toilets by the city council, 'complained that these portable toilets "cause a smell in the houses. It's unhygienic to live with poo inside the house... It remains in that container and that's why it causes that smell"' (Robins 2014: 1). Subsequently, to draw attention to their 'poo'

76

plight, community activists from Khayelitsha took their 'politicisation of shit' to strategic public places around the city of Cape Town. As Robins recounts, they were 'hurling portable toilet containers filled with faeces onto the N2 highway, in the departures section of the Cape Town International Airport, and on the steps of the provincial legislature.' By so doing, the 'faeces flingers from the urban periphery literally dragged the stench from the shantytowns to Cape Town's centres of political and economic power', compelling, as one of them put it, 'the people who are living in those nice [upper middle class] areas like Constantia to feel how poo can damage your life when it is next to you' (Robins 2014: 1). Maxwele reiterated this when he reposted following condemnation of his smearing of Rhodes's statue with excrement. Responding to a journalist, he said: 'We want white people to know how we live. We live in poo. I am from a poor family; we are using portaloos. Are you happy with that?'.... 'I have to give Cecil John Rhodes a poo shower and whites will have to see it'.[14]

To Maxwele and his generation, the idea of 'Freedom' as Fairbanks writes, 'was an illusion, a promise heard but not truly experienced – fresh new clothes that concealed the dogged persistence of humiliations from the past.'[15] A black South African politics student at UCT who was no stranger to protests, Maxwele, regarded as a most inconvenient youth in many a conservative circle, saw himself as a spokesperson for an intellectually and emotionally wounded black community of students, and by extension the rest of black South Africans who were yet to feed on the purported fruits of liberation. Whether or not the anger and frustration and demand for which he served as a vehicle was 'the result of an inculcated sense of entitlement born of expectation',[16] Maxwele and his fellow student protesters were determined to break their long silence and make themselves heard by whatever means necessary.

As Kuseni Dlamini, a Rhodes Scholar, captures it, the 'protests reflect South Africa's unfinished business', reminding South Africans of 'the burden of our history that could not be wished away with the ushering in of the new constitution which guarantees everyone freedom and equality', and 'tell us that fundamental freedoms without inclusion and benefit from the economy and society are insufficient to guarantee all citizens a feeling of belonging and empowerment'.[17] Maxwele was acting on behalf of the black majority described by journalist Greg Nicolson as still having a most raw deal in the new South Africa. He writes that statues of figures such as Rhodes and Paul Kruger are only 'a symbol of all that remains to be done, of real transformation':

> We still operate on the unequal and bigoted socioeconomic conditions generally talked about in the past tense. In schools, universities and workplaces black people still face hurdles that white people don't and many whites refuse to adjust their perceptions of race to put themselves on an equal footing. Despite hundreds of years of oppression against blacks, whites often see affirmative action initiatives as an injustice, even though the large majority of black people still face systemic challenges just trying to work towards a sustainable and dignified life.
>
> Over 20 years into democracy, after hundreds of years of brutality, things haven't changed fast enough. The ANC [African National Congress] could have done better, clearly, but spaces described as the avenues to opportunity, universities and professional workplaces, remain white, exclusive, often only tolerating a rainbow-nation-trickle of blacks who face extra hurdles. If they fail, their performance reflects a race. If they succeed, well, what an exception!
> [....]
> While almost everyone seems to want change, they want it without fuss, without shaking the status quo. They want to open a conversation (maybe an inquiry?) within the current system while their symbols of being remain untouched. But that leads to stasis, as it has, with the idea of transformation dropped into white noise.[18]

Maxwele and his fellow protesters recognised the importance of symbols as 'vessels of identity and knowledge of the collective and its power', and as things that 'emotionally [tie] us to who we think we are, where we've come from, and what we represent.'[19] In his repeated statements on the apparently disgusting gesture, Maxwele reiterated that pouring excrement on the statue was intended as a metaphor 'to explain our collective black pain', and to express 'our collective disgust'[20] at the resilience of colonial education and symbols and institutional racism at UCT and in the country at large. He had acted for those perplexed by the fact that, so little transformation had taken place in a university that claimed post-apartheid credentials and loved to portray itself as Africa's premier university[21]. Indeed, the situation had remained the same[22] – some would say it had worsened – since Mahmood Mamdani's experience (1996–1999) of the institution's lack of an Africa-focused intelligentsia and hostility to Africa-focused thought (Mamdani 1998a, 1998b), captured in the following words:

> At the University of Cape Town, I witnessed a university administration that paid lip service to 'transformation' but was so terrified of losing control of the process of change that it came to see any innovative idea as a threat to its position and power (Mamdani 2007: xiii).

A talk presented at the University of KwaZulu-Natal (UKZN) is particularly revealing of the resistance and uphill battle that Mamdani faced while trying to go beyond a lip service approach to teaching and studying Africa in a predicament-oriented fashion at UCT. An excerpt of the talk reads:

> I was appointed as the A.C. Jordan Professor of African Studies at the University of Cape Town in September of 1996, and then as Director of its Centre for African Studies in early 1997. I spent my first year startled that I had only one colleague and no students in the social sciences. I wondered to whom I was supposed to profess. When I shared this thought with a senior administrator, suggesting that surely the decision to appoint a Professor of African Studies must have been taken as part of a larger decision to create a core faculty in African Studies, he did not disagree, but advised me to wait until one of the people in the larger departments in Arts either died or retired to press for more intellectual resources. The thought did occur to me that I may have been hired as an advertisement, a mascot for the Centre for African Studies, and that I should not take myself too seriously. But I shoved this thought out of my mind as soon as I became conscious of it.
> The Centre, I realised, was mainly an extra-curricular affair. I could and did organise conferences where South African intellectuals could meet counterparts from the equatorial African academy, as in March and October of 1997, but this left untouched the key problem of the Centre: that it was totally marginal to the real work of the university, teaching and research.
> Then came an opportunity that I thought would surely provide me a way out of this dilemma. It was October 1997, and I was by now over a year old at UCT. I was approached by the Assistant Dean of the Faculty of Social Sciences and Humanities, Associate Professor

Charles Wanamaker from the Department of Religious Studies, who informed me that the Faculty was taking a bold new step to design a Foundation Semester, one which would be compulsory for all entering social science students. The core of the Foundation Semester would be a course on 'Africa'. He requested that I design the syllabus for this course. It seemed a golden opportunity to step out of extracurricular preoccupations and get involved in the mainstream of social science teaching. I decided to seize it with both hands.

I put one request before the Assistant Dean at the outset. I said that even though I considered myself a historically informed social scientist, I would need the help of a historian to do the work well. I added that though UCT had a large Department of History, I think 14 in established posts, it had only one person whose research focus was outside of southern Africa. That was Dr. Shamil Jeppie, whose research interest was Sudan. I concluded that I would need to get the assistance of a historian from the University of Western Cape, and that this person would have to be paid. The Deputy Dean agreed. I went on to secure the support of Dr. Ibrahim Abdullah as a consultant, requesting that he provide me with bibliographical assistance, directing my reading on issues where I felt particularly weak. And then I began work, on the average 6 hours a day for 6 days a week, with a passion that I would say I had not experienced since I left Kampala for Cape Town in late 1996.

In mid-October, I presented a draft outline, called 'Problematizing Africa' to the relevant faculty Committee, and followed with a revised outline on October 30. With the acceptance of the outline, I was asked to come up with appropriate readings and to liaise with a Working Group of three (Digby Warren, Mugsie Spiegal [sic] Johann Graaf) for purposes of implementation. The tussle that followed with the Working Group and the Deputy Dean was one for which I was totally unprepared. As it unravelled, it highlighted issues that I think go beyond my personal predicament: the relationship between the defence of academic freedom and the pursuit of academic excellence, administrative decision-making in academic affairs, and the relationship of pedagogy to content. It is because I believe these issues to be of general concern that I have decided to elaborate them before presenting my review of the substitute course that was put together under the leadership of the same team.[23]

Over a decade after Mamdani had given up and left, Siona O'Connell, a lecturer at the Michaelis School of Fine Art at UCT, expects management to take transformation beyond 'renaming campus roads and commissioning memorials of slave burial sites on

UCT property.'[24] Writing in September 2014, O'Connell argues that as a campus at odds with itself, UCT is:

> trying to make sense of a multicoloured landscape with a dogged determination using the tools, frames and languages of the past. It is a university that has been home to many messy affairs of particularly darker shades, including the Mafeje affair of 1968, the Mamdani affair of 1998 and the Centre for African Studies affair of 2011[25]. One can't help but see a pattern that draws attention to the inability of this university to transform itself as an institution that values all its various publics in a contemporary South African moment that demands a radically new way of thinking if we are to escape a repeat of the likes of Marikana.[26]

Law professor Evance Kalula, director of the UCT International Academic Programmes Office (IAPO), agrees. He regrets the failure by UCT to develop effective support mechanisms to ensure diversity in its programmes and staff. Writing in 2013, Kalula notes that newly recruited promising women and black staff are often 'thrown into the deep end, to sink or swim'. In the Law Faculty where he taught from 1992-2012, the result is that there has been very little effective transformation for twenty years. Black members of staff who have left in frustration have often cited among their reasons for leaving 'a non-supportive environment which at best ignored, undervalued or marginalised them, and in some respects was hostile'. To Kalula, this prevalent 'sense of alienation, marginalisation, exclusion and grievance' shared by black and women staff, creates 'a perception that some colleagues are judged by different yardsticks' – a situation that breeds 'inexplicable mistrust between those perceived as insiders and those who feel they are outsiders' (Kalula 2013: 18-19).[27] As Njabulo Ndebele, argues, it is only by envisioning transformation as the consolidation, deepening, mainstreaming and projection of the 'black' interest in the national life of South Africa, could UCT and all other universities inherited from the apartheid era begin to get right the imperative of inclusive citizenship through an inclusive higher educational system (Ndebele 2007: 165-169).

According to Martin Hall, a professor in the Department of Archaeology when Mamdani was at UCT and who responded in defence of the institution to one of Mamdani's critiques of UCT turning African studies into a new home for Bantu education (Hall 1998), 'Mr Maxwele's protest has electrified longstanding resentments about the ways in which the past is remembered and celebrated. …. Wearing a brightly coloured safety helmet and two placards – 'Exhibit White Arrogance UCT' and 'Exhibit Black Assimilation UCT' – Mr Maxwele emptied his bucket in front of the press, who had been tipped off to attend.' Quoting Nelson Mandela, Hall observes that it is hardly surprising, that South African museums and national monuments should be seen as alien spaces when they have excluded and marginalised most South Africans. It was Mandela's hope that democracy would afford South Africans 'the opportunity to ensure that our institutions reflect history in a way that respects the heritage of all our citizens'.[28]

If one insists that Maxwele was an individual in his action, he was no ordinary individual. His individuality had been crushed by a history of repressive encounters with the violence of dominance which Rhodes and UCT had come to incarnate. The violence of colonialism and apartheid had denied him the luxury of fulfilling his ambitions as an individual. He belonged to that amorphous, homogenous and voiceless darkness whose purportedly primitive savagery and unenlightened circumstances offered a perfect licence for others to invade and conquer with the benevolence of civilised savagery. Such ambitions of dominance did not allow him or any other black man or woman to aspire to be an individual – at least, not on their own terms. How then could he be anything but a collective? If the term 'individual' had to be applied in his regard at all costs, he was more of a composite individual, whose agency, whatever it was, could not rise and shine because others insisted he did not deserve the status of a human being, regardless of what he thought of himself or what he looked like. Whatever he was or wasn't, is or isn't, is aptly captured by the title of Bloke Modisane's book: *Blame Me on History* (Modisane1986 [1963]).

It is thus hardly surprising that Maxwele's views were shared by a 'collective of students and staff working to purge the oppressive remnants of apartheid in pursuit of a truly African university.'[29] Maxwele's reference to *collective black pain* and *collective disgust* was not to deny individual agency and diversity among black South

Africans. Indeed, as Olaf Zenker reminds us of how strategic essentialism was deployed and enacted under apartheid, not all blacks were victims of apartheid to the same degree, just as not all whites were beneficiaries of apartheid in reality, even if in principle apartheid favoured them (Zenker 2015). Similarly, Maxwele's reference to collective black pain was intended as a strategic essentialism (in the struggle for equality, restitution, reparation or redistribution) in the same spirit that essentialisms were strategically deployed in the colonial and apartheid pasts by the imperial and settler white minority as a technology of exploitation, dispossession, debasement and domination (Maldonado-Torres 2007). In many respects, for black South Africans to recognise their own pain, is to have come of age. Under apartheid, survival depended precisely on not dwelling on such pain that fed the repressive machinery of the violent regime and those it benefitted. In the following passage, Modisane gives us insight into how many a black South African coped with such mass produced and zealously disseminated pain under apartheid:

> I have no use for human feelings, I stripped myself of them that day I looked upon the battered remains of the man who was my father; I pushed down the pain, forced it down, refused to cry and never cried since; every pain, every hurt, every insult I pushed down and held down like vomit; I have graduated bloody well, I cannot feel anything, I have no emotional responses, I am incapable of being humiliated, I have long ceased to experience the sensation of feeling a hurt. I am a corpse (Modisane 1986 [1963]: 77).

For blacks actually to own up to pain on the bodies which are 'monuments of centuries of torture'[30] in the way Maxwele speaks about can only be explained by the likelihood that they must have invested much hope and aspiration in the declaration that apartheid had come to an end and that its victims could now dream about reactivating their humanity. To feel pain is to have hope, and to believe that human agency can result in creative innovations. And to endure pain is to be able to look beyond your reality and to be willing to seek out a better version of the present. Yet, if such hope is repeatedly frustrated even as freedom is celebrated, one is entitled to pinch oneself every now and again with the question, 'Are you free or are you dumb?' in the manner of the Vodacom advert for its Night Shift subscription service.[31]

This is how Mbembe understands the current urgency and impatience in clamours for decolonisation by the RMF and related movements, spearheaded by the eruption of rights-claiming and rights-denying wounded bodies, piling up, swearing and cursing, speaking with excrements and in allegories and analogies, demanding to be heard. Thus to Mbembe, what we are hearing from the protesting students 'is that there has not been enough meaningful, decisive, radical change, not only in terms of the life chances of the black poor, but – and this is the novelty – in terms of the future prospects of the black middle class.' The students are impatient about the fact that, more than 20 years into the so-called free and new dispensation, South Africans have yet to disrupt 'enough the structures that maintain and reproduce "white power and supremacy"', and which ensure that the mostly black majority continue to be 'trapped in a 'bad life' that keeps wearing them out and down.' They are revolting against the terms of engagement dictated to them, terms that have only compounded their predicament.[32] The students are voicing in no uncertain terms their dissatisfaction with the lacklustre manner in which those in charge have gone about the business of transforming a skewed, racialised South Africa into an inclusive, egalitarian country.

To Mbembe, the anger and impatience of South African youth should be read as an accusation that those charged with transformation:

> have not radically overturned the particular sets of interests that are produced and reproduced through white privilege in institutions of public and private life – in law firms, in financial institutions such as banking and insurance, in advertising and industry, in terms of land redistribution, in media, universities, languages and culture in general.
>
> 'Whiteness,' 'white power,' 'white supremacy,' 'white monopoly capital' is firmly back on the political and cultural agenda and to be white in South Africa now is to face a new-old kind of trial although with new judges – the so-called 'born-free'.[33]

Rhodes's statue was attacked as a symbol of Eurocentric, narrow-minded racism, and as a way of drawing attention to the unfinished – and sometimes altogether untackled – business of transformation beyond symbols.[34] Jonathan Jansen, VC of the University of the Free State (UFS) recognised this when he acknowledged in a newspaper column that the protests are about a deeper transformation of universities – including the complexion of the professoriate – that remains largely unchanged.[35] Singling out the English-speaking universities, Jansen elaborates:

> The three English universities in upheaval – Rhodes, UCT and Wits – struggle with second-order challenges of transformation. Having enabled access to black students over the years – also not without a struggle, despite their liberal pretences – the students now rightly demand greater recognition through who teaches them, what is taught, how the past is remembered (symbols such as statues, for example) and how they are made to feel (institutional culture) at universities where they still roam around campus like visitors. This is the heart of transformation, and these universities are only now beginning to realise what anger simmered below the epidermis of the superficial politeness of English culture, and boiled over with #RhodesMustFall.[36]

When in February 2016 the UFS which Jansen heads erupted in violent protests by black students demanding an end to racism, a replacement of Afrikaans with English as the main language of instruction, and his resignation as rector of the university, Jansen issued a detailed and carefully worded statement which he concluded as follows:

> The events of Monday night represent a major setback for the transformation process at the UFS[37]. While we have made major progress in recent years—from residence integration to a more inclusive language policy to a core curriculum to very successful 'leadership for change' interventions for student leaders—we still have a long way to go.
> One violent incident on a rugby field and we again see the long road ahead yet to be travelled. As I have often said before, you cannot deeply transform a century-old university and its community overnight. We acknowledge the progress but also the still long and difficult path ahead. We will not give up.
> We have 32 000 students on our campuses; the overwhelming majority of them are decent and committed to building bridges over old divides as we have seen over and over again. So many of our students, black and white, have become close and even intimate

friends working hard to make this a better campus and ours a better community and country. Like all of us, they are gutted by what they saw on Monday, but the hundreds of messages I received from parents, students, and alumni this past 20 hours or so said one thing—keep on keeping on. And we will.[38]

Adam Habib, VC of Wits, was in agreement that the protests around the Rhodes statue pointed to deeper concerns about race, racism and marginalisation:

> The Rhodes statue was simply a trigger point for a broader unhappiness about race, racism, and marginalisation at the University. The universities, particularly the historically white ones, have been immersed in a bubble. They assumed that their intellectual atmosphere and their middle class constituencies protected them from a social explosion around race. But this was not to be because there is legitimacy to the criticisms of the students. How can there not be when there are universities 20 years after our democracy that still have more than two thirds of their students white? How can there not be unhappiness when there are universities that are organised around racialised federal principles, which when an incoming vice-chancellor tries to change, he becomes subject to attack by external right wing organisations including AfriForum and Solidarity? How can these students not feel offended when even in the more liberal and historically English speaking universities like UCT and Wits, the curriculum is not sufficiently reflective of our history or speaks to our historical circumstances.[39]

In an open letter posted on the UCT website on 19 March 2015, several students wrote that removing the statue would 'end the unreflective public glorification of Rhodes at the expense of the legitimate feelings of those the statue offends on a daily basis.'[40] Social activist and film-maker Gillian Schutte[41] criticises the tendency by the privileged class to react with 'shock and outrage', 'decry the animalistic behaviour of the filthy-bodied, filthy-mouthed, uneducated poor', and criminalise the desperation of the protesting black majority, instead of opening up to understand and address the very conditions of hardship and inequality that have caused the protests, however outrageous. It is all too common, she argues, for the elite of this privileged class to 'use elitist theory to delegitimise the intellectual premise for black protest in supercilious articles brimming with white supremacy masquerading as academic thought.' She labels as 'top-down' and 'infantile' reactions that seek 'to criminalise black struggle and to silence black rage', and condemns the deft insistence by the privileged class on their own meanings and values when black people, suffocated by excessive repression resort to poo protests.[42] On the use of human faeces by historically repressed blacks to make their point to the economically and politically powerful, Schutte writes:

> At a time in our history where the collective is brutally suppressed and black anger is presented on mainstream media as the ultimate violence, the marginalised masses find new and inventive ways to make their grievances heard.
> If this means spewing the human waste which they are forced to live in into the sanitised public spaces of the well-heeled, then we should applaud their bravery and inventiveness.
> In a neo-colonial world order where democracy and human rights for the rich means 'shoot to kill' for the poor, it stands to reason that protest becomes a desperate cry for the recognition of the collective and individual humanity of the disenfranchised.
> Like it or not, defecation is the most visceral and inevitable aspect of being human no matter what your class, race or gender.
> By importing the unfettered faeces of the poor collective, who live with dismally inadequate sanitation, into the deodorised spaces of those who are able to flush their own faeces away in toilets, they are successfully exposing the extreme and dehumanising cruelty of a capitalist system which privileges some and entirely deprivileges others.[43]

Xolela Mangcu, an Associate Professor in the Department of Sociology at UCT[44], has been at the forefront of the call for the injection of a significant number of black South African academics into UCT and other universities in post-apartheid South Africa.[45] At the University assembly to discuss the Rhodes Statue and Transformation at UCT he told the VC: 'Max, I find it racially offensive that whenever the issue of black professors comes up and you are asked about it, the issue of standards must come in.'[46] Nhlapo[47] and many others have subsequently based their arguments on statistics provided by Mangcu. At UCT where by 2013 there were only 48 black South African academics out of a total of 1405 – that is 3 percent, and where not a single full professor is a black South African woman –, black students and staff are expected to bear institutional racism with a stiff upper lip, and to be subservient to the call of an intellectual tradition and logic of practice steeped in colonial symbolism and the celebration of primitive savagery as an essence of being black and African. In a country where by 20 July 2014 only 4 per cent – 194 out of 4000 – of the professors were black South Africans[48], it is hardly surprising that 'one hundred and fifty years of Black intellectual thought remains outside the social theory curriculum in South Africa.'[49]

Mimicry and hypocrisy are central to the game of keeping up appearances in order to be remotely visible as a black member of staff or as a black student. White privilege and arrogance reward with token inclusion those who are able to discipline their true feelings and embrace what they are fed without question. As Amina Mama, former head of the Africa Gender Institute at UCT, argued during a meeting with the 'RMF writing and education subcommittees', given that most vehicles for scholarly communication in South Africa and globally continue to be owned and controlled by whites, it becomes very difficult for writing that challenges colonial thinking and models to be tolerated and made visible.

This predicament was reiterated by 15 RMF students when the Johannesburg Workshop in Theory and Criticism, housed at the Institute for Social and Economic Research (WISER) at Wits made the pages of its *Salon* available to them.[50] T. Gamedze and A. Gamedze titled their introduction to its volume 9 'Salon for what?' and argued that 'to be a radical African intellectual is to challenge, on fundamentally personal, institutional and societal levels', the 'form of alienation that colonial education encourages', and that it is somehow ironic for the RMF students to have to resort to a publication named 'The Salon' to express themselves. That notwithstanding, it is important that they are able to write what they want to write, the way they want:

> We write to assert our humanity as Black people, and to assert that, while the imagination that stems from this unrecognised, in-between condition is indeed flashy, exciting, 'avant-garde'(in its un-investigated-ness) our humanity is at its root. ... we [must] continue to write, and while we must navigate the inevitable 'Salon' of Western

knowledge structures, we are aware that we are writing in ways that these knowledge structures have not prescribed.[51]

We just have a feeling that there is something about writing that allows us to subvert the structures that have oppressed us and continue to do so, and while this space of writing is contested, we are armed to enter this contest in ways that cannot and do not occur to our oppressors. We write different, and so we feel that writing is important. It is important to write ourselves, to write our own story. We know that many, who are not us, have BEEN writing about us and have painted us in many different ways, of which none are creative nor imaginative enough. We are here to represent ourselves and share our thoughts on our situation and on what we are up against. We are thinking about how we might create something new: how we might pursue writing in a way that represents and humanises us as energetic and hurt bodies.[52]

Transformation can only happen, UCT senior lecturer Shose Kessi argues, if black academics and students can unapologetically foreground black pain as a legitimate concern:

The idea of logical reasoned argument outside of affect is nonsensical and serves to legitimise the idea that intellectual projects and academic freedom exist outside of historical structural analyses. It serves as a smokescreen that invisibilises whiteness or white feelings. I cannot count the number of times I have been in classrooms, meetings, and committees where the feelings of white students and staff dominate the space in suffocating ways that exclude and silence — under the guise of 'logical reasoned argument'. The burden of black academics in these spaces is often one of appeasing and negotiation for fear of being dismissed and labelled as irrational, at best, or, at worst, for fear of the white backlash that typically spirals out of control. Black pain and anger is pathologised and condemned whereas white people's anger is cajoled, understood, and considered rational.[53]

Black pain and white privilege are two sides of the same coin. Both are the result of particular encounters in a hierarchized world shaped by ideologies around factors such as race, place, class, gender, education, cultivation and civilisation. In such a world, the pain, poverty and discomforts of the one are actively produced or co-produced by the privilege, pleasure and power of the other. They feed into each other and cause deep wounds to fester (Nyamnjoh

2012a, 2012b, 2013b). White South Africans may not be a unified bloc, but the edification of biological and cultural racism under apartheid made it possible for their collective interests to be privileged, regardless of class, gender, status or the resistance of some against the structures in place (Steyn 2001, 2008). It is in this sense that while appreciating the spotlight on black pain occasioned by RMF and related protests, anthropologist Sakhumzi Mfecane observes that in South Africa, black pain must not be discussed in isolation from the white privilege that makes it possible:

> Black pain is a direct product of white privilege; which makes me wonder why those whites who are supporting black struggle are not speaking out openly about their privilege and its effects on blacks. I just worry that if our analysis focuses simply on black pain, it may reproduce the same problem of rendering blacks as easy anthropological objects of analysis and render whiteness – again – invisible to the anthropological or sociological gaze.[54]

Notwithstanding the merits of Mfecane's remark about privileged whites who pay lip service to solidarity with black pain, once in a while, a privileged white South African speaks out against the comforts of privilege which most seem to take for granted. Justin Foxton, columnist and founder of The Peace Agency, shares a personal account of what it means to be white and privileged in South Africa, when he writes[55]:

> I am tired of the way I view the world as a white person. The more time I spend with people of different colours and cultures the more one-dimensional, overly-simplistic and irrationally self-righteous I realise my worldview can be. To add to this - or perhaps to protect myself from these hard realisations - I have created a life for me and my family that ensures that our access to other cultures is limited at best.
> I am tired of the fact that I say how much I love this country but I have spent so little time actively exploring and participating in the rich and diverse heritage of our people. Opting for the comfort and safety of what is known and familiar I basically live on a cultural island. And yet when I do venture into the unknown and actually spend time interacting outside of my norms, I am humbled - to be honest, broken - by how petty, parochial and self-absorbed I am. My decidedly Western, dualistic view of the world and my neat, judgement-laden boxes labelled things like 'religion', 'meditation',

'time', 'marriage', 'ancestors' etc. are squashed in an instant when I let go and spend some time being with those different to me. And I discover how much I have to learn. This is uncomfortable as I have always viewed myself as 'the teacher'.

I am tired of belonging to a group that feels constantly hard done by. Why can we not see that we deserve to be last because we were first for so long (we still are if we are to be honest)?[56]

Anthropologist Patience Mususa[57], lecturer at UCT until September 2015, agrees with Mfecane when she argues that it is unrealistic to continue to expect the oppressor to undo oppression, with the token evangelical do-goodism of some who have clearly benefitted from the comforts of oppression. Indeed, by mobilising around black pain, and by pushing for recognition of these feelings as a strategy to urge for the change that has not happened, seems to have been the catalyst bringing together multiple experiences of blackness, across class. However, by directing the energies of the cumulative violent history of oppression, once more towards the black body, as a way to legitimate an experience that is clearly materially apparent, she worries is to risk further psychic self-annihilation. In addition, by calling on a genealogy that has most benefitted from this oppression to recognise this suffering, is to legitimate a characteristic of this relationship that is most problematic, as it is one that has continuously sought to deny black humanity. In Mususa's estimation, it is not enough to point out racist discourse or practice. Rather, it is important to put mechanisms in place to make such perspectives much less comfortable. Over and above the bandwagonism of hashtags, Facebook posts[58] and sympathising with black pain, there has not been an adequate enough discussion on how to achieve broad based justice[59] – and on what forms it should take, beyond just free education and nebulous calls for transformation. It is not realistic to hope that co-optation alone of blacks by a powerful hyper-capitalist appeal to consumption, would surface as a solution to the inequalities and injustices plaguing post-apartheid South Africa. Mususa would expect, that – in the manner of one who has tired of their living arrangements, being cramped in a corner, suffocated by the edifice of all that is pressing into them – black South Africans would, instead of crouching further in, disrupt what is crowding

91

them in, and re-arrange for themselves the furniture, rather than waiting for the very people who most gain by an unjust system to direct the process. Also, how does one go about doing so, without adding to the weight of the same sort of dehumanising practices that the institutionalisation of racism has done over the years? She calls for the creation of a just society that does not just re-arrange the furniture to squash some other bodies in the corner, through co-optation of a few into the privileged circles framed by race, place, class, gender and generation, among other factors.

Mususa's argument brings to mind appeals for a universal humanism by thinkers and social critics such as Frantz Fanon, Stephen Bantu Biko, Robert Mangaliso Sobukwe, Winnie Madikizela-Mandela, Miriam Makeba and Fela Anikulapo Kuti that presupposes recognition of black humanity not through the benevolence or magnanimity of the oppressor, but through collective action in struggle. For an oppressed black who cannot rise to challenge his or her oppression is akin to a slave who condones servitude for fear of risking death in quest of freedom.

As Kopano Matlwa's novel *Coconut* demonstrates, growing up black in white suburbs in post-apartheid South Africa is no easy feat or fix as racialized differences and hierarchies are actively contested and reinforced (Matlwa 2007). According to Panashe Chigumadzi, the founder and editor of *Vanguard* magazine, being what is generally referred to in South Africa as a 'coconut' is no reason for one to lose sight of, ignore or dismiss the reality of racism and the protection it affords white privilege to the detriment of blacks seeking redemption for their humanity. Drawing on her personal experience, she explains:

> At the age of six I had already begun the dance that many black people in South Africa know too well, with our names just one of the many important sites of struggle as we manoeuvre in spaces that do not truly accommodate our blackness. I had already taken my first steps on the road to becoming a fully-fledged coconut, that particular category of 'born free' black youth hailed as torchbearers for Nelson Mandela's 'rainbow nation' after the fall of apartheid; the same category of black youth that are now part of the forefront of new student movements calling for statues of coloniser Cecil John Rhodes to fall, and for the decolonisation of the post-apartheid socioeconomic order.

We all know what a coconut is, don't we? It's a person who is 'black on the outside' but 'white on the inside'. This term came into popular South African usage in apartheid's dying days as black children entered formerly white schools. At best, coconuts can be seen as 'non-white'. At worst, they're 'Uncle Toms' or 'agents of whiteness'.

I've chosen to appropriate the term and self-identify as a coconut because I believe it offers an opportunity for refusal. It's an act of problematising myself – and others – within the landscape of South Africa as part of the black middle class that is supposed to be the buffer against more 'radical elements'.

Instead of becoming the trusted mediators between black and white, we are now turning to conceptions of blackness and mobilising anger at the very concept of the rainbow nation. The fantasy of a colour-blind, post-racial South Africa has been projected onto us coconuts, but our lived experiences are far from free of racism.[60]

Anthropologist, Kharnita Mohamed, echoes Chigumadzi's point that admitting to being or being seen as a 'coconut' in South Africa does not and should not blind one to the racism at play, and the fact of whiteness and blackness as social constructions for particular political expediencies. In a blogpost titled, 'I See Coconuts Everywhere', Mohamed argues that:

whiteness and blackness are both lies, that they do not have a real basis in physiology but are socially and culturally constituted. What is also true, is that every one of us is not a real anything but have been forced to act in ways that allow us to be recognised as real. Make no mistake, the white man, during Apartheid, wielding power and using his sjambok and teargas to fatal effect whilst stilling his compassion and empathy or the white woman treating her black maid like an object, is no less wounded than the black body in the crowd and the objectified black woman separated from her family so they may live another day. What is real are the effects of racism and inhumanity. What is real is that we have the agency to become. What is real is that the anti-apartheid struggle was not intended to allow us to become trapped by an opposing racial classification. We live in a world where we are able to transcend racial classifications and not be expected to have our bodies determine our pleasures, dislikes, moralities or even the way we relate to our cultural others, be they coconuts or peaches.[61]

Regardless of the blackness one targets, global or local, national or pan-African, to object to the reference to black pain is to want to erase a history in which blacks were defined and confined through

93

particular encounters as a collective body and not simply as individuals by their colonisers who were armed with ambitions of dominance that were sometimes veiled or disguised by claims of *mission civilisatrice* (civilising mission) and continue to be rationalised by the nebulousness of claims to modernisation, development and globalisation. However loud the silence of some in their apathy to black pain may be, to proclaim this silence in public is to deny that universalisms, if not arbitrarily imposed (such as 'All lives Matter' or '#ColourBlind' in response to 'Black Lives Matter'), are always negotiated and navigated through the encounters of particularisms. Common denominators come not from hiding the personal but from taking personal experiences to the emotive public distilleries of contextually relevant forms of rationality. In the case of South Africa, to doubt black pain is also to force black South Africans to live a post-apartheid lie that the playing field has been levelled and that race and the benefits it accords and denies are no longer important, even as no concerted effort has been made, in real terms, to right past wrongs (Bhana 2014; Gobodo-Madikizela 2003; Haffajee 2015; Mangcu 2015; Soudien 2010, 2012).[62] If a painful past cannot be undone, as Mamphela Ramphele argues, and rightly so, how does one or a collective transcend such a past in a manner that restores and maintains dignity, as well as safeguards a passion for freedom for all and sundry (Ramphele 2013)?

As a numerical majority, black South Africans are miffed by their incapacity to assert themselves in the age of freedom[63]. They are impatient and flabbergasted that whiteness continues to be such a powerful force and to impose its vocabulary of provocation and victimhood on blacks despite political independence. Of the multiple pains blacks succeeded in freezing under apartheid, post-apartheid South Africa seems to have mitigated little more than the pain of political disenfranchisement. It has reawakened material desires and aspirations that had been numbed *à la* Bloke Modisane who is cited above describing numbing as a survival strategy in the days when freedom was an extravagant illusion. Little wonder that the language of black pain now proliferates, especially among those who feel they have invested effort enough at schooling themselves in the values enshrined by the whiteness that has dominated them – body, mind and soul – for so long. What use is it to be termed

94

middle class in post-apartheid South Africa only to be differentiated as 'black' in that middle-classness (Southall 2016) since one, however corrupt in one's capacity to accumulate in a hurry, can hardly measure up to the traditional middle class (white remains firmly white) because of decades (if not centuries) of accumulation and the passing down of wealth through successive generations of the family? And how can black South Africans born post 1994 celebrate the generic category of born-free – those 'raised with almost no direct memory of apartheid's terrors'[64] – when they cannot freely compete with their white counterparts because of persistent material and structural inequalities (Bhana 2014)?[65] If this freedom generation remains committed to a united South Africa, irrespective of continued material and structural inequalities, as Newman and De Lannoy (2013) argue, what would it take for them to fulfil their vision of unity when the wounds of the past refuse to heal? To speak of collective black pain and collective black disgust is to demonstrate that one is not duped by hollow claims of a common humanity and equality for all in a world structured by and around interconnecting global and local hierarchies informed by considerations or categories such as race, place, class, culture, gender and generation. The persistence of racial inequality and racism even among the born-free, the middle classes, and the culturally and racially mixed in South Africa, like elsewhere, shows how deeply embedded and embodied are the concepts of whiteness and blackness, and how they are reproduced or camouflaged with changing contexts (Fanon 1986 [1967b]; Clarke and Thomas 2006; Pierre 2013; Wade 1993).

Bearing this in mind, one can understand how and why Rhodes's statue along with an untransformed UCT was seen by the protesting students as a chilling reminder of a history steeped in blood and ruthless indifference to the humanity of black South Africans. To Maxwele, his generation of black South African students is ready to succeed where its parents failed in tackling white power and privilege until satisfactory concessions are made. Hence, theirs is both a new struggle and the continuation of the struggle for dignity that the previous generation undertook.[66] If a letter addressed to the chairperson of the UCT Council, Archbishop Njongonkulu Ndungane, by another student

Rekgotsofetse 'Kgotsi' Chikane[67], who describes himself as 'a student who wants transformation he can see', is anything to go by, Maxwele's dramatic 'poo' intervention was meant as shock treatment for an institution that has systematically resisted transformation. The letter begins with a series of what the author terms plaguing questions, among which are the following:

> Why must it be that a student at the University of Cape Town (UCT) is pushed to the point of having to throw faecal matter over the statue of Cecil John Rhodes in order to have a conversation about transformation at UCT? How is it that we are now at this point?

Chikane is frustrated by the absence of a plan for real, palpable, honest and meaningful transformation on campus. He is worried about the 'disconcerting' silence of the chair of the UCT Council, a black South African like himself and a man of God, over the 'institutionalised racism' that continues to stand in the way of transformation at UCT. To him, neither the VC nor the UCT Senate can be trusted to lead the process of 'meaningful transformation' in the institution, as the discussion around the transformation of curricula and race relations 'is largely ignored or recklessly diluted by those in decision-making positions.' Policies purportedly aimed at bringing about racial transformation are yet to yield tangible outputs and to have a meaningful impact. UCT has not only failed to transform, it has achieved little in opening itself up to represent black South African aspirations in any significant way. Chikane describes as 'weak' the VC's repeated defence that the university cannot attract quality black South African academics because it cannot afford to offer competitive salaries to entice young black graduates to continue studying. The university is seriously in need of the injection of black academics and African perspectives to disabuse itself of the reputation among students of 'being a European university stuck at the bottom of Africa.' The 'systemic' and 'subliminal' form of institutionalised racism at UCT is, in Chikane's estimation, worse than that in any other university in South Africa. He elaborates:

It is the form of racism that makes you ignorant about your subjugation because you are never challenged to seriously engage on critical matters. It's the form of racism that allows those who enter UCT from a position of privilege to never have to question their privilege. The privilege of being able to walk past a statue of Saartjie Baartman in the library and have no idea that simply placing her on display, with no justification, is an insult to her legacy and painfully offensive to many students.

Like his fellow students, Chikane was totally frustrated with the excesses of the conquering *amakwerekwere* represented by Rhodes and his mocking imperial defiance of black humanity. How could those who had abundantly inherited his tremendous wealth and outlandish privileges and impunities continue to be insensitive to the screaming revulsion the students were displaying to their plight in an institution in which they felt like perfect strangers, *Uitlanders* or *amakwerekwere*? The statue of Rhodes, erected to celebrate an oppressor and imperialist who was able to buy his way into prominence with land and wealth he acquired through dispossession of their forefathers and foremothers, was a symbol of oppression and white privilege – an impediment to real transformation. It was neither here nor there that some of the protesting students had benefited from funding by the Rhodes estate, or that the university was built on land bequeathed to it in Rhodes's will. The protesters were sick and tired of the arrogance of *amakwerekwere* like Rhodes who had turned the bona fide sons and daughters of South Africa and earlier generations of migrants into beggars and strangers, maids and gardeners, miners, garbage collectors and jobless in their own land. Instead of opening up to the idea of a truly inclusive and reconciled post-apartheid South Africa in the spirit of the 'rainbow nation' propagated by the Truth and Reconciliation Commission (TRC), the white establishment had, in the estimation of the protesting black students, clung to their privileges in a business-as-usual sort of way, while paying lip service to transformation.[68] The outcome has been, as comedian Trevor Noah puts it in one of his sketches: 'We [in South Africa] used to be the 'rainbow nation'; now the colours are going their own way'.[69]

UCT Professor of Politics Anthony Butler believes that by 'speaking out frankly about the shortcomings of UCT's transformation strategy', black students were demonstrating 'why they are better placed than their lecturers to understand their own experiences of being black.'[70] They were also offering their fellow undergraduate white students the opportunity to be introspective and contemplate their often taken-for-granted privileges. These privileges include not just their 'affluent suburban backgrounds, well-resourced schools, and the societal dominance of their home languages', but also, and perhaps more importantly, the:

less obvious aspects of their advantage: an expectation that when they underperform it will not be attributed to their race; a capacity to succeed that is not attributed by others to affirmative action; a happy expectation that potential employers will assume they are competent because of their skin colour; and an ease in negotiating the legacies of colonialism and white domination.[71]

The protest spread as more and more students joined, and as politicians, and the media (both conventional and social) became part of the fray. In a statement issued by ANC Secretary General Gwede Mantashe, the ANC National Executive Committee (NEC) 'unequivocally' expressed support for the protesting 'students in their determined demands for transformation at universities across the country.' The NEC declared: 'We appreciate that statues are mere symbols of our racist history and believe that the transformation needed must be concerned with entrenching fundamental and far-reaching structural, systematic and cultural change; reflective of the aspirations and realities of our democratic and non-racial order.' Twenty years into democracy, transformation is a non-negotiable matter of urgency.[72] Higher Education and Training Minister Blade Nzimande, for example, notwithstanding what some might term his modest track record at effecting meaningful transformation of the country's universities, vowed to turn 2015 into a year in which he would 'uncompromisingly' push for the transformation of the country's universities, adding: 'There remains an urgent need to radically change the demographics of our professoriate; transform the curriculums and research agendas; cultivate greater awareness of Africa; eliminate racism, sexism and all other forms of unjust discrimination; improve academic success rates and expand student support.'[73]

Speaking in her capacity as shadow Minister of Higher Education for the Democratic Alliance (DA), Belinda Bozzoli, former DVC for Wits, admits that South Africa still has a long way to go in eradicating racism, and that 'proper reconciliation hasn't been truly achieved yet.' In her view, 'reconciliatory ideas vanished from politics with Nelson Mandela's death', and the purported lack of money for new academic posts in South Africa would make it difficult for universities to open up any time soon to the inclusion of more black South African academic staff.[74]

Meanwhile Mbuyiseni Ndlozi, spokesperson for the Economic Freedom Fighters (EFF) called for the reconstruction of public monuments in non-oppressive ways, adding that the party would continue to 'agitate' and provide 'ideological perspective' on the removal of colonial and apartheid-era statues and monuments. Inspired by the RMF protest, a statue of Paul Kruger was allegedly defaced by members of the EFF in Tshwane, and a memorial statue in Uitenhage Market Square in the Eastern Cape was reportedly set alight by members of the EFF. The student protests had given the party's campaign to remove colonial and apartheid statues and monuments added impetus. It was only logical, Ndlozi argued, that with the end of apartheid, public spaces configured in the image of the repressive forces of the apartheid era be reconfigured to reflect the dreams and aspirations of the new South Africa. Such reconfiguration is all the more imperative, especially in Cape Town where many public spaces continue to reflect grand reminiscences of yesteryear.[75]

Anglican Archbishop Thabo Makgoba of Cape Town was of the opinion that: 'the campaign against symbols of the injustice of our past, along with service delivery protests and public outrage over corruption, reflect the anger of South Africans at the inequalities that continue to plague us.' He called on all and sundry to 'harness the energy being poured into protest into rigorous self-examination and action to expand the current campaigns into a creative, society-wide drive for real transformation.'[76]

The demonstrators mounted an RMF campaign on Facebook and other social media, along with a Twitter account:

#RhodesMustFall.[77] Tanja Bosch, a UCT media and communication scholar, observes that in the RMF campaign Twitter was particularly effective to students as they sought to set the agenda on socio-political issues, participate in discussions on social transformation, and develop a new biography of citizenship marked by individualised forms of activism around a collective project of resistance (Bosch 2016). The 'Rhodes Must Fall' Facebook page – which described the campaign as 'a collective student, staff and worker movement mobilising for direct action against the institutional racism of UCT'[78] – attracted sympathetic posts from far and wide including from student movements in universities across the world.[79] It must be added, however, that not all of the posts were positive, as some students at the University assembly made evident by reading out some of the derogatory posts – posts referring to blacks as monkeys, pigs, primitive savages and morons because 'you can take them out of the bush but you can't take the bush out of them'.[80]

Transformation[81] became the catchword, catchall and catchon about the unfinished recalibration of the hierarchies of humanity that had informed relations, privilege and poverty in apartheid South Africa. In this way, the Rhodes statue was merely an entry point for a series of demands seeking recognition and representation for those who felt hard done by because of the privileges of the white *amakwerekwere* that presided over their destinies, diminishing the self-esteem and sense of identity of especially black students and academics who felt they deserved better especially within a new and purportedly free South Africa.

It is thus significant that many white students initially drawn to the protest persuaded by the general outcry in favour of mental decolonisation and the transformation of curricula and relations within the institution, and the removal of the statue of Rhodes as a symbolic gesture, soon found themselves being made to feel that they were more than a family mourning the death of a loved one. Those who sought to become more deeply involved, were made to understand that their role was strictly limited to one of solidarity and support in a struggle that was clearly black. In other words, they questioned, or were made to question, how it is possible for a *makwerekwere* in the image of Rhodes – a white, born-free or not, local or foreign – to seek to convince anyone that he or she could feel the pain of the oppressed black other, or claim to be in the same boat?

To some black students, whites who joined the protest were merely keeping up appearances, acting as if Cecil Rhodes and his excesses were all that is to blame for the predicaments of black South Africans and black Africans on campus in general. Did they really think that all that was needed was to name and shame Sir Cecil John Rhodes (as an individual, as if he had lived his life entirely as an island with neither ancestry, kin, progeny or relationships with others) – the white *makwerekwere* who debased, humiliated and undermined Africans with impunity so as to appropriate their resources? If Rhodes, however iconic, was the only problem, why did his excesses and material superabundance appear to have trickled down through the ranks and generations, as if flowing in the blood of his white brethren to contaminate even the post-apartheid generation of so-called born-frees? Why did his legacy of a highly concentrated monopolistic economy persist? Why is the economy still firmly under white control? Could the fact – as evidenced by the '#RhodesMustFall', '#FeesMustFall' and '#End Outsourcing'[82] student protests which subsequently rocked universities countrywide[83], dubbed by Achille Mbembe as 'South Africa's Fanonian moment'[84] and by Heike Becker as 'South Africa's 1968 moment'[85] – be blamed entirely on the incompetence and corruption of the new ANC mostly black elite in power as some have tended to insinuate? Is it really satisfactory merely to claim that one is only a beneficiary (reluctant or not) of a history of unequal encounters for which one is absolutely not to blame? As UCT emeritus professor Martin Hall reminds us, in a post-apartheid South Africa with a high and growing level of unemployment and arguably one of the most unequal countries in the world, the 'disruption of teaching, damage to buildings and facilities, clashes and widespread protests' by angry students and overworked and underpaid support staff of public universities cannot be satisfactorily accounted for outside of the history and legacy of apartheid that 'taints all aspects of public life'.[86]

Rhodes may have been 'the incarnation of British imperialism', which he inspired as much as he was inspired by it, and the methods and policies of which he corrupted as much as he was corrupted by them (Marlowe 1972: xiv). However, if Rhodes was an imperialist, his imperialism was not merely a common cold to be wished away with his passing. His imperialism was an entire way of life – an economic, political and cultural system – and way of defining and prioritising humanity in accordance with yardsticks stipulated by the superior civilisation and values of the British race, which Rhodes, in his messianic pretensions, never tired of believing was a truly divine blessing to the world it was preordained to govern (Brown 2015: 103). It was a deliberate policy of Rhodes to acquire new territories where the British could migrate not only for economic opportunities, but to introduce and enforce the superior values of Britain, as a civilising mission both for the colonies and the working and underclasses of Victorian Britain (Magubane 2004). The British migrants or *amakwerekwere* of yesteryear, however much they blame Rhodes for the sins of the past, are still very much part and parcel of post-apartheid South Africa (Haffajee 2015), and many still assume (albeit with the required sensitivity imposed by political-correctness or a desire to fall in line) the purported burdens of spreading civilisation and the superior values of being human to the less endowed of their countrymen and countrywomen in the townships and rural areas.

Notes

[1] See http://www.news24.com/SouthAfrica/News/UCT-students-in-poo-protest-against-white-imperialism-20150310-2, accessed 1 October 2015.

[2] On his return, Price issued a statement on 18 March, detailing the measures and programme of action on the Rhodes statue protests and transformation. See http://www.uct.ac.za/dailynews/?id=9034, accessed 5 October 2015. This is an excerpt of his statement:

> Last week's student protests have resulted in a massive outpouring of anger and frustration – much about the issue of the statue, much more about experiences of institutional racism, aggravated by students' perceptions that they are not being heard, or that their demands are not achieving the response they seek.

There are also similar frustrations experienced by a number of our members of staff. There have also been many voices critical of both the mode of the student protest, and the view that the statue should be removed. Given this recent escalation of debate and protest, I think it appropriate to replace our original programme with a more accelerated process to facilitate a more rapid decision about the statue.

[3] See http://www.iol.co.za/news/uct-rhodes-statue-protest-both-sides-1.1831688#.VfWLGpce4TZ, accessed 17 September 2015.

[4] Adekeye Adebajo http://www.bdlive.co.za/opinion/columnists/2015/03/23/debate-over-rhodes-is-one-of-transformation, accessed 2 October 2015.

[5] See Eve Fairbanks's article with excerpts of an interview with Chumani Maxwele, http://www.theguardian.com/news/2015/nov/18/why-south-african-students-have-turned-on-their-parents-generation, accessed 23 November 2015.

[6] Adekeye Adebajo http://www.bdlive.co.za/opinion/columnists/2015/03/23/debate-over-rhodes-is-one-of-transformation, accessed 2 October 2015.

[7] See Eve Fairbanks's article with excerpts of an interview with Chumani Maxwele, http://www.theguardian.com/news/2015/nov/18/why-south-african-students-have-turned-on-their-parents-generation, accessed 23 November 2015.

[8] See Eve Fairbanks, http://www.theguardian.com/news/2015/nov/18/why-south-african-students-have-turned-on-their-parents-generation, accessed 23 November 2015.

[9] See http://m.news24.com/news24/SouthAfrica/Local/Peoples-Post/Dont-invite-bin-miners-20151102, accessed 7 December 2015.

[10] See http://m.news24.com/news24/SouthAfrica/Local/Peoples-Post/Dont-invite-bin-miners-20151102, accessed 7 December 2015.

[11] See Eve Fairbanks, http://www.theguardian.com/news/2015/nov/18/why-south-african-students-have-turned-on-their-parents-generation, accessed 23 November 2015.

[12] Dr Crystal Powell obtained her PhD in Social Anthropology from the University of Cape Town in 2014. This description is excerpted from her field notes, 'Visiting the Shacks. Notes from the field, Langa township, 15 August 2011.

[13] See Steven Robins, http://www.iol.co.za/capetimes/toilets-that-became-political-dynamite-1.1089289#.VlaTlL-3ud8, accessed 26 November 2015.

[14] See Steven Robins, http://www.iol.co.za/news/back-to-the-poo-that-started-it-all-1.1842443#.VlvZRb-3ud8, accessed 30 November 2015.

[15] See Eve Fairbanks,

103

http://www.theguardian.com/news/2015/nov/18/why-south-african-students-have-turned-on-their-parents-generation, accessed 23 November 2015.

[16] Simon Lincoln Reader, http://www.bdlive.co.za/opinion/columnists/2015/03/27/one-monument-cannot-capture-all-countrys-ills, accessed 3 October 2015.

[17] See http://www.iol.co.za/sundayindependent/rhodes-scholars-play-a-vital-role-in-sa-1.1843802#.VfWkSJce4TZ, accessed 3 October 2015.

[18] Greg Nicolson http://www.dailymaverick.co.za/article/2015-04-09-op-ed-statues-of-thought-and-symbols-of-resistance/#.VfWKb5ce4TZ, accessed 3 October 2015.

[19] Greg Nicolson http://www.dailymaverick.co.za/article/2015-04-09-op-ed-statues-of-thought-and-symbols-of-resistance/#.VfWKb5ce4TZ, accessed 3 October 2015.

[20] http://america.aljazeera.com/articles/2015/4/6/anti-racism-protesters-in-south-africa-take-aim-at-a-statue-with-poop.html, accessed 17 September 2015; see also Chumani Maxwele, 'Black pain led me to throw Rhodes poo', http://www.bdlive.co.za/opinion/2016/03/16/black-pain-led-me-to-throw-rhodes-poo, accessed 16 March 2016.

[21] Amid the protests to bring down the statue, UCT retained its position as the highest ranked university in Africa, giving it the status of the Harvard or Cambridge of Africa, both universities respectively ranked first and third globally, as well as being first-ranked universities in the US and UK respectively. See http://www.destinyconnect.com/2015/05/27/uct-still-africas-top-ranked-university/, accessed 3 October 2015.

[22] See Siona O'Connell, 'UCT: A Campus at Odds with Itself', http://mg.co.za/article/2014-09-08-uct-a-campus-at-odds-with-itself, accessed 17 October 2015.

[23] See http://ccs.ukzn.ac.za/files/mamdani.pdf, accessed 26 October 2015.

[24] Siona O'Connell, http://www.iol.co.za/capeargus/what-uct-s-not-telling-their-first-years-1.1806441#.ViKF1ise4TZ, accessed 17 October 2015. The Rhodes Must Fall protests led to further renaming of buildings, an ongoing process, as evidenced by an update issued on 30 March 2016, 'VC Desk: Naming of Buildings', http://www.uct.ac.za/dailynews/?id=9646, accessed 2 April 2016.

[25] This was when a decision was taken to create a new unit bringing together four departments as sections of the unit – School of African and Gender Studies, Anthropology and Linguistics – a decision widely criticised on Facebook and in the print media by those who perceived it as a ploy to further marginalise African Studies at UCT (see also Ntsebeza 2012).

[26] See Siona O'Connell, 'UCT: A Campus at Odds with Itself',

http://mg.co.za/article/2014-09-08-uct-a-campus-at-odds-with-itself, accessed 17 October 2015.

[27] For a recent debate on transformation in the Law Faculty that echoes Evance Kalula's views, see Yusuf Omar, 'Live Debate on Transformation in Law', http://www.uct.ac.za/dailynews/?id=9552, accessed 28 March 2016.

[28] See Martin Hall, http://www.bbc.com/news/business-31945680, accessed 1 October 2015.

[29] See http://mg.co.za/article/2015-05-14-this-is-the-year-varsities-will-transform-blade, accessed 30 September 2015. See also Eve Fairbanks, http://www.theguardian.com/news/2015/nov/18/why-south-african-students-have-turned-on-their-parents-generation, accessed 23 November 2015.

[30] This is how a female student at the UCT University Assembly: The Rhodes Statue and Transformation described it in a poem when she took the stage to express her frustration at being repeatedly told and expected to forgive and forget her white exploiters and debasers. See https://www.youtube.com/watch?v=eWVJnBVnyPc, accessed 7 October 2015.

[31] The Vodacom advertisement entitled 'Night Shift', which ends with the words: 'Recharge and get 60 minutes free between 12 am and 5 am all week', has an announcer beating an armpit or talking drum, who asks those on a night shift whether they are 'free' or 'dumb'.

[32] See http://africasacountry.com/2015/09/achille-mbembe-on-the-state-of-south-african-politics/, accessed 1 October 2015.

[33] See http://africasacountry.com/2015/09/achille-mbembe-on-the-state-of-south-african-politics/, accessed 1 October 2015.

[34] See Eve Fairbanks, http://www.theguardian.com/news/2015/nov/18/why-south-african-students-have-turned-on-their-parents-generation

[35] http://www.news24.com/SouthAfrica/News/UCT-students-to-protest-over-racial-transformation-20150319, accessed 1 October 2015.

[36] See http://www.timeslive.co.za/thetimes/2015/09/04/The-Big-Read-The-storm-rages-unabated, accessed 3 October 2015.

[37] For the Monday night incident referred to, see Jonathan Jansen, http://www.timeslive.co.za/thetimes/2016/02/25/The-Big-Read-An-assault-on-transformation, accessed 28 February 2016. This is an excerpt of Jansen's report:

> An incident on Monday evening in a Varsity Cup rugby match between the Madibaz of the Nelson Mandela Metropolitan University and the Shimlas of the University of the Free State shocked us to the core. A small group of protesters, students and outside people, broke through a closed entrance to the stadium

and about 17 minutes into the match walked onto the field to disrupt the game in progress.

Sensing danger, because of the main security dispatch still being outside the stadium, I rushed back to the parking lot to retrieve my cell phone from the car. By the time I returned, the last seconds of a terrible scene unfolded before my eyes as spectators, community members from outside the university and some students (not all white), chased down and beat up some of the protesters. Before we could even move, it was over and a few injured protesters were treated on the field and in the medical facility inside the grounds.

[38] See Jonathan Jansen, Statement by Prof Jonathan Jansen, Vice-Chancellor and Rector of the University of the Free State (UFS) about the situation on the Bloemfontein Campus, http://www.ufs.ac.za/template/news-archive-item?news=6670, accessed 28 February 2016. For related declarations in the media by Jansen, see http://www.iol.co.za/news/crime-courts/jansen-laments-ufs-violence-abuse-1988779, and http://www.politicsweb.co.za/news-and-analysis/protesters-rights-trampled-at-ufs-rugby-match--jon, accessed 1 March 2016. Many people called for Jansen's dismissal, following the incident. As one student, Ntutli, put it: 'The University of the Free State in 2016 is the same as the University of the Free State in 1997.... The university still has a white Afrikaans policy. The university still has oppressive policies', see Greg Nicolson, http://www.dailymaverick.co.za/article/2016-03-01-report-days-of-violence-and-thunder-at-the-university-of-free-state/#.Vtb-2ObCBV8, accessed 2 March 2016. Jansen also received death threats. He declared: 'I have been accused of putting black student's interests above the white students, and I am also accused of putting white student's interests above blacks. It is all lies, and I think it is the kind of things people say to unsettle you.' See http://www.news24.com/SouthAfrica/News/i-have-received-death-threats-jonathan-jansen-20160224, and http://www.sabc.co.za/news/a/5ee909804bcd49bfac3dac96fb2bb898/Angry-UFS-students-call-for-Jansen-to-step-down-20162402, accessed 1 March 2016.

As Robert Morrell has observed, Jonathan Jansen, like many other vice chancellors are learning to cope with and offer leadership at a very challenging moment in the lives of the institutions they head. He recalls not too long ago, Jansen was a hero when he 'dealt decisively, yet sensitively, with the problem' of the Reitz Residence scandal in 2008, which brought public scrutiny to bear on the UFS's vacillation with 'shrugging off its racial past'.

106

See http://www.dailymaverick.co.za/article/2015-11-11-op-ed-treasure-or-curse-south-africas-university-vice-chancellors/#.VtVX8ebCBV8, accessed 1 March 2016.

[39] Adam Habib, http://www.wits.ac.za/newsroom/newsitems/201504/26107/news_item_26107.html, accessed 5 October 2015.

[40] See Open letter from former SRC presidents: 'Rhodes must fall', http://www.uct.ac.za/dailynews/?id=9037, accessed 6 October 2015; see also http://allafrica.com/stories/201503230163.html, accessed 1 October 2015.

[41] Schutte is a founding member of Media for Justice, a social justice and media activist as well as a documentary film-maker.

[42] See Gillian Schutte, http://www.iol.co.za/sundayindependent/becoming-a-master-of-subterfuge-1.1907710#.VfWmypce4TZ, accessed 1 October 2015.

[43] See Gillian Schutte, http://www.iol.co.za/sundayindependent/becoming-a-master-of-subterfuge-1.1907710#.VfWmypce4TZ, accessed 1 October 2015.

[44] Xolela Mangcu was subsequently promoted to full professor later in 2015.

[45] See Xolela Mangcu's 'Ripping the veil off UCT's whiter shades of pale University's move to "downgrade" race fails to hide the truth about inequality', 6 July 2014, *Sunday Times*, p. 18. See also: http://www.bdlive.co.za/opinion/2014/11/03/sas-black-academics-are-getting-raw-deal, accessed 6 October 2015; Xolela Mangcu, '10 steps to develop black professors', *City Press*, 20 July 2014.

[46] See University assembly: The Rhodes statue and transformation, https://www.youtube.com/watch?v=eWVJnBVnyPc, accessed 7 October 2015.
On this point Mangcu was echoing a point made emphatically by Jonathan Jansen at the 21 October 2014 public debate on transformation in higher education held at the Baxter Concert Hall, namely, the idea of standards is often mobilised to exclude those not wanted, as very few universities in South Africa, UCT included, can demonstrate the standards they often claim when challenged to be more inclusive. See https://www.youtube.com/watch?v=thiiUDeIySw, accessed 8 October 2015.

[47] Tokelo Nhlapo, http://www.dailymaverick.co.za/opinionista/2015-03-11-ucts-poo-protest-violence-is-a-perfect-reaction/#.VfXL4Jce4TZ, accessed 4 October 2015.

[48] See Xolela Mangcu, '10 steps to develop black professors', *City Press*, 20 July 2014; Max Price, 'Addressing the shortage of black and women professors', http://www.uct.ac.za/dailynews/?id=8891, accessed 6 October 2015.

[49] See Xolela Mangcu, 'What a less Eurocentric reading list would look like', http://www.uct.ac.za/dailynews/?id=9275, accessed 6 October 2015.

[50] See http://www.jwtc.org.za/the_salon/volume_9.htm, accessed 12 October 2015.

[51] See http://www.jwtc.org.za/the_salon/volume_9.htm, accessed 12 October 2015.

[52] See http://www.jwtc.org.za/the_salon/volume_9.htm, accessed 12 October 2015.

[53] Shose Kessi, http://thoughtleader.co.za/blackacademiccaucus/2015/09/25/of-black-pain-animal-rights-and-the-politics-of-the-belly/, accessed 1 October 2015.

[54] Excerpt of an email reaction by Sakhumzi Mfecane to an earlier version of this book.

[55] Although whites in South Africa are encouraged to be sensitive in how they position themselves and reflexive in the stories they tell about the black other and especially about themselves, it is not uncommon that their accounts are likely to be considered as 'self-flagellation' propelled by 'a desire to consume the other and their creativity', which is how the present account was described by one of my non-white South African readers of an earlier draft of this book.

[56] Justin Foxton, http://beta.iol.co.za/news/the-burden-of-being-white-in-sa-1927777, accessed 11 October 2015.

[57] In an email comment to an earlier version of this book.

[58] The UCT: Rhodes Must Fall Facebook page has remained active since its creation at the start of the protests in 2015. A cursory look suggests that the RMF is using the Facebook page as a platform to highlight larger social issues facing students, this includes predominantly racial issues about black bodies and their institutional oppression, but it also covers gender issues quite extensively. What is however striking is that all posts and responses to comments are seen as coming from RMF as a collective, even when they are very clearly biased or derogatory. This means that accountability falls on the collective movement. On the other hand, those who engage with the posts do so, for the most part, under their own name. The visceral responses are a testimony to deep-seated anger from some students, a desire to discuss the issues from others and a very blatant display of aggression and name-calling from a minority. I am grateful to Mohini Baijnath, MA student researching transformation of teaching and curricula at UCT, since RMF movement began in 2015, for kindly distilling for me how the UCT Rhodes Must Fall Facebook page is used.

[59] For echoes of similar protests and campaigns in the USA, where black student activists are challenging white supremacy and institutional racism on university campuses, see Peniel E. Joseph,

http://www.theroot.com/articles/culture/2015/11/black_student_activis ts_stand_against_racist_cultures_on_campus.html, accessed 5 December 2015.
[60]Panashe Chigumadzi, http://www.theguardian.com/world/2015/aug/24/south-africa-race-panashe-chigumadzi-ruth-first-lecture, accessed 3 October 2015.
[61] See http://transformingtraditions.blogspot.co.za/2011/11/i-see-coconuts-everywhere.html, accessed 19 February 2016. See also her related Youtube interview, 'Why South Africans don't get the question of the coconut', https://www.youtube.com/watch?v=HsPNqkcYGGM, accessed 19 February 2016.
[62] How can one quibble about black pain in what Mbembe describes as the only country in which a revolution took place which resulted in not one single oppressor losing anything? See http://africasacountry.com/2015/09/achille-mbembe-on-the-state-of-south-african-politics/, accessed 1 October 2015.
[63] See https://medium.com/@tomolefe/a-long-comment-on-mbembe-s-state-of-south-african-politics-5cd1030a1990, accessed 1 October 2015.
[64] See Eve Fairbanks, http://www.theguardian.com/news/2015/nov/18/why-south-african-students-have-turned-on-their-parents-generation, accessed 23 November 2015.
[65] According to a survey of born-frees conducted in the course of the Rhodes Must Fall campaign, many born-frees declared they were likely to resort to violent protests because of the persistence of inequalities in the country.

According to the report, 'unemployment rates are higher among younger people, women and Africans.' On the expanded definition of unemployment, the rate among African males aged 15 to 24 years is 67% compared with 75% of African females.

Violent protests in SA have almost doubled in the last three years and it is suspected that the economically disenfranchised youth may play a huge part in it.

Born frees are also receiving poor quality education, said the report, with literacy and numeracy scores in Grade 3 in this group barely above 50%. This has a major ripple effect later on as only 51% of matric candidates pass their final school-leaving exam.

The report found that 'people aged 14 to 25 years old account for 29% of the country's prison population.'

See 'Born free but still in chains: South Africa's first post-apartheid generation', http://www.biznews.com/briefs/2015/04/29/sas-born-frees-likely-to-drift-into-violent-protests-says-report/, accessed 3 October 2015.

[66] See Eve Fairbanks, http://www.theguardian.com/news/2015/nov/18/why-south-african-students-have-turned-on-their-parents-generation, accessed 23 November 2015.

[67] See http://www.iol.co.za/news/uct-rhodes-statue-protest-both-sides-1.1831688#.VfWLGpce4TZ, accessed 17 September 2015. For a similarly critical open letter on the Rhodes Must Fall Movement addressed to the President of UCT Convocation Barney Pityana, by Leigh-Ann Naidoo, a PhD student in Education at the University of the Witwatersrand, Johannesburg, see http://www.dailymaverick.co.za/opinionista/2015-04-14-open-letter-to-barney-pityana-on-the-rhodes-must-fall-movement/#.VfWVl5ce4TZ, accessed 17 September 2015. Naidoo concluded her letter with this call to action: 'Don't stand by and watch these students and their message and action be criminalised. They are speaking truth to power as you once did. And you know what it feels like to be served with legal papers, bannings, trials, and police harassment. Perhaps Max Price will go to sleep at night feeling accomplished to have contained and shut down the possibility for real change driven by brave black staff, students, workers and alumni. But will you?' In his defence, Professor Barney Ptiyana reportedly said, 'amid a chorus of boos and jeers': "It is untrue that I said the statue must stay [...] I said it is important to raise this issue at all levels and to think about how to handle history ... the only reason why I am here is to facilitate debate ... if my presence is not helpful I am more than happy to step down." See http://www.bdlive.co.za/national/2015/03/26/pityana-replaced-as-co-chair-of-rhodes-debate, accessed 2015. See also 'University Assembly: The Rhodes Statue and Transformation', https://www.youtube.com/watch?v=eWVJnBVnyPc, accessed 7 October 2015.

[68] See http://america.aljazeera.com/articles/2015/4/6/anti-racism-protesters-in-south-africa-take-aim-at-a-statue-with-poop.html, accessed 17 September 2015. See also Eve Fairbanks, http://www.theguardian.com/news/2015/nov/18/why-south-african-students-have-turned-on-their-parents-generation, accessed 23 November 2015.

[69] See Trevor Noah, 'It's My Culture Full Show', https://www.youtube.com/watch?v=DBYgnTIaG4c, accessed 6 October 2015.

[70] See http://www.bdlive.co.za/opinion/columnists/2015/03/27/uproar-at-uct-has-only-been-good-for-it, accessed 17 September 2015.

[71] See http://www.bdlive.co.za/opinion/columnists/2015/03/27/uproar-at-uct-has-only-been-good-for-it, accessed 17 September 2015.

72 See http://www.politicsweb.co.za/party/anc-nec-backs-rhodes-statue-protests-at-uct, accessed 2 October 2015.
73 See http://mg.co.za/article/2015-05-14-this-is-the-year-varsities-will-transform-blade, accessed 30 September 2015.
74 See http://allafrica.com/stories/201503230163.html, accessed 1 October 2015.
75 See http://www.bdlive.co.za/national/politics/2015/04/07/eff-calls-for-public-spaces-to-be-reconstructed, accessed 2 October 2015.
76 See http://www.news24.com/SouthAfrica/News/UCT-protesters-vow-to-continue-occupation-of-building-20150410, accessed 2 October 2015.
77 See http://allafrica.com/stories/201503230163.html, accessed 1 October 2015.
78 See https://www.enca.com/south-africa/cecil-rhodes-statue-should-be-moved-uct-vice-chancellor, accessed 5 October 2015.
79 See for example, http://www.news24.com/SouthAfrica/News/American-students-support-RhodesMustFall-Campaign-20150326, accessed 17 September 2015.
In a message of solidarity posted on the Rhodes Must Fall Facebook page, members of the Black Student Union at the University of California, Berkeley, wrote: 'We write to express to you our strongest solidarity as you embark in the courageous struggle to take down one of Africa's biggest enemies, and colonizer, Cecil John Rhodes.' 'We believe that, when we as Black students and youth organize ourselves in a disciplined manner, the decolonization of our education and the total liberation of our people is inevitable.' Other displays of support came from universities within South Africa, and also from universities outside of South Africa such as Oxford University and the University of the West Indies. See http://mg.co.za/article/2015-03-26-rhodesmustfall-protest-spreads-to-other-campuses, accessed 5 October 2015.
80 See University assembly: the Rhodes statue and transformation, https://www.youtube.com/watch?v=eWVJnBVnyPc, accessed 7 October 2015. The students who read out these posts requested management to disengage itself through positive action to demonstrate that they were not complicit in perpetuating such racist innuendos.
81 In his email reaction to an earlier version of this book, already referenced above, Sakhumzi Mfecane writes:

For me, the issue of academic transformation is not achievable while it is still led by black academics only – and students. It seems to me that whiteness gives people more power to change things and reorder society and institutions as they please. I'm reminded of the case of Human Sciences Research Council (HSRC). When Mark Orkin took over as the CEO his main

111

mission was to transform the institution and have more black representation. Most whites simply obliged; they did not resist him. I don't think he would have succeeded the way he did if he was black. So, yes your imaginary character in chapter 6 has much in common with Rhodes, but what he lacks is Rhodes's skin colour.

[82] It is significant that the decolonisation of space has been taken into the digital realm, thereby transcending the political, cultural and economic constraints of the palpable and the physical, and making it more effective in furthering the cause in a context where power and privilege continue to stand firmly in the way of meaningful transformation. The student supported struggle to end outsourcing was meant to improve conditions for university workers whom Tinyiko Maluleke describes as 'the nameless people who stand guard at the gates, serve the food, mow the lawns and keep the toilets clean', but who 'have long been invisible', see http://mg.co.za/article/2016-01-28-current-heat-is-forging-a-new-university/, accessed 17 February 2016.

[83] See discussion in Chapter 5 titled 'Lessons from Rhodes Must Fall' below.

[84] See Achille Mbembe, 'The State of South African Political Life', http://africasacountry.com/2015/09/achille-mbembe-on-the-state-of-south-african-politics/, accessed 1 October 2015.

[85] See Heike Becker, 'South Africa's May 1968: Decolonising Institutions and Minds', http://roape.net/2016/02/17/south-africas-may-1968-decolonising-institutions-and-minds/, accessed 20 March 2016.

[86] See Martin Hall, 'Why are South African students so angry?' http://www.bbc.com/news/business-35883919, accessed 30 March 2016.

Chapter 3

Not Every Black is Black Enough

It is commonplace to be caught betwixt and between anywhere and everywhere in the world, especially in South Africa where it is all too easy to be crushed by the giant compressors of the regressive logic of ever diminishing circles of inclusion (February 1991; Adhikari 2005). Colonialism and apartheid functioned best through hierarchies of humanity and their multiplicities of agentive possibilities (Mandaza 1997). It was the ideal form of divide-and-rule. Even in the post-apartheid era South Africans are in no hurry to give up on categories that have served them so well. So, it is hardly surprising that in the current clamour for decolonisation epitomised by RMF, some attitudes and declarations leave one in little doubt that not every black is black enough, both among nationals and foreigners. Just as there is a hierarchy of whiteness (since Rhodes and his British imperial times when the Boers and others were put in their places as inferior whites), so too is there a hierarchy of blackness, which, in some cases has resulted in violent ethnic cleansing and could degenerate into genocide.

Through its policy of inventing indigenes or natives, colonialism created or reinforced hierarchies among the native populations of its African colonies, whereby Africans who came closest to Europeans either through physical attributes or culturally through educational achievements and mimicry, were placed at the top of the hierarchy of the subjected. This arbitrary racist and administrative system of categorisation was internalised and reproduced at independence by the postcolonial states, to give rise to a lethal cocktail of competing identities. Privileging divide and rule, the system thrived on freezing individuals into citizens and subjects, depending on whether their lives were governed by the civic regime of laws or by culture and tradition (Mamdani 1996), hardly providing for the reality of those straddling both regimes in their daily lives. Even in the world of total subjection to the registers of culture and ethnic tradition, the craving to divide and rule was such that there was all to gain in polarising or freezing identities, by ensuring that invented ethnic (cultural) citizens and ethnic (cultural) strangers put asunder by colonial racism and administration shall never meet and work in harmony (Mamdani 1996, 2001, 2010; Nnoli 1998; Gourevitch 1998; Akinyele 2000). While every national can assert their legal citizenship, some see themselves or are seen by others to be less authentic claimants. The growing importance of cultural identity politics and more exclusionary ideas of citizenship are matched by the urge to detect difference and to distinguish between 'locals', 'nationals', 'citizens', 'autochthons' or 'insiders' on the one hand, and 'foreigners', 'immigrants', 'strangers' or 'outsiders' on the other, with the focus on opportunities, economic entitlements, cultural recognition and political representation (Geschiere and Nyamnjoh 2000; Geschiere 2009; Bahi 2013).

In the case of Rwanda, which was later to turn genocidal in 1994, the colonial and postcolonial authorities refused to recognise the age-old cultural conviviality of the Hutus and Tutsis that they were so determined to keep asunder. They would not acknowledge, until it was too late, the sociology of the Hutus and Tutsis who had come to speak the same language, follow the same religion, intermarry, and live intermingled, without territorial distinctions, on the same hills, sharing the same social and political culture in small chiefdoms (Maquet 1961; Gourevitch 1998; Mamdani 2001). Current tensions over belonging and citizenship in South Africa are not dissimilar to the humble beginnings of what eventually built up to explode as genocide in Rwanda, and as Mamdani (2010) would argue with reference to Darfur, in Sudan.

Neighbouring Botswana, which went through similar debates on citizenship, belonging, rights and entitlements in the late 1990s and early 2000s, captures in a fascinating way the complexities and intricacies of belonging and attitudes towards citizenship and foreigners which South Africa is currently experiencing, and from which South Africans can draw vital lessons for a future of inclusion. In a study I did of citizenship and belonging in Botswana in the late 1990s and early 2000s, I noticed that identity politics was growing in importance, alongside more exclusionary ideas of nationality and citizenship, as minority claims for greater cultural recognition and plurality were countered by majority efforts to

114

maintain the status of an inherited colonial hierarchy of ethnic groupings. Minority clamour for recognition and representation were countered by greater and sometimes aggressive reaffirmation of age-old exclusions informed by colonial registers of inequalities amongst the subjected. While the rhetoric clearly emphasised democracy as an individual right, the reality was one that sought to bridge individual and group rights, thereby making Botswana democracy far more complex than was often acknowledged. While legal provisions might promise citizenship to all in principle, the practice was one of inequality in citizenship among individuals and groups. I observed a hierarchy of citizenship fostered by political, economic, social and cultural inequalities, such that it made some individuals and groups much more able to claim and articulate their rights than others. Being a rights-bearing Motswana was a matter of degree and power relations, and some were less Batswana than others, even when they had a national identity card (*Omang*) and were inspired or protected by the same constitution. In the past, and still very much the case when I did the study, in certain circles, for example, Tswana had to various degrees claimed for themselves the status of landlords, of whom others (ethnic minorities) were tenants who, for one reason or another, had earned recognition and entitlements over time. However, in times of crisis, uncertainty or anxiety over entitlements, when survival or comfort could imply sacrificing the interests of some, the politics of belonging was crucial in determining whose interests were to be sacrificed first and whose protected (Nyamnjoh 2002, 2006, 2007c).

Parallel with this hierarchy among Batswana nationals was another hierarchy among foreigners or immigrants. Whites, in their various gradations were at the apex while blacks from the rest of Africa, in their various gradations as well, constituted the bottom of the hierarchy. I observed that not all outsiders were welcome, and not all who were welcome were accorded the same respect, privileges or rights by Batswana. Some were more likely to lose privileges or have their rights violated than others. Again, it was all a matter of degree, subject to renegotiation and the caprice of changed circumstances. Nothing was fixed, not even the rhetoric of rights, which was appropriated and articulated differently by individuals and groups, depending on context and issues at stake. I

115

suggest that the hierarchies of humanity, of nationals and citizens, among foreigners and between nationals and foreigners observed in Botswana offer a useful framework for South Africa, where there is the added complexity of a racialized hierarchy among white and black citizens and/or nationals, which are in turn refracted onto foreigners (Nyamnjoh 2002, 2006, 2007c).

In view of these observed diminishing circles of inclusion among citizens or nationals of Botswana, between them and various categories of foreigners, it is important to take a closer look at the fact that the RMF protests which started in Cape Town were occurring concomitantly with an upsurge in violent attacks on *amakwerekwere* from Africa north of the Limpopo, that originated in and around Durban. Seen together, both events would suggest a determined effort by black South Africans from both ends of the social spectrum (top and bottom) to strip themselves of perceived constraints to fulfilling fantasies of and efforts at whitening up since first encounters with Europe and its *mission civilisatrice* or unilinear model of modernisation. In other words, the cigarette of black South African modernist ambitions was lit from both ends. The cigarette was lit on the one end (that of the impoverished masses) by the burning hurdles posed by an ever surging influx of *amakwerekwere* – the present-day 'homo caudatus', 'tail-men', 'cavemen', 'primitives', 'savages', 'barbarians' or 'hottentots', who remind South African blacks of the naked savagery from which they are desperately seeking to graduate (Nyamnjoh 2006: 39) – from the heart of darkness north of the Limpopo following the end of apartheid. It was lit on the other end (that of the emerging 'black' middle classes) by the inconvenience of resident *amakwerekwere* of yesteryear who had remained like the residue of a purportedly fallen apartheid to continue to thwart black dreams of the good life inspired by whiteness, for which they have aspired since first contact with whites. For this emerging black elite, it is an extra irritation that their purported white compatriots are recruiting and co-opting black Africans (elite *amakwerekwere*) from Africa north of the Limpopo, to thwart their dreams and aspirations for whiteness. Hence, I would like to insert a brief description here, of those parallel but complementary protests and how they unfolded, before returning to RMF, so we are able to see correlations that are not immediately obvious when the two events are treated as disconnected.

In the early months of 2015, just before the RMF protests, the atmosphere in South Africa was an amalgamation of fear and anxiety resulting from a series of attacks which many observers and commentators associated with earlier patterns of xenophobia that have come to characterise post-apartheid South Africa, and to which I referred at the beginning of this book (Adam and Moodley 2015; Alhaji 2015; Crush et al. 2015; Landau 2011; Mangezvo 2014; Mano 2015; Neocosmos 2010; Nyamnjoh and Shoro 2014; Steinberg 2015; Owen 2015; Powell 2014). Others, including the South African government, were hesitant to term the attacks xenophobic, preferring to characterise them instead as criminal, as if xenophobia and criminal activity are mutually exclusive occurrences, or as if they do not feed on each other.[1]

It is hardly surprising that *amakwerekwere* as a derogatory word has traditionally been used by the black South African masses in townships, in informal settlements and at city-centre spaces to designate black immigrants from the African continent competing with them for scarce opportunities to get by, given that these immigrants are most likely to share spaces and places with the South Africans who refer to them as *amakwerekwere*. We tend to name what we are familiar and interact with on a regular basis. This does not imply that the phenomenon we name may not be present among distant unfamiliar others with whom we have little in common. In contrast, because white foreigners are unlikely to reside in townships and informal settlements, or find themselves competing with black South Africans for pavement spaces at the city-centre, they are spared the label of *amakwerekwere*, not because their reality is necessarily different, but because different social circles elicit different vocabularies. When addressed by their black hosts, who are more likely to be middle class – 'coconut' or not, white and other non-black foreigners in South Africa tend to be treated differently, often referred to as 'expats' or simply categorised as 'tourists', and assumed (often falsely) to be bringing more into the South African economy than taking out. It is with this nuance in mind that some have referred to the 2015 spate of attacks as Afrophobia (as opposed to xenophobia) because the main targets

117

were African immigrants[2] – and a particular type at that, those most likely to rub shoulders with South African blacks in the townships and other informal settlements and spaces. Those African immigrants insulated from the obvious Afrophobia spaces of the masses, were, as we would see shortly, in turn targeted within the framework of the RMF protests as not being black (South-Africanly speaking) enough. To some, these xenophobic, Afrophobic or criminal attacks arise from a 'cultural propensity to hate foreigners; opportunistic manipulation of the unemployed by local entrepreneurs who cannot cope with growing competition posed by foreign businesspeople; provocation of locals by elements who are part of the diaspora; the absence of good organisation and leadership on the ground; and indecisiveness on the part of the government'.[3]

Whatever the causes, the attacks of early 2015 left at least seven dead and thousands displaced. Violence and looting targeting black foreigners and/or their businesses erupted in Durban, Johannesburg and KwaZulu-Natal. In addition to heavy police presence, the army was brought in to help in the volatile areas affected by the violence.[4] A reported 307 people were arrested in connection with the attacks.[5] More than 1000 shops owned by black foreigners were looted in Soweto, as large gangs moved between townships, taking airtime, cigarettes and cash. In Durban and Johannesburg, gangs targeted black foreign-owned shops before gradually shifting their attacks to black foreigners in general.

Several countries on the continent expressed concerned with what was going on in South Africa, with some issuing cautionary travel notes. Mozambicans received the brunt of the attacks.[6] In Ghana, four men threatened to set fire to the South Africa High Commission, while the South African diplomatic mission in Lagos was shut down following picketing by protesting Nigerians[7], and the Nigerian government recalled its High Commissioner for consultation.[8]

Within South Africa, civil society organisations and other spontaneously assembled groupings marched in protest against xenophobia, accompanied or led in some instances, by moral religious authorities such as Anglican Archbishop Thabo Makgoba.[9]Thousands of South Africans, including activists, unionists, students and academics, turned out for the march against xenophobia in Johannesburg. Five kilometres of marchers, representing a body of individuals from different classes, nationalities and races, stomped through Hillbrow to Newtown, under the banner 'People's March against Xenophobia'. The marchers could be heard chanting '*Sisonke!*' (We are together) and 'We want peace' – in the hope that the march would bring hope to black foreigners in the country.[10]

Leaders of trade unions and opposition parties added their voices to the condemnation. The General Secretary of the National Union of Metalworkers of South Africa (Numsa), Irvin Jim, openly blamed the ANC's failure to implement the Freedom Charter and make fundamental changes to the economy that would transform the lives of all South Africans as the cause for the attacks.[11]Blaming the ANC for the country's struggling economy and for the attacks, EFF leader Julius Malema stated:

'If we took all the foreigners away you would still be unemployed. It is the ANC ...so don't blame our brothers and sisters from Africa ... If you are angry, vent that anger on the ANC and not foreign nationals ... Blame the ANC for your suffering. You are in shacks with no water and power. Your children are not properly educated. The ANC is responsible for that. If you are looking for the criminals stealing your houses and jobs, look at the penthouse called Luthuli House'.[12]

The ANC government could not remain indifferent to rising indignation across the continent and globally. Deputy Police Minister Maggie Sotyo admitted that 'it was embarrassing that South Africans were turning against African countries, which assisted our freedom fighters when they were in exile', and wondered what Nelson Mandela would think of these current xenophobic attacks if he was alive today.[13] To these alleged allegations, ANC spokesperson Keith Khoza defended his party against criticism by Numsa's Irvin Jim, in particular, saying:

It is fashionable that when we are faced with challenges that need all of us, people start pointing fingers. You can't use the ANC as a scapegoat. The ANC government has been working hard to resolve the socioeconomic challenges in the country. We all have a role to

119

play to change the economy. Numsa too has a role. Playing a blame game does not make them look better. Transformation is a national project. It cannot be an ANC preserve.[14]

The National Prosecuting Authority (NPA) worked closely with the police to help quickly prosecute the perpetrators of attacks. Special courts and magistrates were dedicated to some of the affected areas.[15]

Equally singled out for criticism, indeed, more than anyone else, was Zulu King Goodwill Zwelithini[16], a close ally of President Zuma's. He was accused of inciting the violence when he stated in a speech, held in Pongala on 15 March, a month prior to the attacks that 'foreigners must pack their bags and go home'[17]. King Zwelithini reportedly said:

> ...Most government leaders do not want to speak out on this matter because they are scared of losing votes... As the king of the Zulu nation, I cannot tolerate a situation where we are being led by leaders with no views whatsoever... We are requesting those who come from outside to please go back to their countries... The fact that there were countries that played a role in the country's struggle for liberation should not be used as an excuse to create a situation where foreigners are allowed to inconvenience locals... I know you were in their countries during the struggle for liberation. But the fact of the matter is you did not set up businesses in their countries.[18]

Zwelithini claimed that he was unfairly misquoted, noting that the statement was made in isiZulu and was misconstrued during translation. He insisted that he meant only that illegal immigrants should be deported, as it was unacceptable that locals were being made to compete for the few economic resources available with people from other countries.[19]

South African President, Jacob Zuma's son, Edward Zuma, did not help matters when he, in support of Zwelithini's (however misinterpreted) statement, stated that 'Foreigners need to leave the country'.[20] He sought to shame the South African government saying that they need to stop 'unnecessarily accommodating foreign nationals'.[21] In an interview with News24, Edward Zuma justified this sentiment, stating:

We need to be aware that as a country we are sitting on a ticking time bomb of them [foreigners] taking over the country…The reason why I am saying that is because some of the foreigners are working for private security companies where they have been employed for cheap labour. These companies are running away from complying with South African labour laws.[22]

Making it clear that his views were independent from his father's[23], Edward Zuma also claimed that foreigners were carrying guns illegally as they did not have the required gun licenses and that they were fuelling the drug problem in South Africa.[24] Mr. Zuma remained unapologetic of his views claiming that they were his personal views that he would stick with and die with. Though he did not blame South Africans for being angry at the overwhelming presence of foreigners living among them, he did, however, condemn the recent attacks against foreigner, asserting that those found responsible should be dealt with accordingly. It was not his wish to be seen as 'xenophobic'. Rather he wanted to emphasize that the country has a problem.[25] It is worth adding that these comments were made in April 2015, long before the Guptas, strongly associated with the Zumas, and accused of having infiltrated and taken over the government, including influencing the appointment and strategic positioning of ministers to do their bidding, issued a statement in March 2016 claiming they were victims of xenophobia.[26] Edward Zuma's xenophobia was clearly not aimed at biting the finger that fed him, but rather, at the mostly black African migrants rubbing shoulders in informality in impoverished townships and overcrowded city centres (Adam and Moodley 2015; Alhaji 2015; Crush et al. 2015; Landau 2011; Mangezvo 2014; Mano 2015; Neocosmos 2010; Nyamnjoh and Shoro 2014; Steinberg 2015; Owen 2015; Powell 2014).

Compelled to apologise or recant, King Zwelithini organised an anti-xenophobia imbizo in Durban, at which he denied accusations that he was the cause of xenophobic violence against black foreigners.[27] He claimed that if he had given an order to kill foreigners, 'this country would be reduced to ashes'.[28] Further aiming to clarify his intentions Zwelithini stated:

The speech that I made at Pongola was directed to peace but I cannot see it in any newspaper or on the radio. But what I see is that people are being fed just an excerpt, a small part of what I said, and also out of context, which is actually ludicrous and laughable. Even now I still challenge the media: let them come forward with the entire speech that I made. This speech has become central and very important. It has become even more important now than when it was given.[29]

In an apparent volte face, Zwelithini concluded that a 'real war' was needed; 'a war to ensure that all foreign nationals in South Africa, regardless of which country they come from, are protected'.[30]

During the anti-xenophobia imbizo in Durban, Inkatha Freedom Party (IFP) leader Mangosuthu Buthelezi, accused of fanning the flames of xenophobia when he was Minister of Home Affairs from 1994 to 2004 (Nyamnjoh 2006: 36-37), publicly apologised to black African nationals who were attacked in Durban. This apology followed the controversy that erupted around King Zwelithini's statement. Maintaining that King Zwelithini's statement and the attacks were not related, Buthelezi however asked for forgiveness: 'Please forgive us, because what has been done to you has broken our hearts'.[31] He further stated:

> How can South Africa be in 2015 the most xenophobic country on this continent? Our neighbours in Africa gave sanctuary to all political exiles as we struggled for decades to secure democracy. They stood by us, they supported us and they gave us refuge. They didn't isolate us and ask what we were doing in their countries. They didn't victimise us.[32]

President Jacob Zuma, similarly condemned the violence and organized a team of ministers to put an end to it. The condemnation of the attacks was perceived as passive. He was criticised because he had not provided immediate and sustained protection to those affected. The views expressed by his son also put him in an unflattering light. His administration was further accused of provoking the xenophobic attacks by creating strict anti-immigration laws and policies, limiting the rights of both legal and illegal immigrants.[33] During the 2015 Freedom Day Celebrations at the Union Buildings in Pretoria, President Zuma acknowledged the historic moment on 27 April 1994 when the country first held a democratic election. He celebrated triumph over 'institutionalized racism, repression, state-sponsored violence and the enforced division of our people based on race or ethnicity'.[34] He called for a remembrance of the solidarity, sacrifice and friendship among 'peace-loving nations and peoples from Africa'. He spoke of the country's continued attempts to implement programmes that would induce economic freedom in addition to political freedom, acknowledging Africa's crucial role in the country's economic growth and development, welcoming its economic contribution. Further along in his Freedom Day speech, he publicly condemned the attacks stating:

> We strongly condemn these attacks. They have no place in a democracy where people are free to express their unhappiness about any issue. We also urge our communities to isolate criminal elements who perpetuate such horrendous crimes against fellow human beings. They should be reported to the police.[35]

President Zuma applauded South Africans for coming out in the thousands to march and register their condemnation of such violence. He claimed that the marches demonstrate how South Africans are 'peace loving people who believe in human dignity, human rights and Ubuntu' and 'opposed to xenophobia, racism and all other related intolerances'.[36] He explained that authorities were working hard to ensure that all the foreign-born victims of the violence were positively identified and extended condolences to all the families and compatriots of the deceased.[37] He went on to say:

> We have to address the underlying causes of the violence and tensions, which is the legacy of poverty, unemployment and inequality in our country and our continent and the competition for limited resources... It is also important to emphasise that not all foreign nationals are in the country illegally. Many live here legally and contribute to the socio-economic development of the country. It is also not true that all foreign nationals are involved in criminal activities... We are Africans and we are proud of our African identity. We must continue to live in peace and harmony with our brothers and sisters from the continent. Where problems arise, they must be resolved peacefully and constructively.[38]

The immigration policies and practices of the South African state, as well as the xenophobic attitudes of some South Africans, contradict the rhetoric of inclusivity, human rights and ties to the rest of Africa that proliferate in official pronouncements and civil society discourses. Yet we are reminded by ethnographies of everyday lives and living that being and belonging is a permanent work in progress – open-ended, complex and nuanced (Nyamnjoh 2010, 2013a; Alhaji 2015; Owen 2015). It is the duty of South African leaders (political, economic, cultural, intellectual, and others) and media to make this abundantly and repeatedly clear to all and sundry. Good leadership does not go to sleep between eruptions.

The growing obsession with indigeneity in present-day South Africa is not confined to policies, attitudes and practices targeted at 'alien' humans. Equally active are policies and practices aimed at keeping South Africa pure, pristine and beyond contamination by alien flora and fauna (Comaroff and Comaroff 2001). Gone are the 18th and 19th century possibilities that availed themselves to the European settlers like Rhodes, who could shop around the world as they liked for fruit trees, grass and other vegetation to transplant, nurse, proliferate and indigenise without frontiers in South Africa (Beinart 2003; Beinart and Hughes 2009). It is reported, for example, that Rhodes did not hesitate to invite expert agriculturalists from as far afield as California to assist him with the domestication in South Africa of *amakwerekwere* fruit trees and kindred vegetation from elsewhere that had caught his fancy. Here is an account of how Rhodes effected the *makwerekwerisation* of South African landscape, flora and fauna, with a missionary zeal:

> Rhodes took the greatest interest in agricultural matters. In addition to the two blocks of farms in Mashonaland and Matabeleland, where experiments were being carried out for the benefit of the other farmers in Rhodesia, he purchased about a dozen farms in the Stellenbosch and Paarl districts, with the object of producing fruit on scientific lines. He imported several experienced men from California, including Mr. H. E. V. Pickstone, a most able and energetic expert, whom he appointed as general manager. Mr. Pickstone had the greatest success, as a visit to the 'Rhodes Fruit Farms,' as they are called, will amply demonstrate. He has done a great work for South Africa, as he taught our farmers how to grow

fruit, with the result that the large majority of our Western Province farmers are to-day producing fruit on a large scale and are making a very good business out of it. Mr. Pickstone introduced the best varieties of fruit-trees from California, and as a consequence to-day South African farmers are producing as fine and luscious fruit as is produced anywhere in the world. There is a great demand for Cape fruit in the London market to-day and exceptional prices are being realized. Here, again, we have Rhodes as the benefactor of his adopted country. If it had not been for him, if he had not brought these splendid experts over from California, who taught us how to grow the choicest fruit, and how to pack it so that it should reach the consumer in the best possible condition, we should now probably still be following the same old lines, and be growing the same old varieties on the same small scale. There is no doubt that Pickstone and his men gave a tremendous impetus to the fruit industry in South Africa. I think I am within the mark when I say that where twenty years ago one fruit-tree was growing, to-day there are a hundred, and of the finest varieties. If Mr. Pickstone were to publish the number of young fruit-trees that he has sold to farmers in South Africa, I am sure his figures would astonish the world. His name is well known amongst farmers all over South Africa, including Rhodesia, and even in the remotest parts, hundreds of miles from the nearest railway, one finds Pickstone's trees thriving most beautifully.

Rhodes used to like nothing better than to discuss with Mr. Pickstone the prospects of his fruit-farms, and had him down to Groote Schuur almost every week-end. He liked Pickstone, because he said he had a level head and that he could always rely on his figures. Pickstone at the commencement of operations on these farms gave him an estimate of the cost per month, which he never exceeded. That pleased Rhodes immensely. He was so interested in farming that others who heard him talk were inspired with equal keenness. *Wherever he travelled, if he came across a good class of stock, or if he saw a pretty and useful tree, his first thought was, will this animal or this tree thrive in South Africa?* If, after inquiries and consideration, he thought that South Africa would be benefited, he spared no effort or money in acquiring specimens of his particular fancy and sending them out to South Africa. He spent large sums on these experiments (Jourdan 1910: 209-211, emphasis mine).

The current upsurge in environmental autochthony stands to jeopardise whatever achievements Rhodes and his fellow *amakwerekwere* of yesteryear claimed in appropriation, domestication and naturalisation of foreign flora and fauna. As recently as February 2016, a participant at a workshop in Cape Town, Amanda Underwood, shared with me her concerns, when she heard my presentation on xenophobia in South Africa. She remembers with utter disgust, a period when the conservation unit of the Department of Environmental Affairs cut down some 70,000 hectares of trees considered alien to the country. And she recalls a period when motorists were constantly confronted with posters urging them to 'kill', 'strangle' and 'hack' alien plants, accompanied with pictures of the offending trees. Even Jacarandas came under attack, and were only saved by an outcry from the population inspired by their beautiful blooms. She recounts how the Department of Environmental Affairs has rekindled the aggressive campaign to eradicate all alien vegetation (including trees such as the Eucalyptus and the Blue gum), regardless of their local adoption, adaptation and appropriation. Scant regard is paid to the fact that these trees give much needed shade and rest in summer to humans and cattle alike. The onslaught is justified with the need to 'save water' and 'protect the natural environment', a campaign that has led to the extensive use of poison, to the extent that the land looks burnt and totally desolate. Paradoxical as it might seem, in the name of 'biological control', imported 'alien predator insects' are employed to kill certain trees (the Port Jackson and the Prickly Pear, for example) regardless of the fact that people make a living from harvesting and selling them, as is the case with the Prickly Pear in the Eastern Cape (Beinart and Wotshela 2012). A consequence is that the trees are laden with hideous tumours containing highly destructive alien predators. There seems to be little official concern that deforestation might lead to desertification, with fewer trees to attract rain. Under the guise of protecting the environment, thousands of birds' nests have been sprayed with a deadly blue poison that targets reeds. Underwood concludes her lamentation thus:

> Where there was once life and beauty, there is now desolation and death. There is no moderation, or love of nature, or respect for God's creation to be detected in such policies. Just a blanket policy of applying poison everywhere. And what is more, there is very little water to show for this devastation either. That these conservation practices are now a staple menu in school curricula does not augur well for our future, as there is the likelihood that a new generation of

children are growing up with no care for nature, or any aspect of nature labelled as 'alien'.

Will the environmentalist purist stop in time their apocalyptic obsession with nurturing the nation through selective inclusion, before they have totally jeopardised South Africa's rainbow nation of nature (Comaroff and Comaroff 2001; Beinart 2003; Beinart and Wotshela 2012)?

If whitening up is the order of the day, every now and again, those in pursuit of whiteness must stop, take stock, and deal with the hurdles on their way to achieving the promise of whiteness. For South Africans in townships and informal settlements, the tendency is to look for scapegoats in their circles, among those who share the same spaces and with whom they compete on a daily basis for the lure and allure of elusive whiteness, or at least, for someone to blame. Those much further up in terms of social visibility are often too far up to be pulled down easily. One learns to cut one's coat of blame according to one's cloth. With this in mind, let us again turn our attention to RMF and the liberation struggles of the ivory tower.

In the current RMF and transformation debates, by insisting frequently that the Rhodes statue was only a symbol or metaphor for the wider lack of transformation at UCT, the protesting students echoed and were echoed by academic staff with similar concerns about the predominantly white reality of the institution despite the allegedly post-apartheid landscape of the country. Mangcu wrote several pieces featured by the national media, complaining of the snail's pace of transformation at UCT, an institution where whites dominate teaching positions and there are too few black South African academics at professorial level. He makes a distinction between black South Africans, coloureds and Indians, as do fellow South African academics and the state as well. Here is an excerpt from one of his articles on the matter:

Of the 174 South Africans who are full professors at the university, there are only five black South Africans (2.8%), six coloured males (3.4%) and two coloured females (1%). There are 10 Indian male full professors (5.7%) and only one Indian woman (0.5%). In short, Steve Biko's Blacks – blacks, coloureds and Indians

127

– constituted just about 12% of the full professors at UCT who were South African in 2013. As Biko pointed out, the fate of coloureds, Indians and Africans in South Africa will always be interconnected on the margins. Yes, you guessed it right, 85% are white South Africans (148 out of 174). The parallels with the Land Act of 1913 could not be more striking.

In my faculty at UCT, the humanities, where you would expect pioneering research about our future, there are only two black South Africans who are full professors. There was a 100% increase with the appointment of a new dean of the humanities to bring us to a whopping two out of 47 full professors in the humanities. And they are in one department, sociology.[39]

Put differently, Mangcu was complaining that UCT was dominated by *amakwerekwere* of yesteryear (whites, coloured, Indians) – some of whom have divided loyalties by virtue of carrying more than one passport – and that those claiming the status of bona fide black native sons and daughters of the land had yet to feel genuinely integrated into an institution that was supposedly theirs. Instead, the university authorities resorted to filling the place up with *amakwerekwere* of another kind, blacks from north of the Limpopo, as if every black was black enough in the South African context.

This nuance was aptly pointed out by Professor Sakhela Buhlungu, Dean of the Humanities Faculty at UCT (who, in recognition for his demonstrated leadership on drawing attention to the unfinished business of transformation, has earned the reputation of champion of transformation[40]), when he denounced as 'most dishonest, most hypocritical and cynical' the common practice by universities in South Africa to 'cop-out' from expectations of redress, equity and access by counting as 'equity candidates' for recruitment 'international scholars, who just happen to be black.' At the risk of unsettling a number of his fellow academics, Buhlungu subscribes to 'three categories of academics: white South African academics, black South African academics and international scholars', and calls for 'balance across the categories.' In other words, he recognises the *amakwerekwere* within the category of South African (white South Africans, who happen to be mostly those playing 'tricks' and being hypocritical about transformation and to whom one black equals another, South African or not) and

128

the obvious *amakwerekwere* in their varying degradations (non-South African whites and non-South African blacks – those who are recruited to the detriment of meaningful equity and redress and whose recruitment is often justified/rationalised with arguments to the effect that South African universities need to be competitive internationally).[41] At an assembly on transformation held on 6th August 2015 by the Humanities Faculty of which Buhlungu is Dean, 'it was suggested' that:

- UCT should cap the employment of foreign academics at a percentage of all full-time posts.
- UCT should require that all academics have a certain proportion of black African South African students at PhD and Postdoc levels or not be confirmed after their probationary period. This should also be a condition of continued employment if possible.
- The Faculty should put a moratorium on employing foreign academics in GOB positions and create an alternative five year contract for foreign academics who should have to raise their own grants to fund their positions further.[42]

It is unclear the extent to which the category of 'black African South African' is open to negotiation and to new membership. How possible, for example, is it for someone like Law professor Evance Kalula – a Zimbabwean-born Zambian, who has served UCT since 1992 and actively campaigned for transformation as the pursuit of an enabling environment for diversity beyond a mere chasing of targets[43], who carries a South African heart (as a result of a transplant)[44] as well as a South African passport, and who sees himself as 'a product of the southern realisation of Cecil John Rhodes's "Cape to Cairo" dream, the Southern African migrant system' – to rewrite the nationality laws enough to qualify as a black South African by Buhlungu's categorisation, given that he feels himself a bona fide citizen of the Southern African Development Community and as settled and belonging in Cape Town and South Africa (Kalula 2013: 6-20)?

The emphasis on a particular type of victim of colonisation begs a few questions about 'decolonisation', the label that has found traction with the current RMF campaign. Since context matters, decolonisation cannot be articulated in abstraction. What is the context in which current clamours for decolonisation are inserted?

If African, and guided by an aspiration to Africanise, what would Africanisation amount to? When does decolonisation entail Africanisation?[45] And when does it mean South-Africanisation only, without the whiteness? When does decolonisation as Africanisation enter into a meaningful conversation with decolonisation as whiteless-South-Africanisation?

Above all, when does decolonisation as whiteless-South-Africanisation and Africanisation enter into worthy epistemological conversations with decolonisation as a universal aspiration *à la Frantz Fanon* (1967a, 1986 [1967b]) and *à la Steve Biko* (2004 [1978])? This is an important question (as neither South Africa nor Africa can claim monopoly over victimisation by colonisation, imperialism and apartheid as a racialized technology of subjugation and domination). Decolonisation as a universal aspiration may or may not coincide with being African or with being South African, in both the general, generous and inclusive sense and the exclusionary, parochial and autochthonous sense of these identities.

This teething problem of decolonisation is a replay of the debate in the 1960s in the rest of Africa, the time most countries on the continent gained a semblance of independence[46], even if South Africa's predicament is that decolonisation is happening at the same time as accelerated globalisation and the resurgence of imperialism (Saccarelli and Varadarajan 2015), which complicates the situation remarkably, through the mass production of black migrants by the collapsing economies of many African states (Crush et al. 2015; Nyamnjoh 2015a). But even in the 1960s, as Fanon notes in *The Wretched of the Earth*, the narrow nationalism inherited from the erstwhile colonialists was already inciting nationals to violence against foreigners while calling for ever diminishing opportunities to be confined to citizens (Fanon 1967a: 125-126). Caught between continued exploitation by *amakwerekwere* of yesteryear who remain firmly in charge as privileged and powerful nationals and as mediators between multinational corporations and local opportunities on the one hand, and the influx of sweet footed Africans (Alhaji 2015) and men of good hope fleeing the hardships of warzones and failed states (Steinberg 2015), South African blacks who mainly remained hemmed in in townships and at the margins of the economy twenty years into the end of apartheid (Pillay et al.

2013), have every reason to feel consumed and suffocated, and to erupt every now and again in the jingoism they inherited from Rhodes. These are legitimate existential conditions that fuel sentiments of exclusion, which, paradoxically, only serve to further divide-and-rule the very already marginalised black lives that should be busy creating solidarities of steel to fight off oppression and exploitation with reckless abandon by the global evangelists for the doctrine of profit over people.

This raises some critical questions. When is decolonisation more than simply opening out to engage with African and South African issues, knowledge and epistemology? What reason is there to quibble about making knowledge production focused on South Africa and Africa the central concern of a university that purports to be South African and African, and therefore to imply that it thinks, teaches and relates to the world from that vantage point of being South African and African? What manner of transformation is sufficiently accommodating of the complexities and nuances of being African or South African in a nimble-footed world where everyone is a potential *makwerekwere*, powerful or not, and where autochthony makes sense only in terms of how ready one is able to include history beyond that which is convenient for one and the interests one is defending for the moment?[47] If decolonisation is to entail a self-critical struggle for meaning (Hountondji 2002) that frowns on institutionalised prejudice and spurious justifications of socially cultivated indifference, past and present (Herzfeld 1992), what degree of nuance and care do we need in navigating and negotiating the myriad intricacies involved, in order to get it right?

In a Facebook post reacting to Mbembe's article 'State of South African Politics', Mojalefa Murphy – 'a South African born Nuclear Physicist' and 'skilled generalist and activist' – echoes Buhlungu's sentiments. He argues that to keep postponing the redressing of past injustices and the provision of equal citizenship for black South Africans, university authorities in South Africa who remain predominantly white, prefer to reach out to and co-opt black African academics from the rest of the continent (such as Mbembe) to provide token black presence on campuses in order to give the impression of racial reconfiguration in the name of transformation. Murphy may be right that it is no secret that foreign black Africans

131

'are generally preferred for employment in white managed South African outfits both in the public and private sector', possibly to foster the white supremacists' agenda of 'exploiting the economy corruptly to feather nests abroad.' In reward for their support, foreign African academics in 'white institutions of higher learning' in South Africa are known to 'sail through with ease' while many black South African academics are 'overlooked for promotion to senior and professorial positions.' It is wrong, he concludes, for whites and their black conformists in South Africa to 'interpret the justifiable anger at whiteness as hatred for whites.' Black anger is nothing but an expression of collective black psyche as informed by black people's lived traumatic experiences of centuries of racial assault by white supremacists.[48] Such divide-and-rule practices as described by Murphy, if truly intended, ought to be condemned without mitigation. It is equally in the interest of those invested in decolonisation as both a local and global pursuit to understand and circumvent the game of divide-and-rule championed by an ideological predisposition to a world of interconnecting local and global hierarchies informed by factors or considerations such as race, ethnicity, place, class, gender and generation.

While some non-South African blacks may be perceived to be co-opted to serve the interests of white supremacists, a prioritisation of transformation as redress and equity for South African blacks exclusively, however justified contextually, disenfranchises or delegitimises any compelling claims to black pain that non-South African black academics may experience at UCT as an institution dominated by the privileged interests and taken-for-granted perspectives in tune with the *habitus* of being white in South Africa. Such exclusionary or selective indicators of blackness and black pain give the impression that black pain at UCT is experienced by degree, on which hierarchical continuum South African blacks experience greater pain. It gives the impression as well that, however much solidarity non-South African blacks bring to the struggle, their black pain – the pain of black *amakwerekwere* or outsiders within – is always susceptible, a priori, to being defined and related to as inferior to the pain of black South Africans who overtly or covertly consider themselves as authentic sons or daughters of the native soil. Accordingly, if black pain and black lives matter, the geography, nationality, ethnicity, gender (or whatever other determinant of importance) of black pain and black lives matters even more. Black South Africans who think and act thus, feel they really should have been in charge, had not the white *amakwerekwere* of yesteryear, epitomised by Rhodes, conquered and tamed them with violence and superior technology, injecting and implanting themselves and their progeny as a more or less permanent blot on the native landscape.

Thus, being black or white is not all there is to the transformation debate, which is also, and often more importantly, about rights and entitlements as nationals and citizens of a specific nation-state. In such localised autochthonous struggle for social visibility, resources and power, the new generation of *amakwerekwere* who are black, often powerless and dispensable, and who hail from Africa north of the Limpopo, matter very little whatever the magnitude of their own frustrations with the deeply colonial nature of the university institutions that have hired them, or where they are students. They are caught between forces that often know little compromise. Seen in these terms, such *amakwerekwere*, their commitment to genuine transformation notwithstanding, could easily find themselves in awkward situations (not dissimilar to those in which so-called born-free white students have found themselves when they have come out to show solidarity with their protesting black colleagues) where they are perceived and related to as if they were perfect strangers at a funeral weeping more than the owner of the corpse, or as fighting fights in which they have no stakes. Paradoxically, it seems to matter little what non-South African blacks think or feel, as they are open to caricature either way in the game of narrow nationalism that South African blacks find themselves compelled to play, systematically stifled as they have been by the callous indifference of whites and whiteness.

In this light, Shose Kessi's critical reaction to Mbembe's article discussed above needs qualification and nuance to reflect the ever-diminishing circles of inclusion even when race is a common denominator. Kessi, a black senior lecturer of Tanzanian nationality in the Department of Psychology at UCT, is keen to highlight an all-black predicament in the institution. She presents herself as belonging to 'the Black Academic Caucus' at UCT – 'a group of over 80 black academics representing all faculties … engaging in institution-wide conversations and actions to address the exclusion of black experiences and scholarship in the area of curriculum, research, staff recruitment and development, and institutional culture'. She identifies with the struggle to the extent that it is inclusive of all blacks, and expresses what to her are all-black concerns. To her, black scholarship, whether by black South Africans or by *amakwerekwere* from beyond the Limpopo and in the diaspora, should prioritise the needs and aspirations of blacks. It should be scholarship that takes into account the social and historical contexts of blacks, and in the particular case of South Africa and the continent, 'the material, symbolic and structural conditions brought about by colonisation and apartheid.' Important in such scholarship are 'the affective and bodily experiences' of black scholars and black people. It is a scholarship that seeks to 'dismantle the racist masculinist culture of our institution (city, country and continent) and … whiteness and patriarchy in the lived experiences of black staff and students.' It is a scholarship that challenges a tendency in 'rational' talk to portray black people as always the 'problem' – either as helpless passive victims or as people whose sense of judgement is eternally clouded by too much emotion. To Kessi, it is precisely such emotion that is needed to understand the objectification, undermining, and experiences of exclusion of black bodies in the institution. Emotions awaken consciousness of how the past invades the present and how to move forward. Kessi argues that far from closing off dialogue, expressing 'black pain' can be instructive on the workings of 'oppressive power … and the intricate levels and dimensions at which it operates.' To her, 'Engaging with black pain develops a new level of consciousness where the affective experiences of exclusion are at the root of how critical reasoned argument can emerge and lead to decolonising and transformative practices.'[49] She illustrates her point thus:

> When black students protest at being silenced in classroom debates, at being taught with materials that exclude or devalue their bodies and cultures, at having to live through the rape culture of our residences, these painful experiences inform the learning, teaching, and cultural practices that need to change. When black staff protest at

being denied promotion, at being rejected by ethics committees, or at being depicted as incompetent simply because of their race or so-called 'black accents,' these experiences inform the teaching, research, and governance practices that need to change. In fact, all of these experiences tell us of the ways in which the dominant white male culture at UCT is perpetuated at the expense of black, women, and LGBTQ experiences and intellectual excellence. As an academic institution that is forging and inspiring the minds of future generations, challenging these dynamics is fundamental to creating a society that fosters inclusivity, dialogue, and wellbeing.[50]

Although Kessi mentions women and LGBTQ experiences and intellectual excellence as victims of patriarchy in passing, these require a full length study in their own right. An intersectional approach to decolonisation is of critical importance, one that takes on board how hierarchies premised on factors beyond race – factors such as gender, class, ethnicity, nationality, geography and generation – render more complex and layered the form decolonisation should take to be meaningful to all and sundry social categories seeking it. Women students and staff have played a major and sustained role in the RMF at UCT. The internet, Facebook, YouTube, Twitter and related social media platforms are full of evidence in this regard. Women students were at the forefront of the occupation of Bremner building and along with their male counterparts staged many protests to summon university management to address transformation concerns, including patriarchy and sexism at the institution and nationally. Before the erection of what was dubbed 'Shackville' on campus to draw attention to the plight of UCT students without accommodation in March 2016, the women of RMF actually kicked all the men out of the organisation because of patriarchy.[51] This point was reiterated by the Trans Collective when they disrupted an exhibition to mark the anniversary of RMF that appeared to trivialise the contributions by women.[52] Indeed, patriarchy is rife across university campuses.[53] As recently as April 2016, the Wits University SRC distanced itself from the homophobic and sexist attacks that took place during a demonstration organised by RMF and the EFF student command at the Braamfontein campus of the university. The SRC statement read:

We take issue with blatant patriarchy, displays of antiqueer and anti-transgender politics as well as aimless acts of violence and intimidation of students and in particular women students. We believe these acts fundamentally undermine the very values that the student movement seeks to embody.[54]

The story of the day at UCT that black women sat and stood-still around campus with tape over their mouths to demonstrate how they feel silenced by the male dominated university deserves to be written in a volume beyond the few brushstrokes here. Exemplary kindred studies to inspire a scholarly documentation of RMF from a woman and feminist perspective include *Rape: A South African Nightmare* by Pumla Dineo Gqola (2016) and *Engendering African Social Sciences* edited by Ayesha Imam, Amina Mama and Fatou Sow (1997).

A focus on resistance by university students and staff in South Africa accords us the possibility to see the operations or workings of power inherited from the likes of Rhodes and the narrow individual and collective interests they sought to defend in the name of a co-opting civilising mission (Abu-Lughod 1990). The students' protests reveal a fascinating diagnostic of the continued overt and convert oppression and exploitation by whiteness as experienced by the so-called born-frees, who, at face value and as Newman and De Lannoy (2014) largely argue, should be an epitome of a deracialised and seamlessly inclusive post-apartheid dispensation. The tensions and divisions in such protests demonstrate how refuge to parochial definitions or shifting indicators of citizenship and belonging are indicative of the extent to which the myth of the sovereign postcolonial state has been internalized and uncritically reproduced by citizens of South Africa, university professors included. It reveals as well how much the myth of whiteness as a catalogue of power, privilege and opportunity continues to serve as a 'charter' for social action on the part of the oppressed, who are preponderantly black. If myth serves a powerful social function – namely to justify current social arrangements of power, privilege and hierarchies – then the resort to such parochialism in fact legitimates the myth of white power, privilege and superiority. In other words, it vindicates and immortalises Cecil John Rhodes and all he represents in contemporary South Africa.

Blackness as an attribute of being a particular type of human, whether ascribed, achieved or imposed, is not the monopoly of any particular African country, nor of the continent. It calls for a conceptualisation and articulation of the decolonisation of knowledge production and consumption that is carefully nuanced to provide for the complex intersections of race, ethnicity, geography, class, gender and generation. Even at our most legitimately aggrieved, we cannot afford to resort to the zero-sum games of dominance of the oppressors, as this would only compound our subservience and predicaments.

Notes

[1] Kwanele Sosibo, http://mg.co.za/article/2015-04-23-xenophobia-what-did-we-learn-from-2008, accessed 4 March 2016.
[2] Elyas Mulu Kiros, http://allafrica.com/stories/201504250205.html, accessed 5 March 2016.
[3] Fholisani Sydney Mufamadi, http://mg.co.za/article/2015-04-23-proactive-solutions-need-to-be-found-to-solve-the-problem, accessed 4 March 2016.
[4] Qaanitah Hunter & Mmanaledi Mataboge, http://mg.co.za/article/2015-04-23-police-minister-missing-as-sa-burns, accessed 4 March 2016.
[5] David Smith, http://www.theguardian.com/world/2015/apr/20/south-africa-xenophobic-violence-zulu-king-goodwill-zwelithini, accessed 6 March 2016.
[6] Kwanele Sosibo, http://mg.co.za/article/2015-04-23-xenophobia-what-did-we-learn-from-2008, accessed 4 March 2016.
[7] Qaanitah Hunter & Mmanaledi Mataboge, http://mg.co.za/article/2015-04-23-police-minister-missing-as-sa-burns, accessed 4 March 2016.
[8] Jean-Jacques Cornish, http://ewn.co.za/2015/04/26/Nigeria-officially-recalls-its-ambassador, accessed 7 March 2016.
[9] See for example, http://www.sabc.co.za/news/a/a146fd0048216b3eb3bbbb99b16eb747/SouthundefinedAfricansundefinedmarchundefinedagainstundefinedxenophobia-20152404, accessed 7 March 2016.
Ashoka Jegroo, http://wagingnonviolence.org/2015/04/thousands-of-south-africans-march-against-xenophobic-violence/, accessed 7 March 2016.

[10] Sarah Evans, http://mg.co.za/article/2015-04-23-today-we-are-all-african, accessed 5 March 2016.

[11] Matuma Letsoalo, https://unitedfrontsa.wordpress.com/2015/04/24/irvin-jim-lays-xenophobia-at-ancs-door/, accessed 5 March 2016.

[12] Jeff Wicks, http://www.news24.com/SouthAfrica/News/Malema-changes-tune-to-kissing-the-Boer-20150427, accessed 5 March 2016.

[13] See http://www.news24.com/SouthAfrica/News/SA-media-in-firing-line-for-xenophobia-coverage-20150424, accessed 4 March 2016.

[14] Matuma Letsoalo, https://unitedfrontsa.wordpress.com/2015/04/24/irvin-jim-lays-xenophobia-at-ancs-door/, accessed 5 March 2016.

[15] Thulani Gqirana, http://mg.co.za/article/2015-04-24-dedicated-courts-appointed-to-deal-with-xenophobic-cases, accessed 5 March 2016.

[16] See https://www.youtube.com/watch?v=5RgSqDaH7QY, accessed 12 March 2016.

[17] David Smith, http://www.theguardian.com/world/2015/apr/20/south-africa-xenophobic-violence-zulu-king-goodwill-zwelithini, accessed 6 March 2016.

[18] Clive Ndou http://citizen.co.za/349347/foreigners-must-go-home-king-zwelithini/, accessed 6 March 2016.

[19] Clive Ndou, http://citizen.co.za/349347/foreigners-must-go-home-king-zwelithini/, accessed 6 March 2016.

[20] Amanda Khoza, http://www.news24.com/SouthAfrica/News/Zumas-son-wants-foreigners-out-of-the-country-20150331, accessed 6 March 2016.

[21] See http://www.news24.com/SouthAfrica/News/Zumas-son-Govt-must-stop-unnecessarily-accommodating-foreign-nationals-20150414, accessed 6 March 2016.

[22] Amanda Khoza, http://www.news24.com/SouthAfrica/News/Zumas-son-wants-foreigners-out-of-the-country-20150331, accessed 6 March 2016.

[23] See http://www.news24.com/SouthAfrica/News/Zumas-son-Govt-must-stop-unnecessarily-accommodating-foreign-nationals-20150414, accessed 6 March 2016.

[24] Amanda Khoza, http://www.news24.com/SouthAfrica/News/Zumas-son-wants-foreigners-out-of-the-country-20150331, accessed 6 March 2016.

[25] See http://www.news24.com/SouthAfrica/News/Zumas-son-Govt-must-stop-unnecessarily-accommodating-foreign-nationals-20150414, accessed 6 March 2016.

[26] See South Africa's Guptas hit back in Zuma finance minister row, http://www.bbc.com/news/world-africa-35846831, accessed 19 March 2016.

[27] See https://www.youtube.com/watch?v=kzJj7I1-WZ8, accessed 12 March 2016.

[28] David Smith, http://www.theguardian.com/world/2015/apr/20/south-africa-xenophobic-violence-zulu-king-goodwill-zwelithini, accessed 6 March 2016.

[29] David Smith, http://www.theguardian.com/world/2015/apr/20/south-africa-xenophobic-violence-zulu-king-goodwill-zwelithini, accessed 6 March 2016.

[30] David Smith, http://www.theguardian.com/world/2015/apr/20/south-africa-xenophobic-violence-zulu-king-goodwill-zwelithini, accessed 6 March 2016.

[31] Vusi Khumalo, http://www.sabc.co.za/news/a/c736648047e4865ea076f74405f77b26/IFP-leader-apologises-to-foreign-nationals-for-xenophobic-attacks-20150404, accessed 6 March 2016.

[32] Vusi Khumalo, http://www.sabc.co.za/news/a/c736648047e4865ea076f74405f77b26/IFP-leader-apologises-to-foreign-nationals-for-xenophobic-attacks-20150404, accessed 6 March 2016.

[33] Elyas Mulu Kiros, http://allafrica.com/stories/201504250205.html, accessed 5 March 2016.

[34] See http://www.thepresidency.gov.za/pebble.asp?relid=19584, accessed 6 March 2016.

[35] See http://www.thepresidency.gov.za/pebble.asp?relid=19584, accessed 6 March 2016.

[36] See http://www.thepresidency.gov.za/pebble.asp?relid=19584, accessed 6 March 2016.

[37] See http://www.thepresidency.gov.za/pebble.asp?relid=19584, accessed 6 March 2016.

[38] See http://www.thepresidency.gov.za/pebble.asp?relid=19584, accessed 6 March 2016.

[39] See Xolela Mangcu, 'Ripping the veil off UCT's whiter shades of pale University's move to "downgrade" race fails to hide the truth about inequality', 6 July 2014, *Sunday Times*, p. 18. See also: http://www.bdlive.co.za/opinion/2014/11/03/sas-black-academics-are-getting-raw-deal, accessed 6 October 2015; Xolela Mangcu, '10 steps to develop black professors', *City Press*, 20 July 2014.

[40] See, for example, Public debate: Transformation in higher education, https://www.youtube.com/watch?v=thiiUDeIySw, accessed 8 October 2015.

This debate, which took the form of a panel discussion, was titled 'The University and Society' and took place at the Baxter Concert Hall on 21 October 2014. The debate was chaired by Sakhela Buhlungu; participating panellists were Dr Max Price, UCT VC; Professor Jonathan Jansen, rector and VC of the University of the Free State; and Professor Mamokgethi Phakeng, vice principal, research and innovation, University of South Africa.

[41] See http://mg.co.za/article/2015-03-06-brazen-trickery-in-transformation, accessed 30 September 2015.

[42] See page 4 of report on 'Humanities Faculty Assembly on Transformation', circulated by the Dean via email to 'hum-everyone-l@lists.uct.ac.za' on 18 March 2016.

[43] Not that the achievements of such targets should be ignored. In her auto-biography, Mamphela Ramphele recounts among her successes as VC of UCT both the change in institutional culture and in the demographics of the university. She writes: 'In the early 1990s a third of the student body was black and during my term this increased to the point where nearly half were black. Equally encouraging, by 2006, the female component of the student body stood at 51%' (Ramphele 2013: 308). Another change was in the attitude of black students who did not have to feel ridiculed and embarrassed for excelling as black students – unlike in the 1980s, when black students who excelled in the examinations were obliged to cross out their marks on the results lists pinned up on notice boards, because to 'achieve high percentages was seen as making yourself white' – (Ramphele 2013: 307).

[44] Of his new South African heart Evance Kalula writes: 'I am eternally indebted to the donor's family for the ultimate gift of life. It is the most generous gift one can receive. I gratefully embrace it in trust, to use and to put this second chance to the service of others' (Kalula 2013: 50).

[45] For further reflections on this issue, see, for example, Achille Mbembe, Decolonizing knowledge and the question of the archive, http://wiser.wits.ac.za/system/files/Achille%20Mbembe%20-%20Decolonizing%20Knowledge%20and%20the%20Question%20of%20the%20Archive.pdf, accessed 9 October 2015; http://wiser.wits.ac.za/content/podcast-achille-mbembes-public-lecture-decolonizing-university-12046, accessed 9 October 2015.

[46] Many African countries have since regretted the fact that they obtained token political independence – usually derogatorily referred to by critics as 'flag independence' to the detriment of the economic independence they ought to have sought vigorously in order to avoid the excessive economic dependence on former colonial masters and the West at large in the postcolonial era. Kwame Nkrumah's slogan – Seek ye first the political kingdom and all else shall follow – was an extravagant illusion to which the post-apartheid ANC government seem to have fallen prey.

[47] See http://www.destinyman.com/2015/04/23/ucts-latest-move-towards-transformation-may-not-be-the-best-way-forward/, accessed 3 October 2015.

48 See http://www.mediaforjustice.net/achille-mbembes-state-of-south-african-politics-undermines-black-south-africans/?fb_action_ids=10154170807341124&fb_action_types=og.likes, accessed 1 October 2015.

49 See Shose Kessi, 'Of black pain, animal rights and the politics of the belly', http://thoughtleader.co.za/blackacademiccaucus/2015/09/25/of-black-pain-animal-rights-and-the-politics-of-the-belly/, accessed 1 October 2015.

50 See Shose Kessi, 'Of black pain, animal rights and the politics of the belly', http://thoughtleader.co.za/blackacademiccaucus/2015/09/25/of-black-pain-animal-rights-and-the-politics-of-the-belly/, accessed 1 October 2015.

51 See for example, 'How UCT's system failed student after sexual harassment case', http://city-press.news24.com/News/an-art-school-gender-protest-20160103, accessed 6 April 2016.

52 See Ashraf Hendricks, http://www.dailymaverick.co.za/article/2016-03-11-groundup-rhodes-must-fall-exhibition-vandalised-in-uct-protest/#.VuPbznrCAdw, accessed 12 March 2016. See also Yusuf Omar, 'Trans Collective stops RMF exhibition', http://www.uct.ac.za/dailynews/?id=9620, accessed 12 March 2016.

53 See for example, http://www.news24.com/SouthAfrica/News/ucts-maxwele-slammed-over-physical-altercation-with-female-wits-student-20160405, http://www.timeslive.co.za/local/2016/04/05/NotMyFMF---sjamboks-and-muscles-in-Wits-gender-showdown, accessed 6 April 2016.

54 See Batandwa Malingo, 'Wits homophobic, sexist attacks condemned', http://www.thenewage.co.za/wits-homophobic-sexist-attacks-condemned/, accessed 9 April 2016.

Chapter 4

UCT Fires on All Cylinders

As the RMF protest grew in intensity and stature, the university authorities went to work, firing on all cylinders, or just about, in an attempt to concoct a solution.[1] The VC and his senior administrators admitted that UCT had tended to test the waters instead of confronting transformation head on. A few quotes by senior management and spokespersons at different points of the protest illustrate this assessment. Gerda Kruger, in her capacity as spokeswoman for the university affirmed that '[UCT] has acknowledged that we have been slow to address certain facets of transformation, such as curriculum reform ... we are committed to listening, discussing, debating and finding answers'.[2] Management held meetings with students and set up white boards around the statue, wrapped in black plastic, where students could write down their opinions. UCT's first response to these calls for action was to issue a circular announcing it would convene a discussion on 'Heritage, Signage and Symbolism' led by DVC, Professor Crain Soudien.[3] But before this discussion could take place, there had been further protests centred on the Rhodes statue, then swathed and taped in black rubbish bags. By the time these first negotiations with the university administration were convened, the SRC's position had hardened.

SRC President, Ramabina Mahapa, said: 'I understand it is part of history, but the institutional representation of black people at this university is negative.'[4] From here, the RMF movement escalated rapidly, culminating in a march and the occupation of the university's administration building, Bremner. VC Max Price responded with university-wide debates and a special meeting of the university senate to consider proposals. Upfront, he said that he and his executive favoured removing the statue, but only the university council could take the final decision. An emergency meeting of the council was called for 25 April. Meanwhile, the stand-off rapidly became a national issue. Students at Rhodes University in

Grahamstown went on protest in sympathy, and minister Blade Nzimande gave his support for moving the statue.[5]

The extended debate at UCT considered various options. One was to leave the statue standing where it was but include a plaque at its base acknowledging the 'injustices of colonial conquest enacted under Rhodes' watch.' In addition, the option to leave the statue where it was would have to be 'accompanied by another artwork to be located alongside Rhodes, to 'speak back' by way of alternative values and convictions.' To the VC, it was the very strategic location of the statue at the focal point of the campus that had attracted connotations of Rhodes being a 'founder, hero, patron, role model and [an] embodiment of UCT's heritage.'[6] Hence his personal opinion that the statue should be moved:

> I just think it should not be there – it should be moved. This will not compromise our ability to record and debate the role Rhodes played in the city's and continent's history. And it will not change our acknowledgment that UCT acquired its site from the Rhodes estate, and the positive contribution it has made to our institution and its students.[7]

Despite his conviction that there was 'a significant view that the statue should be moved', the VC opted for an extended consultation because 'there has never been any formal consultation or organised discussion on this matter, and it would not be appropriate for the UCT executive, or council, to make such a recommendation without undertaking such a discussion'.[8] Adekeye Adebajo, executive director of the Centre for Conflict Resolution at UCT, was among those who criticised the university for being rather officious in its response to the protest, 'with a questioning of the methods of some of the students; an insistence on the need to follow 'procedures' for 'peaceful and safe' protests; encouraging 'open debate and responsible action'; and threatening to take legal steps against any 'unlawful behaviour'.[9] The VC responded to Adebajo, accusing him of distorting his views on Rhodes:

> Adebajo succeeds in completely distorting the view I hold on Rhodes. First, he fails to mention that I, personally, have repeatedly stated that I regard Rhodes as a villain, the perpetrator

of ruthless exploitation of indigenous people, land expropriation, illegal wars and vicious conquest.

Second he fails to remind readers that I, as well as the entire senior leadership group of the university, have publicly expressed our view that the Rhodes statue must be moved.[10]

The VC defended his decision to consult extensively despite his personal conclusion that the statue should be moved, by reiterating the following: 'UCT is an argumentative university. This is an abiding strength: it shows our engagement with the issues of our times and our interest in ideas that matter. Undoubtedly the students are leading a national debate.'[11] While some felt that UCT had wasted time deliberating the obvious, others such as Wits VC Habib, felt that UCT had not deliberated and conversed deeply enough before a decision on the Rhodes statute was concluded.[12]

Following nearly a month of protests and meetings, the university senate voted in favour of moving Rhodes's statue as follows: 181 votes in favour; 1 vote against; 3 abstentions.[13] The decision was endorsed at a special meeting of the UCT Convocation on 7 April 2015. On 8 April the university council decided unanimously to remove the statue and that it be temporarily housed for safekeeping in an unnamed storeroom approved by the Western Cape Heritage Resources Council, pending a formal application to that council to have the statue removed permanently, in accordance with the National Heritage Resources Act.[14] The chair of the UCT Council, Archbishop Ndungane asked for an accelerated and acceptable roadmap of transformation. He credited the students in particular for the historic removal of Rhodes's statue:

> What sparked this was a cry from the students. That transformation needs to be consolidated. Cecil John Rhodes, for the sins of his past, as an imperialist and a racist ... stands in contrast to the values that this university enhances. And so Management of this university got into a process of consulting various structures of the university, including Senate, and terminating in our meeting last night when Council voted unanimously as recognition of what the students are saying and a demonstration of our commitment to transformation.[15]

On 9 April 2015, at 5.37 pm, the contentious 'statue of Cecil John Rhodes was lifted a short distance by a huge crane from its pride of place [and] pelted with whatever members of the gathered crowd could get their hands on, as it was lowered onto its waiting transport', while 'some onlookers stood in silence, a few took selfies and some sang and danced.'[16] As the statue was driven off, the SRC vice-president of external affairs Zizipho Pae said moving it was paving the way for the 'real work' of transforming UCT to begin. Other students concurred, waving banners that read 'We have only just started'. The students had won a victory over a statue, and they would continue to occupy Bremner Building, re-christened 'Azania House', until their demands for racial transformation were met. 'This movement is not just about a statue, it's about decolonizing the colonial structure, the curriculum and everything it stands for', some insisted. On their transformation shopping list were plans to lobby in coming months 'for the promotion of black lecturers and the enrolment of more students from disadvantaged communities', and to follow up on a proposal they had submitted requesting that 'the names of various other 'colonial landmarks' at the university, including Jameson Hall, be changed. Jameson Hall was named after Leander Starr Jameson, a confidant of Rhodes.'

The protests spread to other formerly white universities such as Wits, Rhodes University, Stellenbosch University (SU), and the University of KwaZulu-Natal. But reverberations have also been felt at universities such as North West, Tshwane, Western Cape and Free State.[17] In all of these institutions, as Tasneem Essop, a master's student in Political Studies and the Secretary-General of the 2013 SRC at Wits, puts it, black African students were in 'rage against the forms of institutional racism that students have been told to live with.' The students were protesting and taking to social media to challenge 'the silencing of black students' in colonial institutions that no longer had a place in post-colonial and post-apartheid South Africa.[18]

As Essop argues, in all of these universities the protests spoke to 'a much broader failure in higher education since 1994 and a much deeper problem of exclusion' for black South Africans. She maintains that the increased number of black students and black staff on campus does not matter much if institutional racism and

146

inequality are not tackled at a structural level. 'Having been a student leader at Wits University, I know all too well the consistently frustrating pace of transformation at our institution. Wits, like most other former white universities, has a deep-seated, institutional and systemic form of racism that is swept under the carpet.' It is quite possible, she argues, for the majority of students in a programme to be black, and yet, for a student 'to go through a humanities curriculum without meeting one African, female lecturer and without learning anything outside of a deeply Eurocentric curriculum.'[19]

Faced with such intricacies, transformation requires careful and meticulous thinking through to get it right. Otherwise, current clamours for transformation are likely to end in failure just as did past initiatives in the 1990s, Essop warns. There are fewer black postgraduate students who graduate 'partly because of socioeconomic circumstances outside of universities which force them to enter the workforce earlier, rather than to remain in academia', and partly because of the failures of universities to take seriously the financial, social and academic conditions of black students or to take black students seriously. 'Many black students have had to come to terms with the fact that, despite their relative privilege at universities, they do not benefit from the structures of the academy in the same ways as white students.' As in the case with other RMF campaigners, Essop's sights are set beyond the symbolic: 'Once the symbols – the statues and names – have been removed from our campuses, the same rage that we see now, must be focused on the heart of these academies. That will be the real battle to transform the often invisible structures and mechanisms that sustain institutional racism.'[20]

At Stellenbosch University, which insists on Afrikaans as the principal language of undergraduate instruction (Bottomley 2012: 124-135; van der Waal and Robins 2011), protests to open up the university inspired a film by Dan Corder of Contraband Cape Town, working with Open Stellenbosch titled *Luister* [Listen].[21] Produced in just 17 days, this 35-minute documentary is made up of interviews with 32 students and one lecturer at Stellenbosch University, detailing their experiences of racist abuse, discrimination and exclusion. The film is centred on responses to the question:

147

'What is it like to be a black person at Stellenbosch University?' All 32 student interviews were filmed over six hours on 2 August 2015.[22]

The following pronouncements by students stand out in reviews and discussions of the film in social media and newspapers: 'I feel like it's wrong to be black ... I sometimes ask myself when I'm alone, why did God make me black when a lot can happen in a good way when you're otherwise?'; 'The colour of my skin in Stellenbosch is like a social burden ... I mean just walking into spaces, there's that stop, pause, and stare where people cannot believe that you would enter into this space'; 'Being black within the Stellenbosch community you know that you're not accepted and you kind of ask yourself what's wrong with me, like what did I do wrong?'; 'In the beginning I actually started to assimilate, you know, wanting to lose myself and attain whiteness. Maybe this will work better and they'll accept me more because I'm trying to be like them. And I realised that I cannot do that. I'm not willing to sell my soul to whiteness. I have to be proudly black.' Released on 17 August 2015, the film had attracted over 343,222 views (3,784 likes, 735 dislikes on YouTube) by 5 October 2015, the date I accessed it. It has trended on social media in South Africa, attracting the attention of political leaders of all leanings. Debate over the film reportedly resulted in the suspension of Metro FM host Unathi Msengana, following comments she made about the video[23] and in Stellenbosch University management being summoned to appear in Parliament for an urgent meeting on transformation.[24]

As observed of higher education in South Africa in general (Bhana 2014; MacDonald 2006; Soudien 2010, 2012; Higgins and Vale 2016), the film makes clear that transformation is not merely a case of add a little black and stir, while continuing with the same structure and the same rules. Commenting on *Luister*, Jansen calls on white Afrikaans universities to make peace with the fact that African students are rightly knocking on the doors of learning simply to gain access to public institutions, and to ensure that these students are protected from the risks to which they are exposed in universities where they are a racial minority. Jansen elaborates:

148

As I have said over and over again, in a country shaped by centuries of white supremacy, and with a violent history of trying to push Afrikaans down the throats of black people (Soweto 1976), race will always trump language in the transformation debates. In other words, because of our history the right to access will always take on much more political significance than language rights. The longer leaders of the Afrikaans universities take to accept this simple truth, the more their campuses will be the target of upheavals for years to come.[25]

As a direct result of the protests spearheaded by Open Stellenbosch, on Thursday 12 November 2015, Stellenbosch University management announced its decision to discontinue insistence on Afrikaans as the primary language of instruction with effect from January 2016. Here is an excerpt of the statement:

Language should be used in a way that is oriented towards engagement with knowledge in a diverse society and to ensure equitable access to learning and teaching opportunities for all students. Since English is the common language in South Africa, all learning should be facilitated in at least English to ensure no exclusion due to language. The University remains committed to the further development of Afrikaans and isiXhosa as academic languages.
[....]
The primary language of communication and administration at Stellenbosch University will be English, with Afrikaans and isiXhosa as additional languages. The additional languages may not be used to exclude anyone from full participation at the University. This implies that all communication at Stellenbosch University will be in at least English, including meetings, official documents, and services at reception desks and the call centre, etc.[26]

This announcement was celebrated by the Open Stellenbosch campaign group with a Facebook post that read: 'The Language Policy Has Fallen'.[27] In a BBC report, Milton Nkosi adds: 'Dropping Afrikaans means that, psychologically and symbolically, the walls of apartheid are still crumbling 21 years after racial segregation was officially removed from the statute books.'[28] The decision also inspired similar calls for a switch from Afrikaans to English as the main language of instruction by protesting students at the universities of Pretoria and the Free State in February 2016.[29]

It is worth recalling, as Fiona Ross reminds us, that Afrikaans, like any other language, can hold people together, just as it can divide people and destroy relationships (Ross 2010: 139). 'We inhabit the world through language', which 'pre-exists us', is 'saturated in power', and with which we are 'always already implicated' (Ross 2010: 163). Afrikaans unites and divides along class lines, and also within classes, in how it is used or not used by different individuals in social situations. When people use Afrikaans to navigate their everyday life and articulate their dreams, it is not always the same Afrikaans that is drawn upon or recognised by their interlocutors. While the fight for or against Afrikaans might suggest homogeneity, Afrikaans, just like English, is informed by hierarchies. There is, for example, *Taal*, which is used in the Cape Flats where Ross did her fieldwork and perceived as inferior to *Suiwer Afrikaans* that is seen as purer and closer to Dutch, and that is the preferred variant for lectures at Stellenbosch University. Thus, even as blacks are expected to learn in Afrikaans, the Afrikaans of their everyday lived world is likely to be perceived as an inferior Afrikaans to that of their fellow white (Afrikaner) students and that of their white lecturers at Stellenbosch University.

If status is key in who says what to whom, how, where, when and with what outcome, and if 'Power does not always work through brute force and we are reminded to pay attention to the exertion of language on social forms' (Ross 2010: 160), then it is important to see how social hierarchies are internalised and reproduced through speech. Here again, as Ross reminds us, and as evidenced in the film *Luister*, 'The humiliations of being treated as less than human are sometimes internalised, become so much part of self-identity that when people describe themselves and their lives they automatically use the vocabulary proper to animals' (Ross 2010: 153).

Since encounters with Europe and with the imperatives to whiten up for greater social visibility, hierarchies of languages mean that, as Neville Alexander would put it, South Africans are constantly urged to mind their language until they are completely minded by the language of power to the detriment of the power of languages (Busch and Busch 2014). Internalisations of inferiority-superiority dichotomies are reproduced in everyday language, and are in turn transmitted to children through socialisation in families, schools and related institutions. In such a context, a successful black student in the eyes of the instances of language legitimation is not one who speaks the Afrikaans they have grown up speaking, but rather one who makes an effort to whiten up their Afrikaans, accent and speech mannerisms, in tune with a hierarchy that stretches as far up as the Dutch and The Netherlands[30], where the purest form of humanity, linguistic traditions and creativity are to be found. Little wonder that Afrikaans, irrespective of its local hierarchies, is often referred to by the Dutch as 'Baby Dutch', implying a language that is still to grow and attend adulthood. In terms of its local hierarchies, it seems not to matter much that some black South Africans have grown to think, see, feel, smell, hear and relate with others and the world around them in no other language than their *Taal*, and are neither ready for *Suiwer Afrikaans,* nor Dutch, nor English, as a substitute. For, if whitening up is the order of the day, *Taal* or 'Baby Baby Dutch', is expected to graduate into *Suiwer Afrikaans* or 'Baby Dutch', which in turn is expected to graduate into 'Dutch', the language of adulthood and ultimate social distinction and visibility within the Dutch universe.

If Afrikaans is a symbol of apartheid and class divisions, it is also a symbol of colonialism, albeit contested (Maseko and Vale 2016). If one were to insist on throwing the baby of colonialism out with the bathwater through insisting on total decolonisation – a decolonisation that rejects even the suggestion that Africans, thanks to their presumed agency, have appropriated, domesticated or indigenised inherited colonial languages in ways that they can legitimately and unapologetically consider these languages as their own – one could argue that it boggles the mind for black South Africans seeking such decolonisation to celebrate replacing one colonial symbol of oppression, Afrikaans, with another, English, even if historically, bantu education in Afrikaans for the black majority was primarily intended by the apartheid regime as a way of mass producing servants for servitude. Such radical decolonisation would not condone either, the justification that people embrace English not because they celebrate British colonialism, but rather because English has become an unequalled global lingua franca – a language of trade, science and scholarship[31] –, and gives people involved in emancipatory political projects all over the world the ability to communicate with each other.

Only within a framework where decolonisation is used to front for ulterior motives would it make sense to seek to replace Afrikaans with English, the ultimate global language of whitening up. [32] Seen in these terms, to seek to replace Afrikaans with English creates the impression (and rightly so) of a hierarchy of colonialisms at the top of which was British colonialism from which black South Africans are in no hurry to extricate themselves beyond their rhetorical clamours for decolonisation. In this regard, it could be argued that even the Afrikaners, perhaps because of a memory of a history of persistent attempts at undermining them culturally by Rhodes and the *Uitlanders*, are likely to be guilty of seeking English as a symbol of whitening up themselves vis-à-vis a global landscape in which English, just as Cecil Rhodes had hoped, towers like an overbearing colossus.

In what concerns Afrikaners as a language of higher education in South Africa, if he who pays the piper calls the tune, it remains to be seen whether Afrikaner sponsors or donors would continue to support Stellenbosch University financially should this decision hold. [33] In 1903, the Afrikaner leader General Louis Botha published a letter in the *Times* of London, in which he asked a question that remains relevant, and that many an Afrikaner is probably still asking in post-apartheid South Africa: 'Do you think the Boers will love and admire their conquerors for openly trying to Anglicise their children and for putting their language on the same footing practically as Zulu, Sesutu, or any other foreign language?' (Cited in Bottomley 2012: 129). Afrikanerness has thrived, however precariously, on Afrikaners being able to insist on a contrived purity and 'separateness on the basis of ethnicity' and by simultaneously claiming 'the privileges of dominant Anglo whiteness' and maintaining 'the benefits of whiteness' by resisting being 'lumped with black ethnic others'. [34]

Were the Stellenbosch University decision, which makes English 'to look like it has neither equal nor rival' among the 10 other languages guaranteed virtual equality in the constitution [35] (see also Maseko and Vale 2016), to be effectively implemented [36], it would be like a posthumous victory for Alfred Milner. Echoing

Cecil Rhodes, Milner had always craved and hoped for the day that 'British interests, British ideas and British education' (Brown 2015: 237) would prevail in a region where whites of Dutch descent outnumbered British whites by two to one. We would recall how Rhodes was ready to extend the right to vote to blacks, whom he considered 'not altogether citizens', as 'they are still children' (Plomer 1984 [1933]: 126) – an audacious move that earned him the dubious sobriquet of 'nigger-lover' – in order to challenge the Boer majority in the Cape parliament, where the English were outnumbered by two to one. Committed, like many other associates or acolytes of Rhodes, to a unified and reconciled English-speaking universe for the betterment of the world, Milner was the 'arch-Anglophile and passionate imperialist' of an English mother and a German father who became executor of Rhodes's will and ideals of anglicising South Africa and fulfilling the vision of globalisation the British empire and bringing about 'a new world order' through a secret society of like-minded imperialists and anglophiles (Brown 2015: 237). He reportedly 'remained loyal and true to everything Rhodes believed in, particularly his aim of making southern Africa 'one dominion" (Brown 2015: 241). An ambition of Milner's was to make English the dominant language of instruction in the Boer lands, with Afrikaner children taught directly from English books. To this end,

> Milner endowed English-speaking grammar and diocesan schools, known as the Milner Schools, in the Afrikaner heartlands of the Transvaal, particularly around Pretoria. These, along with schools like Rondebosch Boys' High School in the Cape which Rhodes endowed, are still among the most prestigious schools in South Africa (Brown 2015: 241).

Milner's ambitions for the British Empire were larger than seeking to convert Afrikaners through feeding Afrikaner children a stable staple of carefully designed menus of English imperial content served in the English language. He also had the mission of ensuring that Rhodes achieved immortality in the minds of people by using the money and institutions Rhodes had left behind to manage how Rhodes was remembered and to continue the pursuit of Rhodes's 'Great Idea' (Flint 1974: 227; Plomer 1984 [1933]: 26-

29). As Robin Brown recounts, Milner went on to preside over a newly established Rhodes Trust tasked with administering 'a transparent and prestigious scholarship programme at Oxford, Rhodes's alma mater, endowed from his gold and diamond fortunes'. This was a programme 'designed to provide immortality for Rhodes' (Brown 2015: 248), by providing youth from the colonies and former colonies with the opportunity to use English as their 'winning ticket in the lottery of life' (Brown 2015: 324) to pursue 'the necessary education' to contribute the goodwill and understanding needed for the running of the 'English-speaking and English-dominated Empire' in which both Rhodes and Milner believed firmly as the solution to a world plagued by war, chaos and uncertainty (Brown 2015: 249). The idea was to make of youth the glue and future leaders of the British Empire (and its subsequent mutation into the Commonwealth), and in this regard, both Rhodes and Milner were keen to insist that religion and race would not be a barrier to selection for a Rhodes Scholarship (Brown 2015: 250-251, 318-319). All that was needed initially was a sort of profession of faith in the British Empire as a supreme moral achievement, and increasingly today, a recognition of and commitment to advancing British civilisation, the English language, and British claims to a history of supreme moral achievements as articulated in Rhodes Trust publications such as The Round Table magazine (Brown 2015: 275-276), and propagated by the Royal Institute of International Affairs and its affiliate and sister institutions around the world (Brown 2015: 323-325).

What is aimed at and indeed achieved short of Rhodes's original dream of unifying the British Empire, is 'a global hegemony of like-minded spheres of influence' (Brown 2015: 327), at the centre of which is 'a special relationship with the English language', which 'has rapidly become a universal language, especially in the spheres of commerce and technology, particularly aviation, in a globalising world' (Brown 2015: 324).[37] No one needs to speak English at the same level to be recognised and provided for in this global spread of English, as provision for whitening up is there to ensure that, to quote Chicago University Linguistic professor Salikoko Mufwene, 'native speakers...claim more authority on English' than non-native speakers, are able to 'dictate the norms in publishing and international broadcast', and 'are also less subject to stigmatisation for their grammatical and spoken peculiarities'.[38]

Administered jointly from South Parks Road, Oxford and from Groote Schuur in Cape Town, the Rhodes Trust remains active amid calls for decolonisation, and maintains its letterhead of 'the Zimbabwe bird – a copy of the icon that Willie Posselt had stolen from Great Zimbabwe to decorate Groote Schuur', Rhodes's home in Cape Town (Brown 2015: 249).[39] Current and past beneficiaries from the Rhodes Scholarship are 'moulded in his [Rhodes's] image', 'however slightly' (Brown 2015: 251; see also Flint 1974: 244-247), and are all expected to 'aspire like him to "make public service their highest aim"'(Baker 1934: 135) in 'advancing the highest interest', if not of the British Empire as initially envisaged (Williams 1921: 321), at least, of the remnants of it and the 'Great' that continues to prefix Britain. They are inculcated into what is considered to be the height of 'civilised society' at Oxford and then sent back to their countries of origin to exert their influence in shaping opinion and influencing the direction of social change à l'anglaise. 'Since his death Oxford and its Rhodes scholars have helped to keep his memory green and to further his ideals even beyond the shores of England' (Williams 1921: 4).

Back at UCT, senior management are busy putting together what they deem will be a solid foundation for beginning the serious business of meaningful transformation. They are aiming to engage all constituencies and to be inclusive. The VC is particularly keen to bring on board 'those who have felt marginalised', and 'those who may have unpopular or rather different views on where and how to change the university.' He seeks to provide for co-creation and co-ownership of and unity around the road map for change at UCT, to ensure that the university is truly 'a place where all staff and students feel at home and valued.'[40] In the interest of proceeding with a collective transformation project, the VC announced 'an executive decision to grant an amnesty in respect of all protest-related incidents that occurred between the first protest on 9 March 2015 and 18 May 2015', insisting that 'no disciplinary action will be brought against any student or staff member in respect of these events.' Furthermore, 'I have written to the Student Representative Council (SRC), Rhodes Must Fall (RMF) and Transform UCT, to inform them of the executive decision, and I trust that as a result we will move swiftly to begin meaningful discussions on the way forward.' In addition, referring to a group of students who had occupied a building, the VC wrote: 'We have provided RMF and those occupying Avenue House with a dedicated temporary venue in a hall next to Avenue House, and they will have to leave Avenue House at the latest middle of Monday, 18 May 2015.' He urged that the amnesty should not be seen as a sign of 'capitulation to pressure'.[41]

On the urgent and important business of transformation, the VC outlined the measures taken by the university council at a special sitting on 22 April 2015. The list of things done and planned was not intended to be a comprehensive statement of UCT transformation plans, but rather an indication that things were on the move with renewed energy and devotion. To begin with, several SRC proposals were considered. Council agreed to establish a task team (including student members) to review the names of buildings and works of art across campus, in the interest of creating an environment conducive to diversity[42]. Also established was a task team to review the current function, role and powers of the Institutional Forum and to explore how it could play a more effective role in steering and negotiating transformation. A review of the functioning of DISCHO (the Discrimination and Harassment Office) was scheduled to take place before the end of 2015. Provision was made to extend membership of the Curriculum Review Task Team, a subcommittee of the Teaching and Learning Committee, to students, and a different framework for thinking about curriculum reform was to be developed. A review of the structures, resources and functioning of Transformation Services Office was scheduled. Faculties were encouraged to hold open assemblies and fora where students are encouraged to voice their experience within the faculty, drawing on the example of the faculties of Health Sciences and Law where the initiative was already underway. It was announced that the employment equity plan for 2015 to 2020 had been intensively debated and was scheduled to be tabled in the senate and council in June 2015. A review of the functioning of the system of employment equity representatives, particularly in selection committees, was under way.

Funding was being sought to invest in 'ensuring that the career paths of every black academic in the junior ranks is individually mapped out, with requirements for the next promotion clearly spelled out with a plan for personal development, including pairing up with senior mentors.' It was announced that the composition of promotions committees was undergoing review in all faculties, to provide for greater transparency, rebuild trust and fairness, and ensure that the changes were effective for the 2015 promotions calendar. It was also announced that Transform UCT (a grouping of black academic staff) had participated in the annual Academic Heads of Department (HOD) workshop on the role HODs could play in transformation at department level. A day-long workshop or summit to design the agenda for tackling transformation was planned. The VC concluded with an appeal: 'Once again, I invite all departments, staff and students, the SRC, Transform UCT, RMF, the trade unions and transformation structures to seize this opportunity to plot the course for UCT to achieve leadership and excellence in transformation...'[43]

This programme of action approved by council was followed by the appointment of Associate Professor Elelwani Ramugondo as 'Special Advisor to the Vice-Chancellor on Transformation'.[44] Here is an excerpt of the statement announcing the appointment:

> The Rhodes Must Fall protests, as we know, were about much more than the statue. They reflected deeper underlying frustrations with the pace of transformation. The response of all constituencies within the University of Cape Town – from Council to students, Senate, faculties, professional and support staff, unions, to the Institutional Forum (IF) – has been an overwhelming commitment to take much bolder steps and to focus more energy and resources on the multiple dimensions of transformation that lie ahead.
>
> This needs dedicated attention from my office, and also additional coordination as leadership across the university – the deans, academic heads of department, executive directors, Student Representative Council and IF – all drive new transformation efforts within our respective spheres of governance and influence.
>
> In order to ensure the necessary executive focus on the transformation project over the next 12 months, I am appointing a Special Advisor to the Vice-Chancellor on Transformation, who will work in my office[45], help me keep abreast of all the initiatives and advise me on ways of accelerating the various programmes across the

university. This is since I cannot possibly be directly involved in them all while still performing the VC functions that I must inevitably carry out. While in no way being a gatekeeper to my office, she will also be available to meet with any groups and individuals who wish to raise issues related to transformation policy and practice – whether these are concerns or proposals.

I am pleased to announce that Associate Professor Elelwani Ramugondo has accepted my invitation to become my Special Advisor and will take up the position on 18 June 2015 for a 12-month period.

Associate Professor Ramugondo has been at UCT since her student days, having obtained her BSc Occupational Therapy (1992), her MSc and her PhD here. Her career as a faculty member started as a lecturer in a development contract post in 1998, and she has moved up the ranks, having been promoted ad hominem to associate professor in 2010. She served as head of the division of Occupational Therapy from 2010 to 2013. Associate Professor Ramugondo has supervised or is currently supervising seven PhD and 13 Masters students, amongst whom eight are black South Africans.[46]

Among her many qualifications for the position, Associate Professor Ramugondo was said to have 'led some interesting innovations in curriculum reform within her discipline and profession.' Her portfolio included working with 'the task teams being established to review names of buildings and artworks.' She was expected to 'attend faculty assemblies to hear the issues raised', get 'involved in the reviews of the Discrimination and Harassment Office and the Transformation office', oversee 'the new plans to accelerate employment equity and career development', identify 'issues in the institutional climate that need to be addressed', and time permitting, 'join the expanded curriculum review process.' She was also to serve as 'an assessor member of the IF and University Transformation Advisory Committee'.[47]

In March 2016, the VC Max Price issued an update in which he recounted measures taken to transform UCT, since the RMF. In addition to the appointment of his special advisor on transformation, he listed other achievements, including:

employment equity programmes; creating forums for views not usually voiced; addressing the dominance on campus of the symbols that reflect a particular, white or colonial, heritage; student access;

158

gender and sexual harassment issues; curriculum reform; and insourcing.[48]

Speaking of the UCT community, VC Max Price added:

> I believe most, if not all, of us have been challenged to think more deeply about what institutional racism means and to acknowledge how differently UCT is experienced by many black students and staff compared to their white counterparts. I and others have accepted that the pace of transformation has been too slow on many fronts. Through participating in many meetings with academic leaders, heads of academic departments and managers across the institution, I am also convinced that there is a widespread commitment among this leadership group to accelerate transformation dramatically, to make a decisive break with the past, and to take personal responsibility and be held accountable for driving change.[49]

The VC's optimistic brushstrokes are unlikely to be shared by the RMF movement, whose commemorative exhibition at the African Studies Centre gallery – 'Echoing Voices from Within' – on the same day as the VC's release, was disrupted by members of the UCT 'Trans Collective', an organisation led by students, 'that prioritises the rights of transgender, gender non-conforming and intersex students'. The Collective disrupted the event by smearing red paint across photos, including one of Maxwele throwing human excrement at the Rhodes statue in 2015. The word 'Rapist' was written over it in bold red letters[50]. One of the messages displayed by the protesting Trans Collective read 'We will not have our bodies, faces, names, and voices used as bait for public applause', and another cautioned: 'RMF [Rhodes Must Fall] will not tokenise our presence as if they ever treasured us as part of their movement'.[51] If these intra-student confrontations and acrimony are anything to go by, the future of convivial student relationships and mutual accommodation would depend on the extent to which UCT management is able to recognise and set in place robust structures and a culture of representation, especially for voices and causes that are not always complementary, and that need not always resort to violence, vandalism and disruptions to make their voices heard. This is especially important in a South African context with a proven track record and history of acts of collective violence by politicised disaffected youth (Marks.2001).

Harry Garuba, a Nigerian Associate Professor who heads the School of African and Gender Studies, Anthropology and Linguistics, is sceptical that committees such as those set up by the VC can deliver the rooted transformation of curricula and syllabi needed to definitively banish Rhodes's legacy. 'I don't want the discussion around curriculum reform to die a slow, deliberative death, as so many issues do when landing at the feet of committees.' He labels as 'disingenuous' past explanations advanced by university management for the 'disgraceful paucity of black professors.' Of essence are conversations and debates about the nature and form of a decolonised curriculum in South Africa. Because others have travelled this road before, Garuba argues, South Africa does not need to start at ground zero. There are lessons of earlier debates and conclusions reached on the continent and elsewhere on which to draw. Examples cited include the University of Nairobi, where Ngugi wa Thiong'o and two of his colleagues initiated a transformation debate that challenged the English department to open up its usual continuities in British content to include writings in English from Africa and elsewhere. They demanded the insertion of Kenya, East Africa and Africa at the centre of their research and teaching, and sought to reconceptualise university curricula relevant to their context, and not merely as an extension of the West into Africa. The debate in Kenya, which eventually led to a major curriculum transformation in East Africa, teaches us that curriculum transformation is not simply a question of adding new items to an existing curriculum. It requires a radical interrogation of the very basis for constituting the object of study. [52]

If one takes seriously the 'need for greater recognition of the fact that teaching and learning is not just about knowledge', but also 'an ontological project… about an entire way of being', as Jo-Anne Vorster and Lynn Quinn of Rhodes University argue, then transformation ceases to be merely a question of tinkering with the margins of the structures and conventional assumptions about knowledge and knowledge production in contexts with long histories of social and economic exclusion like South Africa. [53] Transformation should aim to activate and bring into critical conversations and dialogues sensitivities and sensibilities informed by African life-worlds, experiences and predicaments, without necessarily putting them in a contrived hierarchy of importance. Garuba invites us to 'recognise the cultural and scientific production – the knowledge – of previously devalued groups of people.' Borrowing from Edward Said, Garuba argues that a possible way forward could be a contrapuntal approach, which 'takes into account the perspectives of both the colonised and the coloniser, their interwoven histories, their discursive entanglements – without necessarily harmonising them or attending to one while erasing the other.' Such contrapuntal thinking should take place at every level, and should include a pedagogy that seeks to integrate in a significant way the knowledge of the marginalised into what one is teaching. It is not enough to have moved Rhodes's statue. This must be followed up with moving 'the hegemonic gaze of the Rhodes that is lodged in our ways of thinking, in our curricular and pedagogical practices, our professional practices as teachers, academics, scholars and students. We need to take a critical look at our everyday routine.' In short, 'we need to remove the Rhodes that lives in our disciplines and the curricula that underpin them.'[54]

Mashupye Herbert Maserumule, Professor of Public Affairs at Tshwane University of Technology concurs, adding that 'transformation of higher education generally in Africa and specifically in South Africa requires a professoriate with a decoloniality posture', that goes beyond the overly simple tendency to dichotomise between whites and blacks. Because African academics are often schooled largely in Western traditions of knowledge production, which they are expected to reproduce uncritically and often excel at mimicry to the detriment of creative appropriation, being a black academic could be more of a curse than an asset to transformation and decolonisation.[55] For this reason, Maserumule argues that:

> being white does not necessarily mean being anti-transformation. In the same way, being black is not synonymous with transformation. There are white professors whose sense of transformation is more remarkable than that of some black professors. So, reference to black and white is beyond pigmentation. It is, in the logic of the Black

161

Consciousness philosophy, about a state of mind: ideas and attitudes that ought to underpin a strategic gaze to transformation.[56]

Thinking from within the disciplinary confines of architecture, Amira Osman, Associate Professor in Architecture, University of Johannesburg (UJ), suggests ways of how to do more than pay lip service to the transformation of a teaching and practice of architecture steeped in a history or racial segregation that has produced and sustained 'Housing landscapes' of 'sterile, regimented, inefficient settlement patterns'. She calls for 'a major rethink about how cities and housing are planned' by creatively re-imagining and re-imaging South African cities – where the apartheid reality of 'bus and train-loads of black people being brought in to service the elite city early in the morning, then 'shipped out' again just before dark' linger – to provide for 'poorer residents who spend large percentages of their meagre incomes, and a large segment of their day, on commuting.' Such rethinking demands commitment from architects in the academy, regardless of race, nationality or gender, and quibbling about it is more a question of politics than science. It is such complicity with power and the political that makes architecture at the service of elite interests. To Osman, to truly transform architecture in South Africa, requires opening the profession up to young people from diverse backgrounds for a start. It calls, as well, for a transformation of content through a critical deconstruction and reconstruction of a logic of practice in city-building that was 'meticulously conceptualised by built environment professionals who served a particular political dispensation' under apartheid. This involves 'massive spatial restructuring' through 'complex, multi-disciplinary interventions' in which the architectural profession plays a major role. She calls on fellow professionals to 'become critically aware of the power of the built environment', and to 'speak up strongly on how architecture is sometimes complicit in practices that disempower, humiliate, restrict opportunities, destroy livelihoods, damage ecosystems and disrupt economic networks' that 'deepen conflict and reinforce divisions'.[57]

Regardless of discipline and practice, Osman's challenge poses tough questions about knowledge production and consumption

162

with clear implications for how to structure and implement staff development in South African universities, if knowledge acquisition and dispensation must be grounded in the lived experiences of the staff, students and societies involved. As Vorster and Quinn put it, if academic developers are to contribute seriously and meaningfully to South Africa's 'decolonising turn', they would 'need to apply their minds collectively and individually to what it means to 'decolonise' higher education in general and in specific disciplines', and must 'be prepared to engage in courageous conversations' that might challenge their 'deeply held beliefs and their strong disciplinary identities', to provide for 'an environment in which students are heard, listened to, understood and can thrive.' This requires careful critical predicament-oriented introspection by academic developers of their own taken-for-granted practices, attitudes and assumptions that are often sanctioned by power and privilege.[58]

Estelle Prinsloo of the University of Johannesburg calls on the humanities to play a critical intellectual role in decolonisation by subverting 'the current techno-bureaucratic approaches to transformation' in the manner that only they know best (Prinsloo 2016: 164-165). Transformation of curricula would hardly be enough merely encouraging tokenism and the practice of a little African content goes a long way. As Nomalanga Mkhize argues, even in a discipline as the study of African languages, care must be taken to problematize taken for granted conservative notions of culture, which tend to privilege themes that celebrate cultural pride and being what she terms 'Good Bantus', with scant regard for the dynamism of African languages and cultures. To her, there is need 'to bring life into African languages in the academy' through 'aesthetic inventiveness and transgression' and by encouraging 'literary regeneration' as the core business of 'the African language intellectualisation project' promoted by the South African academy (Mkhize 2016: 146-147).

The call for African universities to transform themselves into genuine sites of liberation is by no means new. As the critical writings of scholars such as Okot p'Bitek (1989 [1966]) would demonstrate, the 1960s were already replete with such calls. Three decades ago Fonlon (2009 [1978]) made a plea for African

163

universities as spaces for genuine intellectuals dedicated to the common weal. For African universities and researchers to contribute towards a genuine, multifaceted liberation of the continent and its peoples, they ought to start by joining their people in a careful rethinking of African concerns and priorities, and educational approaches (Ramose 2003, 2004, 2010; Zeleza and Olukoshi 2004a, 2004b; Mama 2007). Current clamours for transformation in South Africa are squarely within a continental tradition, where much is called for in terms of the domestication of higher education but little achieved.

Removing Rhodes, as suggested by Garuba and students of the RMF, might require unlikely but necessary conversations with others who may be more inclined to accept reform than revolution, and who have the means, power and privilege to ignore radical change. This is hinted at by Graham McIntosh, former MP and wealthy UCT alumnus with an 8 figure sum to invest in UCT on condition that his suggested research topics and course content, detailed in an open letter to the university management, are endorsed. McIntosh's list is well worth a closer look.[59] His nostalgia for what he was taught at UCT in his day, cannot simply be dismissed as outmoded content pregnant with colonial prejudice – at least, not by lecturers who are expected to challenge themselves by bringing a critical historical perspective to bear in light of the injustices and inequalities which the production of such knowledge either deliberately ignored or were insensitive to as a result of the privileges and power of the colonial knowledge producer. It calls instead for bringing McIntosh and others outside and within the academy who share his convictions into deep conversation on positionality and reflexivity with those currently seeking transformation within and outside the academy. If the funding challenges posed by the Fees Must Fall protests are anything to go by, UCT may not always be in a position to pick and choose its sources of funding. Rhodes (through the Rhodes Trust and the Rhodes Scholarship[60]), and many a wealthy descendant of rich *amakwerekwere* of yesteryear, may not have had their last say on the RMF. After all, as Mary West reminds us,

The liberal humanist in the history of South Africa's political turmoil has often been the white English-speaking product of a privileged and educated background, an individual who has been allowed the comfort of disapproving of, even resisting, the apartheid regime, but from a position of relative safety, as a result of material privilege and empowerment through education (knowledge) (West 2009: 4).

There is reason to doubt just how ready to turn the page UCT and its tradition of liberal humanism really are. Since the Mahmood Mamdani years (1996-1999), there has been more rhetoric than substance about transformation (Morreira 2015; Nyamnjoh 2012a, 2012b), if the address on the challenges of curriculum transformation to the RMF students by the current A.C. Jordan Chair and Director of the Centre for African Studies at UCT, Professor Lungisile Ntsebeza, is anything to go by (Ntsebeza 2012, 2014).[61] It is equally worrying that despite its offer of amnesty, UCT has not resisted the temptation to spot and discipline those it perceives as scapegoats for the current RMF campaign. In this regard, it has singled out Maxwele (who has dared to think, speak, write and act as he sees fit in the interest of the collectivity for whom he is determined to take leadership on matters of social, intellectual and economic transformation) for exemplary discipline and punishment. In the totalising and often totalitarian logic of systems under attack, it is hardly surprising, given Maxwele's prominence and leadership role in the RMF campaign, that UCT as an institution would seek to undo him in any way it could. For an institution that purports to thrive on consultative democracy even when the problem is the majority white establishment and its logic of practice, the obvious strategy was to resort to legalisms and pro-establishment civilities. Not only was Maxwele accused of having done the unthinkable by smearing Rhodes with human waste,[62] but he was also portrayed as no stranger to insubordination to constituted authority (he purportedly showed President Jacob Zuma's motorcade the middle finger on a Cape Town street in February 2010), alleged to have threatened whites with extinction, and was suspended from the university in May 2015 following an altercation with a female white lecturer over study space on campus during a public holiday.[63] Maxwele was charged, inter alia, with having 'raised his voice at the lecturer; shouted aggressively that 'the

165

statue fell, now it's time for all whites to go'; and showed aggressive behaviour, which included banging on her office door', and to have said: 'We must not listen to whites, we do not need their apologies. They have to be removed from UCT and have to be killed.'[64] The statement suspending him for two months read: 'On May 7, Mr Maxwele was given a provisional suspension order because his continued presence on the campus was considered to pose a threat to the maintenance of good order. This provisional suspension order was made final after a hearing.'[65]

Accusing the university of intimidation and conspiracy and of using his suspension to achieve political ends by silencing the voices of student activists, Maxwele challenged the suspension and released his own version of events, complaining about the tendency in the white world to criminalise black men and treat them as dangerous savages.[66] He was dissatisfied with the manner in which the university had handled his own complaint on the matter: 'My complaint has not been dealt with to date when the complaint against me has been handled with haste and decisiveness', he claimed.[67] The university released a statement refuting Maxwele's[68] claims, an amnesty which Maxwele dismissed as 'purely political'[69], and cited its offer of 'amnesty to protesters for a specific period during which they illegally occupied two UCT buildings and disrupted a council meeting' as evidence of its fair-mindedness in dealing with the RMF campaigners. The suspension was eventually overturned on technical grounds by the independent university student disciplinary tribunal.[70] Disappointed with the outcome, the university resolved to issue afresh a suspension order, and to accord Maxwele a right of appeal within 72 hours, a procedure ignored previously. According to Maxwele, UCT acted without due course when they suspended him a second time, despite his vindication by the discipline appeals committee. Following his resuspension, Maxwele turned to the Western Cape High Court for justice. The court granted an interim order allowing him to register and attend classes and tutorials.[71] It took a High Court ruling in his favour for the suspension to be set aside. To him this was evidence of UCT wanting to silence him at all costs.[72] To interested observers like Nhlapho, the disciplinary proceedings against Maxwele were added proof that 'UCT, a white university, wants black students to submit to white domination without complaint, or that their complaint be processed within the defined legal channels, processed and reduced within a white dominated system, when 47% of whites in South Africa already think Apartheid was 'not that bad'.[73]

It is not only students in South Africa that are protesting institutional racism at their universities. It seems that Rhodes has good company across the Atlantic in the USA, where whites 'share a system of social advantages that can be traced back to the advent of slavery in the colonies that became the United States.'[74] Examples of racialised relations proliferate (Coates 2015), not least in the academy, from Yale to Missouri, Harvard, Princeton, and beyond.[75] Almost as if in consonance with a global ecumene of 'black lives matter'.[76] and the re-affirmation of black humanity (Clarke and Thomas 2006), students at American universities – where the tendency has been to treat blacks as 'outsiders within' (Harrison 2008), in a nationwide context of 'racialized spaces of social death wherein Black lives are rendered less than fully human'[77] – have been asking similar questions to those raised in South Africa. At the University of Texas for example, students led a movement that resulted in the removal in August 2015 of a statue of Jefferson Davis, president of the Confederate States of America, from their campus, saying that the 'statue personifies slavery and oppression and does not belong on the campus.'[78] Students at other universities in the country, such as Harvard, Princeton and Yale, are also protesting the ongoing memorialization of persons who engaged in slavery and reinforced racial segregation as a technology of power and privilege.

In the heartland of the USA, at the University of Missouri, Columbia, on 9 November 2015, the university president stepped down and the chancellor announced his resignation after a vote of no-confidence from the English department faculty[79], student complaints of systematic oppression, the hunger strike of one student and finally, the refusal of the American football team players, backed by their coaches, to play in a game.[80] That is not the first time black athletes on US college campuses engaged in social protest.[81]

On November 12, thousands of students across the USA, from California to New York and Massachusetts, took part in

167

'demonstrations against a culture of racism infecting higher education.'[82] At Yale University, students are reportedly concerned about the paucity of black professors, marginalization of important racial issues, teachers who seem to engage black students far less than nonblack students, classmates who question the intellectual capacity of their black peers, and undue surveillance from police officers. At Emory University in Atlanta, Georgia, students are also concerned with opening the university's classes to black workers at the university as well as the improvement of working conditions, for example of those working in on-campus dining facilities and engaged in maintenance and custodial services.[83] At the University of Missouri, Columbia, students presented the list of demands made in 1950 when the first black students were admitted to the university and claim that little progress has been made to address them. Demands at other colleges and universities across the USA include more spending on scholarships for so-called 'students of color', more instruction on interracial sensitivity, and more resources, such as cultural centres, serving Native American, African-American, Asian, Latino-Americans, LGBTQIA, and other students,[84] as well as recognition of the role that diverse peoples, like African-Americans and Native Americans, have played in developing US universities.[85]

Racial issues and incidents have been 'long-simmering' on US college campuses, some of which have been documented by the *Journal of Blacks in Higher Education* over the last 25 years.[86] Issues being discussed currently include systemic oppression, structural and institutional racism, everyday racism, and white supremacy and privilege. There is debate about media presence at and coverage of the protests, as media is sometimes perceived by some to be as oppressive as the forces being fought.[87] On #BlackOnCampus, students in Canada tweeted to express solidarity with US students. Young black millennials are using twitter and other social media to 'drive the culture forward.'[88] Harvard law professor Randall Kennedy writes how student activists have prompted 'probing conversations' about racial justice and pushed 'dissatisfactions and aspirations of African-American students' higher up on the higher-education policy agenda and also suggests that in the long-run 'reformers harm themselves by nurturing an inflated sense of victimization.'[89] In early 2016, Harvard Law School yielded to protester pressure to change its official seal, after a protest that it had links to slavery. It also decided to discontinue 'using the term 'master' in academic titles, because of connotations of slavery'.[90]

It is definitely the perceived resilience of anti-black racism in American society and institutions, university and otherwise, that pushed Faye Harrison to conclude bleakly:

> The depth, intensity, and pervasiveness of anti-blackness in the fabric of U.S. society compel us to rethink our models of and for social transformation. Those who subscribe to more pessimistic perspectives, such as scholars and activists associated with the Derrick Bell-variety of critical race theory and the intellectual trajectory known as Afro-pessimism, urge us to relinquish our political naïveté in favor of a more critically realistic views of what is, what is possible, and what should be done about them. Whether optimist, pessimist, or somewhere in between, perhaps we can agree that the 'Black Lives Matter', 'Don't Shoot' and 'I Can't Breathe' demonstrations proliferating across the country clearly belie the widespread postracial pretensions and conceit that have denied grievances against racism the legitimacy as well as the political and policy attention they rightfully deserve.[91]

Inspired by his knowledge of the University of Missouri–Kansas City (UMKC), Dr. Stephen Dilks – a white Englishman who grew up in Scotland, self-identifies as Mercian, and is now an American citizen and teaches Irish literature – issued an open letter that resonates with many of the transformation and curriculum challenges facing South Africa, suggesting cautious solutions of his own. To Dilks, for whom diversity must move from 'a talking point' to 'a lived experience', the burdens of 'historical and systematic institutional and cultural racism, sexism, homophobia, xenophobia and other bigotries' cannot be adequately addressed through token 'specially designated courses and programs', needed though such programmes and courses are. Also necessary but hardly enough is the need to recruit and retain academic staff and students who 'more adequately reflect the racial demographics', of the various American communities that feed and draw sustenance from its multiplicity of universities and colleges. In addition, Dilks argues, there is need for academic staff and students 'to reflect critically on their own relationships with identity politics across the board, lived and expressed, felt and imposed, endured and inherited, assumed and questioned.'[92] As he puts it, with reference to Kansas City and the US where blacks or African-Americans are about 30 and 13 per cent respectively of the total population, and on whom, unlike in South Africa where blacks are the majority, the term 'people of color' can be imposed willy-nilly:

> We definitely need to engage in deep analysis of the history and current situation of racial minorities and disempowered groups in our culture, across our state, in our city, on our campus. We also need to critically analyse the history and legacies of state-sanctioned and other forms of slavery and servitude. We need to interrogate all aspects of our lives including the categories of race we use to define ourselves.... And we need to do so in every classroom and discussion-space across campus, in informal and formal conversations, between and among the different groups we associate with.[93]

Students in universities in the United Kingdom have not been indifferent. Many students were sympathetic to the Rhodes Must Fall protests. Even at Oxford University where one would have expected Rhodes to be in particularly good standing – given the fact that he attended Oriel College and became its greatest benefactor[94], was highly regarded in student circles in his day, and kept close associations with Oxford which houses Rhodes House, home to the Rhodes Trust and the Rhodes Scholarship[95] – there have been demonstrations questioning his legacy. Oxford students demonstrated in sympathy with UCT students, and on 6 November 2015, they protested against Rhodes's statue at Oriel College, constructed in his honour following a donation he made to a new building. Basil Williams describes the statue as looking 'proudly down upon The High, taking rank above the sovereigns of his day, as a Founder no less than William of Wykeham, Chichele, Waynflete or Wolsey (Williams 1921: 4). The demonstration which was reportedly attended by more than 250 people was organised by members of the Rhodes Must Fall in Oxford group[96], which aims to 'fight intersectional oppression within Oxford'. The leadership of Rhodes Must Fall Oxford (RMFO) includes Athinangamso Esther Nkopo, Tadiwa Madenga and Roseanne Chantiluke, who are in regular conversation with developments in South Africa.[97] Kiran

Benipal, one of the students who protested, said, 'We are questioning Rhodes' politics and asking if the money he donated came from the enslavement and oppression of black Africans.'[98] Prior to the protest, the campaign orders had issued the following statement:

> The veneration of a racist murderer on our campus violates the University's own commitment to 'fostering an inclusive culture' for its black and minority ethnic students. It is also an overbearing, visual reminder of the colonial apologism rife in one of the world's most esteemed educational institutions. So long as these statues are allowed to stand, we as a society can never begin the process of recognising the violence of our past.[99]

Some in Oxford, including the newly appointed first woman vice-chancellor of Oxford, Professor Louise Richardson, disagree with what they consider a revisionist view of history or what Lord Chris Patten of Barnes, chancellor of Oxford University terms 'pandering to contemporary views' on Cecil Rhodes.[100] 'Our history is not a blank page on which we can write our own version of what it should have been, according to our contemporary views and prejudices', Lord Patten maintained.[101] In a posting titled 'Leave Oxford alone – take anti-Rhodes campaign back to SA', leading British columnist James Delingpole, perplexed by why a student at Oxford would be demonstrating against Cecil Rhodes, especially one who is the recipient of a Rhodes Scholarship[102], writes to the two South African students whom he believes to be behind the anti-Rhodes campaign in Oxford[103]:

> Dear scrotty students,
> Cecil Rhodes's generous bequest has contributed greatly to the comfort and wellbeing of many generations of Oxford students – a good many of them, dare we say it, better, brighter and more deserving than you.
> This doesn't necessarily mean we approve of everything Rhodes did in his lifetime – but then we don't have to. Cecil Rhodes died over a century ago. Autres temps, autres moeurs
> If you don't understand what this means – and it wouldn't remotely surprise us if that were the case – then we really think you should ask yourself the question: 'Why am I at Oxford?'

171

Oxford, let us remind you, is the world's second oldest extant university. Scholars have been studying here since at least the 11th century. We've played a major part in the invention of Western civilisation, from the 12th century intellectual renaissance through the Enlightenment and beyond. [….] We're a big deal. And most of the people privileged to come and study here are conscious of what a big deal we are. Oxford is their alma mater – their dear mother – and they respect and revere her accordingly.[104]

When in January 2016 the governing body of Oriel College 'overwhelmingly' decided that Rhodes's 'statue should remain in place and that the college will seek to provide a clear historical context to explain why it is there', chancellor Lord Patten reportedly advised students who did not embrace freedom of thought to consider going to seek their education elsewhere.[105] Commenting shortly after the decision not to remove the statue, Timothy Garton Ash suggests that the Rhodes Must Fall campaign in Oxford might have had a stronger case if they had directed their attention more at demanding 'more Rhodes scholarships for African students, given that the money originally came from Africa', adding that this is an initiative 'that past and present Rhodes scholars from more privileged parts of the world should support'. The increased number of scholarship would be better served, he argues, by a decolonised curriculum that is much more critical of Britain's colonial past than is currently the case.[106]

These globalised protests which often target controversial monuments and statues and other contested symbols of power[107] are indicative of an interconnected world in which poverty and historical accumulation cannot be understood in isolation from the power and privilege or the lack thereof associated with race, place, class, gender, generation and related determinants of the interconnecting local and global hierarchies that dictate the life trajectories of all and sundry. It is hardly surprising that in a world of interconnecting hierarchies where blacks are systematically represented, sometimes even by themselves, as the scum of the earth, that blacks, regardless of their geography, materialise as Frantz Fanon's 'Wretched of the Earth' (Fanon 1967a) – those preordained to suffer every indignity and dispossession imaginable. As Robin Brown writes, the only way one can begin to understand why Rhodes thought he could simply take Africa, its diamonds and gold from its indigenous inhabitants was that: 'in Rhodes's eyes, the Africans did not realise that God had preordained their fate, or that they were dealing with a man on a secret mission who had no problem driving his evangelistic message home with a Maxim machine gun', and with the full backing of 'Empress Queen Victoria … one of the most beautiful in the world' (Brown 2015: 53).[108]

Notes

[1] See the following statements by VC Max Price, beginning from 18 March, when he returned from Senegal: 'Rhodes statue protests and transformation', http://www.uct.ac.za/dailynews/?id=9034; 'Appointment of Special Advisor to the Vice-Chancellor on Transformation', http://www.uct.ac.za/dailynews/?id=9212; 'UCT and Rhodes Must Fall sign agreement', http://www.uct.ac.za/dailynews/?id=9175; 'UCT grants amnesty to protesters', http://www.uct.ac.za/dailynews/?id=9155; 'Urgent update on the Rhodes statue and Bremner occupation', http://www.uct.ac.za/dailynews/?id=9100; 'Response to Sunday Independent article: "Adebajo distorts Price's view on Rhodes"', http://www.uct.ac.za/dailynews/?id=9068; 'Update on Rhodes statue and occupation of Bremner Building', http://www.uct.ac.za/dailynews/?id=9063; 'Progress in discussing the removal of Rhodes statue', http://www.uct.ac.za/dailynews/?id=9051; 'Price applauds students for bringing transformation issues into focus', http://www.uct.ac.za/dailynews/?id=9042. His deputies and other instances of senior management were equally busy, all accessed 1 October 2015.
For an exhaustive archive on UCT correspondence around #RhodesMustFall, see http://www.uct.ac.za/news/Transform-UCT/, accessed 29 February 2016. The RMF protests grew to include calls to end rising student fees, outsourcing of workers, police brutality and patriarchal practices on campus.
For a detailed archive on UCT correspondence around #FeesMustFall and #EndOutsourcing,
see http://www.uct.ac.za/news/DebatesInHigherEducation, and http://www.uct.ac.za/news/DebatesInHigherEducation/campusupdates/, accessed 29 February 2016.

These archives are evidence of how UCT management increasingly intensified its strategic communication to be seen to be actively engaging with students, academic and support staff and the issues they raised throughout 2015 and the start of 2016.

[2] See http://www.bdlive.co.za/national/2015/04/10/botha-statue-may-be-toppled-next, accessed 17 September 2015.

[3] See 'CT talks: Heritage, Signage and Symbolism', https://www.youtube.com/watch?v=4NgpJ00M5Ho, accessed 6 October 2015.

[4] See Martin Hall, 'The symbolic statue dividing a South African university', http://www.bbc.com/news/business-31945680, accessed 1 October 2015.

[5] See Martin Hall, 'The symbolic statue dividing a South African university', http://www.bbc.com/news/business-31945680, accessed 1 October 2015.

[6] See http://www.iol.co.za/news/south-africa/western-cape/vice-chancellor-statue-should-be-moved-1.1833822#.VfXERpce4TZ, accessed 2 October 2015.

[7] See http://www.iol.co.za/news/south-africa/western-cape/vice-chancellor-statue-should-be-moved-1.1833822#.VfXERpce4TZ, accessed 2 October 2015.

[8] See http://www.iol.co.za/news/south-africa/western-cape/vice-chancellor-statue-should-be-moved-1.1833822#.VfXERpce4TZ, accessed 2 October 2015.

[9] Adekeye Adebajo, 'Debate over Rhodes is one of transformation', http://www.bdlive.co.za/opinion/columnists/2015/03/23/debate-over-rhodes-is-one-of-transformation, accessed 2 October 2015. See also, Justin Parkinson, 'Why is Cecil Rhodes such a controversial figure?', http://www.bbc.com/news/magazine-32131829, accessed 24 December 2015.

[10] Max Price, 'Response to Sunday Independent article: "Adebajo distorts Price's view on Rhodes"', http://www.uct.ac.za/dailynews/?id=9068, accessed 6 October 2015.

[11] See http://www.news24.com/SouthAfrica/News/UCT-leadership-want-Rhodes-statue-moved-20150325, accessed 2 October 2015. See also 'Hello Slaapstad, a video on Rhodes Must Fall', by Yazeed Kamaldien, https://www.youtube.com/watch?v=z2PV5D9LtA0, accessed 7 October 2015.

[12] Adam Habib, 'Race, racism and memorials', http://www.wits.ac.za/newsroom/newsitems/201504/26107/news_item_26107.html, accessed 5 October 2015.

It is ironic though, that Habib would fail to practice the very deep, engaging deliberative conversation when confronted with the case of Mcebo Dlamini, the University of Witwatersrand SRC President, who posted his admiration for Adolf Hitler on Facebook, outraging the South

174

African Union of Jewish Students, among others. Dlamini was summarily expelled from the university, leading him to complain: 'If I was a white student, I wouldn't have been charged.' See http://www.thedailyvox.co.za/if-i-was-a-white-student-i-wouldnt-have-been-charged-dlamini/, accessed 5 October 2015; see also, http://www.news24.com/SouthAfrica/News/SRC-presidents-comments-racist-and-offensive-Wits-VC-20150428, accessed 5 October 2015.

Subsequently, Habib was described as a dictator by striking students protesting 'a 10.5 per cent fee hike', with some referring to him as 'Adolf Habib.' The fee increase was said to affect black students in particular, who continue to feel marginalised and to be plagued by poverty. In the words of Mcebo Dlamini, 'We continue with the struggle to educate black people. Wits must lead society but they neglect us. Our families look up to us to change this poverty cycle.' When the protesting students held VC Habib hostage, the university Council was summoned summarily and the decision to increase tuition and residence fees was suspended, at the end of a meeting that lasted 21 hours. See http://www.iol.co.za/news/south-africa/gauteng/habib-held-hostage-by-students-1.1931589#.ViIShCse4TY and http://mg.co.za/article/2015-10-17-wits-protest-habib-forced-to-hear-student-demands, accessed 17 October 2015; http://www.timeslive.co.za/sundaytimes/stnews/2015/10/18/Victory-for-students-as-Wits-backs-off-on-fees, accessed 20 October 2015. See also a call for affordable university student fees 'to allow for greater access to the poor, poor working class and even middle class families' by Deputy President Cyril Ramaphosa, http://www.msn.com/en-za/news/education/ramaphosa-calls-for-affordable-university-fees/ar-AAfu7Yv?li=AAaxc0E, accessed 17 October 2015.

[13] See statement issued by Pat Lucas of the UCT communication and marketing department, dated 27 March 2015, titled, 'Further Info on UCT Senate vote in favour of moving Rhodes' statue', 27 March 2015; https://www.uct.ac.za/usr/press/2015/SenateVote27March2015.pdf, accessed 28 November 2015.

[14] In September the university issued an announcement that it had sought and obtained an extension of the deadline for submitting the application for permanent removal of the Rhodes statue and heritage statement, from 28 September 2015 to 12 November 2015, in order to allow for extensive comments from all parties concerned. See http://www.uct.ac.za/dailynews/?id=9367, accessed 5 October 2015.

[15] See 'The short rise and long fall of Rhodes statue', https://www.youtube.com/watch?v=Y-rTQrybZpk, accessed 7 October 2015.

[16] See http://www.bdlive.co.za/national/2015/04/10/video-the-short-rise-and-long-fall-of-rhodes-statue, accessed 17 September 2015.

[17] See Kwezilomso Mbandazayo (United Front interim national co-convenor), 'Students should unite in struggle against failed universities', http://www.politicsweb.co.za/politics/students-should-unite-in-struggle-against-failed-u, accessed 5 October 2015.
For a new wave of violent protests in February 2016, see Pontsho Pilane, http://mg.co.za/article/2016-02-25-protest-politics-and-prayers-at-south-africas-universities, accessed 27 February 2016; Robert Morrell, http://www.dailymaverick.co.za/article/2016-02-22-op-ed-the-burning-issue-of-campus-violence/#.Vsv_kfl96Uk, accessed 26 February 2016.

[18] Tasneem Essop http://www.thedailyvox.co.za/student-rage-and-the-battle-for-transformation-at-sas-universities/, accessed 5 October 2015.
For more at University of Witwatersrand where students have joined the revolutionary bandwagon, and 'standing up to the conditions of whiteness their parents accepted, confronting a colonial history manifest in the present', as Greg Nicolson puts it, see his review of a documentary titled 'Decolonising Wits', by Aryan Kaganof, http://www.dailymaverick.co.za/article/2015-07-15-decolonising-wits-a-disconnect-of-content-and-context/#.Vfhblpce4TZ, accessed 5 October 2015.

[19] Tasneem Essop, Student rage and the battle for transformation at SA's universities, http://www.thedailyvox.co.za/student-rage-and-the-battle-for-transformation-at-sas-universities/, accessed 5 October 2015.
For more at Wits, where students have joined the revolutionary bandwagon, and are 'standing up to the conditions of whiteness their parents accepted, confronting a colonial history manifest in the present', as journalist Greg Nicolson puts it, see his review of the documentary *Decolonising Wits* by Aryan Kaganof, http://www.dailymaverick.co.za/article/2015-07-15-decolonising-wits-a-disconnect-of-content-and-context/#.Vfhblpce4TZ, accessed 5 October 2015.

[20] Tasneem Essop, Student rage and the battle for transformation at SA's universities, http://www.thedailyvox.co.za/student-rage-and-the-battle-for-transformation-at-sas-universities/, accessed 5 October 2015.
For more at Wits, where students have joined the revolutionary bandwagon, and are 'standing up to the conditions of whiteness their parents accepted, confronting a colonial history manifest in the present', as journalist Greg Nicolson puts it, see his review of the documentary *Decolonising Wits* by Aryan Kaganof, http://www.dailymaverick.co.za/article/2015-07-15-decolonising-wits-a-disconnect-of-content-and-context/#.Vfhblpce4TZ, accessed 5 October 2015.

[21] See https://www.youtube.com/watch?v=sF3rTBQTQk4, accessed 5 October 2015.

[22] It led to the production of a documentary with the same title, a film exposing South Africa's ongoing racism problem, with Stellenbosch University as a case in point. See http://www.theguardian.com/world/2015/sep/07/luister-south-africa-film-racism-stellenbosch, accessed 5 October 2015. See also Greg Nicolson, 'Stellenbosch: *Luister* could lead to change', http://www.dailymaverick.co.za/article/2015-09-01-stellenbosch-luister-could-lead-to-change/#.VfmAjpce4TZ, accessed 5 October 2015. For the Stellenbosch University appearance before the Higher Education Portfolio Committee in Parliament, see https://www.youtube.com/watch?v=3cufFANkFug, accessed 5 October 2015.

[23] For the said comment and a subsequent apology by Msengana, see http://www.channel24.co.za/The-Juice/Unathi-Msengana-Im-sorry-20150827, accessed 8 December 2015.

[24] It led to the production of a documentary *Luister* [Listen], a film exposing South Africa's ongoing racism problem, with Stellenbosch University as a case in point. http://www.theguardian.com/world/2015/sep/07/luister-south-africa-film-racism-stellenbosch, accessed 5 October 2015. See also, Greg Nicolson, http://www.dailymaverick.co.za/article/2015-09-01-stellenbosch-luister-could-lead-to-change/#.VfmAjpce4TZ, accessed 5 October 2015; for the Stellenbosch University appearance before Higher Education Portfolio Committee in Parliament, see https://www.youtube.com/watch?v=3cufFANkFug, accessed 5 October 2015.

[25] Jonathan Jansen, 'Campuses in SA are in turmoil: What's the root cause of the upheaval?' http://www.rdm.co.za/politics/2015/09/03/campuses-in-sa-are-in-turmoil.-what-s-the-root-cause-of-the-upheaval, accessed 5 October 2015.

[26] See http://www.sun.ac.za/english/Lists/news/DispForm.aspx?ID=3172, accessed 13 November 2015.

[27] See 'South Africa's Stellenbosch University aims to drop Afrikaans after protests', http://www.bbc.com/news/world-africa-34807291, accessed 13 November 2015.

[28] See Milton Nkosi, 'Why South African students want to be taught in English', http://www.bbc.com/news/world-africa-34811562, accessed 16 November 2015.

[29] See Christa Eybers, 'UP shut down after stand-off over Afrikaans', http://ewn.co.za/Media/2016/02/22/Clashes-at-Tuks, accessed 28 February 2016; Reinart Toerien, '#UFS students: "Decolonise our university"' http://ewn.co.za/Media/2016/02/24/Issues-of-transformation-and-wages-stir-tensions-at-UFS, accessed 28 February 2016.

[30] Some would argue that although there is hierarchy that treats 'proper' Afrikaans as more respectable than its creolised versions, Dutch and the Netherlands are not at the top of this hierarchy. They would point to a history of investment by advocates of *Suiwer Afrikaans* in establishing Afrikaans as an indigenous language distinct from, but as respectable as Dutch. Others would go even further to claim that Afrikaans 'is not a white language', and suggest it was 'created by Muslim slaves' – see http://kaganof.com/kagablog/2014/10/08/afrikaans-is-not-a-white-language/, accessed 15 March 2016. To the first group, Dutch and Afrikaans were represented by Afrikaner nationalists as different languages, and Afrikaans was seen as the language of white people who did not necessarily feel any allegiance (politically) to the Dutch. Such aspirations for discontinuities, I would add, do not necessarily imply a radical rejection of overt and subtle continuities. The very fact that the Dutch consider Afrikaans as 'Baby Dutch' is an indication that they see such hierarchies and interconnections.

[31] See Salikoko S. Mufwene, 'English: the Empire is dead. Long live the Empire', https://theconversation.com/english-the-empire-is-dead-long-live-the-empire-55676?, accessed 15 March 2016.

[32] See Salikoko S. Mufwene, 'English: the Empire is dead. Long live the Empire', https://theconversation.com/english-the-empire-is-dead-long-live-the-empire-55676?, accessed 15 March 2016.

[33] See Ra'eesa Pather, http://mg.co.za/article/2016-03-10-right-wing-radicals-back-pretoria-university-protests, accessed 11 March 2016.

[34] See Christi van der Westhuizen, 'How Afrikaner identity can be re-imagined in a post-apartheid world', https://theconversation.com/how-afrikaner-identity-can-be-re-imagined-in-a-post-apartheid-world-56222?, accessed 20 March 2016.

[35] See Tinyiko Maluleke, who is concerned that English, which insinuates itself into 'every linguistic vacuum', is 'Slowly but surely… occupying all formal and informal conversations, even between people who share and speak a language other than English.' http://www.iol.co.za/sundayindependent/english-strangling-indigenous-tongues-1942276, accessed 25 February 2016.

[36] As I finalise this book in April 2016, Afrikaans is still strong in Stellenbosch University. While management and a couple of departments (English and Law) have tried to change to English, they have been blocked by the university council. For an article that tracks the (non)changes to the language policy, see Neil Du Troit, 'Language: Where are we now?', http://www.bonfiire.com/stellenbosch/2016/02/language-where-are-we-now/, accessed 6 April 2016.

[37] See also Salikoko S. Mufwene, 'English: the Empire is dead. Long live the Empire',

https://theconversation.com/english-the-empire-is-dead-long-live-the-empire-55676?, accessed 15 March 2016.

[38] See Salikoko S. Mufwene, 'English: the Empire is dead. Long live the Empire', https://theconversation.com/english-the-empire-is-dead-long-live-the-empire-55676?, accessed 15 March 2016.

[39] As recently as 15 January 2016, UCT released a statement announcing that the Mandela Rhodes Foundation had announced its selection of the 12th cohort of Mandela Rhodes Scholars, 15 of whom will be studying at UCT in 2016. These consisted of students from South Africa, Lesotho, Zambia, Zimbabwe, Malawi, Uganda, Tanzania, Kenya and Egypt. See http://www.uct.ac.za/dailynews/?id=9531, accessed 19 January 2016.

[40] See http://www.uct.ac.za/dailynews/?id=9155, accessed 20 September 2015.

[41] See http://www.uct.ac.za/dailynews/?id=9155, accessed 20 September 2015.

[42] It would appear the task team did not act fast enough to pre-empt the burning of works of art on campus in early 2016. See Shobane, 'The art of hypocrisy: Appeal to re-constitute Shackville', http://m.thoughtleader.co.za/blackacademiccaucus/2016/03/08/the-art-of-hypocrisy-appeal-to-re-constitute-shackville/?wpmp_switcher=mobile, accessed 10 April 2016.

[43] See http://www.uct.ac.za/dailynews/?id=9155, accessed 20 September 2015.

[44] See http://www.uct.ac.za/dailynews/?id=9212, accessed 21 September 2015.

[45] It is worth noting that following fresh RMF protests over student accommodation for black students in February 2016, the VC's office was petrol bombed, along with a car and two Jammie Shuttle buses. See http://www.uct.ac.za/news/DebatesInHigherEducation/campusupdates/, accessed 12 March 2016. See also, https://www.youtube.com/watch?v=Rcilb8b7RDQ, https://www.youtube.com/watch?v=vMuTmkAtH_Y; and https://www.youtube.com/watch?v=cmhSrhN9eaU, accessed 12 March 2016.

[46] See http://www.uct.ac.za/dailynews/?id=9212, accessed 21 September 2015.

[47] See http://www.uct.ac.za/dailynews/?id=9212, accessed 21 September 2015.

[48] VC Max Price, 'VC Desk: On transformation: looking back at 2015' Released: 12h00, 11 March 2016, http://www.uct.ac.za/dailynews/?id=9621, accessed 12 March 2016.

[49] VC Max Price, 'VC Desk: On transformation: looking back at 2015' Released: 12h00, 11 March 2016, http://www.uct.ac.za/dailynews/?id=9621, accessed 12 March 2016.

179

50 In an article titled 'A Rapist State's Children: Jacob Zuma & Chumani Maxwele', Fezokuhle Mthonti writes:

> It is difficult not to see the direct ancestry between him [Chumani Maxwele] and the 'alleged' rapist leading the state. Maxwele's brand of bigoted patriarchal leadership is unfortunately an all too familiar feature of student politics at the moment. His anti-woman, and by implication, anti-LGBTQI brand of politics is the visceral feature of most student movements across the country, where the student revolution has morphed into a crude formulation of 'big man' politics.

See http://www.theconmag.co.za/2016/04/08/a-rapist-states-children-jacob-zuma-chumani-maxwele/, accessed 10 April 2016.

51 See Ashraf Hendricks, http://www.dailymaverick.co.za/article/2016-03-11-groundup-rhodes-must-fall-exhibition-vandalised-in-uct-protest/#.VuPbznrCAdw, accessed 12 March 2016. See also Yusuf Omar, 'Trans Collective stops RMF exhibition', http://www.uct.ac.za/dailynews/?id=9620, accessed 12 March 2016.

52 See Harry Garuba, 'What is an African curriculum?', http://mg.co.za/article/2015-04-17-what-is-an-african-curriculum, accessed 4 October 2015.

53 See Jo-Anne Vorster and Lynn Quinn, http://theconversation.com/how-academic-staff-development-can-contribute-to-changing-universities-51163?, accessed 30 November 2015.

54 See Harry Garuba, 'What is an African curriculum?', http://mg.co.za/article/2015-04-17-what-is-an-african-curriculum, accessed 4 October 2015.

55 See Mashupye Herbert Maserumule, http://theconversation.com/why-africas-professors-are-afraid-of-colonial-education-being-dismantled-50930?, accessed 27 November 2015.

56 See Mashupye Herbert Maserumule, http://theconversation.com/why-africas-professors-are-afraid-of-colonial-education-being-dismantled-50930?, accessed 27 November 2015.

57 See Amira Osman, http://theconversation.com/what-architects-must-learn-from-south-african-student-protests-50678?, accessed 28 November 2015

58 See Jo-Anne Vorster and Lynn Quinn, http://theconversation.com/how-academic-staff-development-can-contribute-to-changing-universities-51163?, accessed 30 November 2015.

59 See Graham McIntosh, http://www.politicsweb.co.za/news-and-analysis/some-suggested-research-topics-for-uct, accessed 9 December 2015. See also, Graham McIntosh, http://www.politicsweb.co.za/documents/uct-should-take-a-stand-against-racism--graham-mci, accessed 9 December 2015.

180

[60] For the birth of the idea of the scholarship, see Jourdan (1910: 73-80) and Flint (1974: 216-217). According to Herbert Bake, Rhodes's architect, Rhodes is supposed to have suspended all work on his Muitzenburg cottage during the last year of his life, due to 'his desire to save all he could for his Oxford Scholarships' (1934: 71). According to William Plomer, by his last will, Rhodes 'left a fortune of several million pounds', of which, among other things, provided for '160 Scholarships to be founded at Oxford of a value of £300 each, to be held by two students from every state of the U.S.A., and three from each of eighteen British colonies. Fifteen other Scholarships of the value of £250 each were reserved for German students, to be chosen by the so much admired Kaiser Willhelm II' (Plomer 1984 [1933]: 167). Selection criteria for the Rhodes Scholar included: '(i) his literary and scholastic attainments; (ii) his fondness of and success in manly outdoor sports such as cricket, football and the like; (iii) his qualities of manhood, truth, courage, devotion to duty, sympathy for the protection of the weak, kindliness, unselfishness and fellowship; and (iv) his exhibition during school days of moral force of character and of instincts to lead and to take an interest in his schoolmates, for those latter attributes will be likely in after-life to guide him to esteem the performance of public duty as his highest aim' (Plomer 1984 [1933]: 167-168). See also Williams (1921: 322-324).

[61] See also Lungisile Ntsebeza, 'Decolonizing the Curriculum', filmed by Wandile Kasibe, https://www.youtube.com/watch?v=JF8KVQSQCnk, accessed 8 October 2015.

In his address, Ntsebeza, who says he is not out to change anyone's course, discusses a university-wide course he envisages on the teaching of Africa, including the possibility of offering a major in African studies. The fact that he is still talking in rudimentary terms is an indication that little of substance, especially structurally, has changed in the teaching of Africa at UCT since the Mamdani years. For additional insights and reflections provoked by RMF, see Cherry Bomb, 'On colonial legacies and the violence of liberal whiteness at UCT – April 2015', http://fleurmach.com/2015/07/14/on-colonial-legacies-and-the-violence-of-whiteness-at-uct-april-2015/, accessed 9 October 2015; Puleng Segalo, 'Reflections on Curriculum Conference 2015 (Rhodes University)', http://www.ru.ac.za/media/rhodesuniversity/content/equityinstitutional culture/documents/Reflections%20on%20Conference%20-%20P%20Segalo,%20UNISA%20.pdf, accessed 9 October 2015.

[62] Clearly revolted by the act, Simon Lincoln Reader represents it as follows:

> Desecrating anything with human faeces is one of the most contemptible forms of protest; in the context of the University of Cape Town debacle, it was worsened by the reality that staff —

181

black staff — were left to sanitise the defiled statue of Cecil John Rhodes. It has been near-impossible to gauge the objective due in part to the blinding incoherence of the protest leader — a troubled boy who has an impressive rap sheet of attention-seeking. See http://www.bdlive.co.za/opinion/columnists/2015/03/27/one-monument-cannot-capture-all-countrys-ills, accessed 3 October 2015.

[63] See detailed UCT press statement on the matter, http://www.uct.ac.za/dailynews/?id=9198, accessed 3 October 2015.

[64] See http://www.news24.com/SouthAfrica/News/Maxwele-My-comments-about-whites-just-allegations-20150608, accessed 3 October 2015.

[65] See http://www.news24.com/SouthAfrica/News/UCT-students-suspension-lifted-on-technical-grounds-20150612, 03 October 2015.

[66] See http://www.news24.com/SouthAfrica/News/UCT-rejects-Maxwele-conspiracy-theory-claims-20150609, accessed 3 October 2015.

[67] See http://www.news24.com/SouthAfrica/News/Poo-flinging-UCT-student-says-suspension-is-politically-motivated-20150511, accessed 3 October 2015.

[68] See http://www.news24.com/SouthAfrica/News/Students-suspension-not-related-to-protests-UCT-20150515, accessed 3 October 2015.

[69] See http://www.iol.co.za/news/south-africa/western-cape/uct-amnesty-purely-political-maxwele-1.1860007#.VfXD8Jce4TZ, accessed 3 October 2015.

[70] See http://www.news24.com/SouthAfrica/News/UCT-students-suspension-lifted-on-technical-grounds-20150612, 03 October 2015.

[71] See http://www.news24.com/SouthAfrica/News/Interim-order-allows-Maxwele-to-attend-UCT-classes-20150722, accessed 5 October 2015.

[72] See http://citizen.co.za/772402/maxwele-wins-case-against-racist-uct/, accessed 4 October 2015.

[73] Tokelo Nhlapo, 'UCT's poo protest: Violence is a perfect reaction', http://www.dailymaverick.co.za/opinionista/2015-03-11-ucts-poo-protest-violence-is-a-perfect-reaction/#.VfXL4Jce4TZ, accessed 4 October 2015.

[74] See Eula Biss, 'White Debt', http://www.nytimes.com/2015/12/06/magazine/white-debt.html?_r=0, accessed 4 December 2015.

[75] For echoes of similar protests and campaigns in the USA, where black student activists are challenging white supremacy and institutional racism on university campuses, see Peniel E. Joseph, http://www.theroot.com/articles/culture/2015/11/black_student_activists_stand_against_racist_cultures_on_campus.html,

accessed 5 December 2015.

[76] Charles R. Larson, Emeritus Professor of Literature at American University, Washington, writing about the US, notes that the very expression 'black lives matter' is indicative of a context where 'black lives do not matter'. Indeed, as he puts it, 'Black lives do not matter but neither does much else, as long as the status quo can be retained and white guys (of all economic and educational levels) can continue to control virtually everything.' See Charles R. Larson, 'Black Lives Do Not Matter', http://www.counterpunch.org/2015/12/21/black-lives-do-not-matter/, accessed 25 December 2015.

[77] See Faye V. Harrison, http://savageminds.org/2014/12/12/reflections-on-the-aaa-die-in-as-a-symbolic-space-of-social-death/, accessed 5 December 2015.

[78] See http://www.mysanantonio.com/news/local/article/University-of-Texas-student-government-votes-to-6161270.php and http://www.npr.org/sections/thetwo-way/2015/08/30/436072805/jefferson-davis-statue-comes-down-at-university-of-texas, accessed 3 December 2015.

[79] See http://www.columbiamissourian.com/news/higher_education/mu-english-department-votes-no-confidence-in-chancellor-s-leadership/article_4c8a52d6-8327-11e5-9ef3-5725103d82ec.html, accessed 3 December 2015.

[80] See Nov. 13, 2015 article titled 'The history of black students' fight for equality at the University of Missouri', http://www.kansascity.com/news/special-reports/article44793585.html, accessed 1 December 2015.

[81] See http://www.npr.org/2015/11/10/455462047/a-deep-rooted-history-of-activism-stirs-in-college-football and http://www.racismreview.com/blog/2015/11/13/black-athletes-and-social-protest-a-long-tradition, accessed 3 December 2015.

[82] See http://www.theroot.com/articles/culture/2015/11/black_student_activists_stand_against_racist_cultures_on_campus.html, accessed 1 December 2015.

[83] See 'demands' from students at Emory University at https://docs.google.com/document/d/1KM_SDc4-QaQKXyl_DYUlDKRjN0DgLN0xVln986LunI/edit, accessed 5 December 2015, and response from university officials along with commentary which characterizes the demands as 'a wish list written by spoiled brats' and their authors as 'arrogant radicalized students', http://www.theamericanconservative.com/author/rod-dreher, accessed 5 December 2015.

[84]See http://www.huffingtonpost.com/entry/campus-racism-protests-didnt-come-out-of-nowhere_56464a87e4b08cda3488bfb4,

and other colleges and universities across the country,
http://fivethirtyeight.com/features/here-are-the-demands-from-students-protesting-racism-at-51-colleges,
accessed 1 and 3 December 2015.
[85] See http://www.thenewjournalandguide.com/national-headlines/803-student-protests-across-nation-launching-changes,
accessed 5 December 2015.
[86] See http://www.cnn.com/2015/11/10/us/racism-college-campuses-protests-missouri and http://www.jbhe.com/incidents,
accessed 1 December 2015.
[87] See
http://www.npr.org/sections/codeswitch/2015/11/11/455615889/a-few-good-reads-on-the-missouri-protestors-and-journalistic-outrage,
accessed 3 December 2015.
[88] In the words of Morgan Debaun who, inspired by her student
experience at Washington University in St. Louis, Missouri, co-founded
Blavity, a 'thriving tech and multimedia company' and source of news and
information with platforms serving black communities and 20,000
followers across social media.
See http://forbes.com/sites/julianmitchell/2015/11/05/meet-morgan-debaun-the-blavity-founder-bridging-the-gap-between-content-and-tech,
accessed 1 December 2015.
[89] See http://www.nytimes.com/2015/11/27/opinion/black-tape-at-harvard-law.html?ref=opinion#story-continues-1,
accessed 11 November 2015.
[90] See Sean Coughlan, Harvard Law School scraps official crest in slavery
row, http://www.bbc.com/news/education-35726878,
accessed 5 March 2016.
[91] See Faye V. Harrison,
http://savageminds.org/2014/12/12/reflections-on-the-aaa-die-in-as-a-symbolic-space-of-social-death/, accessed 5 December 2015.
[92] See Dr. Stephen Dilks http://info.umkc.edu/unews/dr-stephen-dilks-an-open-letter-to-the-umkc-community, accessed 4 December 2015.
[93] See Dr. Stephen Dilks http://info.umkc.edu/unews/dr-stephen-dilks-an-open-letter-to-the-umkc-community, accessed 4 December 2015.
[94] See 'FW De Klerk criticises Rhodes statue removal campaign',
http://www.bbc.com/news/world-africa-35181303,
accessed 26 December 2015.
[95] See http://www.rhodeshouse.ox.ac.uk, accessed 5 December 2015.
[96] See the debate at the Oxford Union
https://www.youtube.com/watch?v=y3aBDBdDIgU,
accessed 27 February 2016.
[97] See 'Skin Deep meets Women from Rhodes Must Fall in Oxford',
http://www.skindeepmag.com/online-articles/skin-deep-meets-rhodes-must-fall-in-oxford/, accessed 5 April 2016.

184

See also https://vimeo.com/143402250, accessed 5 April 2016.
[98] See
http://www.oxfordmail.co.uk/news/13950275.Oxford_students_gather_
to_protest_against_statue_of_politician_Cecil_Rhodes,
accessed 5 December 2015.
[99] See Kim Darrah,
http://www.cherwell.org/news/town/2015/11/07/rmf-to-protest-at-
oriel-following-rhodes-statue-petition, accessed 5 December 2015.
[100] See Javier Espinosa, 'Cecil Rhodes: Lord Patten warns against
"pandering to contemporary views" over statue row',
http://www.telegraph.co.uk/education/universityeducation/12094277/C
ecil-Rhodes-Oxford-University-students-must-confront-views-they-find-
objectionable-says-new-head.html, accessed 28 February 2016.
[101] See Estelle Shirbon, http://mg.co.za/article/2016-01-14-oxford-head-
resists-rewriting-history-over-rhodes-statue, accessed 28 February 2016.
[102] For a repost by Ntokozo Qwabe, the recipient of a Rhodes Scholarship
in question, watch
https://mail.google.com/mail/u/0/#inbox/15327586139dbac2?projecto
r=1, accessed 28 February 2016.
[103] For an idea of the debate on Rhodes Must Fall at Oxford, see
https://mail.google.com/mail/u/0/#inbox/15327586139dbac2?projecto
r=1, accessed 26 February 2016.
[104] See James Delingpole,
http://www.biznews.com/undictated/2015/12/29/james-delingpole-
leave-oxford-alone-take-anti-rhodes-campaign-back-to-sa/,
accessed 28 February 2016.
[105] See Kevin Rawlinson, 'Cecil Rhodes statue to remain at Oxford after
"overwhelming support"'
http://www.theguardian.com/education/2016/jan/28/cecil-rhodes-
statue-will-not-be-removed--oxford-university,
accessed 28 February 2016.
This decision is saluted by Cherly Hudson, a history professor at the
University of Liverpool, in an article titled 'History is not a morality play:
both sides on #RhodesMustFall debate should remember that', see
https://theconversation.com/history-is-not-a-morality-play-both-sides-
on-rhodesmustfall-debate-should-remember-that-53912, accessed 28
February 2016. Her article was republished in the South African *Mail &
Guardian* newspaper,
http://mg.co.za/article/2016-02-01-why-an-oxford-college-was-right-
not-to-take-down-rhodes-statue, accessed 28 February 2016.
For additional coverage on the decision, see Caroline Mortimer,
http://www.independent.co.uk/news/uk/home-news/cecil-rhodes-
statue-will-stay-at-oxford-despite-student-campaign-oriel-college-says-
a6840651.html, accessed 28 February 2016; Javier Espinoza,

http://www.telegraph.co.uk/education/universityeducation/12128151/Cecil-Rhodes-statue-to-remain-at-Oxford-University-after-alumni-threatens-to-withdraw-millions.html, accessed 28 February 2016; Tom Witherow and Lucy Crossley, http://www.dailymail.co.uk/news/article-3421866/Oriel-College-pledges-controversial-statue-Victorian-imperialist-amid-fears-lose-100m-donation-bowed-campaign-remove-it.html, accessed 28 February 2016.

[106] See Timothy Garton Ash, 'Rhodes hasn't fallen, but the protesters are making me rethink Britain's past', http://www.theguardian.com/profile/timothygartonash, accessed 4 March 2016.

[107] See Finlo Rohrer, 'When is it right to remove a statue?', http://www.bbc.com/news/magazine-35161671, accessed 24 December 2015.

[108] Some South African students following these student protests elsewhere in the world, were struck that blacks the world over are plagued by similar racism and were convinced of the urgency of their struggle to affirm that black lives matter and against white supremacy. See for example, http://www.pri.org/stories/2015-12-04/south-african-students-say-protests-us-campuses-validate-their-battles-against, accessed 6 December 2015.

Chapter 5

Lessons from Rhodes Must Fall

What lessons can be learnt from the RMF campaign? How much are *amakwerekwere* of yesteryear ready to accommodate the vanquished in their victories and rethink and rework the present and the future? And how willing are South Africans, not to mention others, genuinely frustrated as they are by the pace of change, willing to embrace transformation as an inclusive idea? To what extent are those frustrated sons and daughters of the native soil (however contested their claims of legitimacy to the land may be) ready to interrogate radically the very foundations of what constitutes present-day South Africa? To what extent does it make sense to resort to a regressive and exclusionary logic of citizenship and belonging in a country where everyone is an outsider, *Uitlander*, *makwerekwere* or stranger in one form or another, given the histories of incessant mobility in the region? How useful is it to expend energies on such questions as: 'What if there were no whites in South Africa?' (Haffajee 2015) in a hierarchized context of histories of myriad encounters where the next oppressor or exploiter is always a level below or above the current one, be these levels determined by race, place, class, gender, generation or other (Landau and Kaspin 2002; Terreblanche 2002)? Is there reason to listen to those who argue that transformation, however radical, cannot afford to ignore the positive outcomes of the unequal encounters of the past? If oppression is perfected by the subservience of its victims, what is the significance of providing for co-implication by the vanquished and victor in the production of victimhood and of imperial arrogance? What does it mean to imagine and realise a dream of a common humanity for intimate strangers trapped in a post-traumatic society in which mutual accommodation holds the only prospect for recalibration of relationships of the hierarchies championed by factors such as race, place, class, gender and generation (Gobodo-Madikizela 2003; Mangcu 2015).

Ashwin Desai, a former student activist and a professor of sociology at the University of Johannesburg, claims that a rejection of Rhodes amounts to a rejection of Mandela, because Mandela 'rescued' Rhodes. In his estimation, Mandela gave Rhodes legitimacy when he allowed his name to be associated with the Rhodes Scholarship. Desai recounts how at the launch of the scholarship, Mandela is supposed to have said: 'Rhodes would be happy with how we are running the economy.'[1] Desai maintains that:

> A rejection of Rhodes is a rejection of the negotiated settlement that gave rise to the Truth and Reconciliation Commission (TRC). The TRC said it was only interested in what happened during apartheid, when the contours of South African history were shaped by what happened way before 1948. Mandela et al., in their zeal to win over the white minority, allowed entities like De Beers, the manifestation of Rhodes' legacy, not to come to the TRC and account.[2]

Mandela did explain further his rationale for opting to be associated with Rhodes when the Mandela Rhodes Foundation, a leadership development programme for Africa, was established in 2003 in Cape Town by agreement between the Nelson Mandela Foundation and the Rhodes Trust.[3] Indicating he had no reason to doubt the commitment to transformation and reparations by those who had exploited black South Africans and their resources (diamond and gold in particular) with reckless abandon under colonialism and apartheid such as Rhodes and the Oppenheimers, Mandela reiterated his position:

> We are sometimes still asked by people how we could agree to have our name joined to that of Cecil John Rhodes in this Mandela Rhodes initiative. To us, the answer is easy, and we have explained the logic of our decision on a number of occasions. We have referred to our constitution's injunction for us to come together across the historical divides, to build our country together with a future equally shared by all. [....]
> We see The Mandela Rhodes Foundation as a significant initiative within that broader framework of South Africans taking responsibility for the transformation of their society, so grievously skewed by a history of colonialism and apartheid. We shall once more take hands across historical divides that others may deem unbridgeable.[4]

In a keynote address at the Rhodes Trust centenary celebrations in January 2003, Njabulo Ndebele, the VC of UCT at the time, noted what Rhodes and Mandela had in common thus:

> We learn from Howard Philips' history of the University of Cape Town that the new South African Union government of 1910 'with the emphasis on English-Afrikaner reconciliation, was keen to implement an idea first mooted by Cecil John Rhodes in 1891, to establish a national, teaching university on his estate at Groote Schuur, where English and Dutch-speakers could mingle during their student years, thus laying a foundation for future cooperation.' *Is it not remarkable that Rhodes' dream of inter-ethnic cooperation should, at this time in world history, combine with Mandela's dream of reconciliation, the latter encompassing a much more complex human environment?* The combination resonates with new possibilities not only for South Africa but for our entire world (Ndebele 2007: 190, emphasis mine).

By lending his name and support to the partnership with the Rhodes Trust on leadership, Mandela was buying into the hope that young South Africans with high thoughts and aspirations, and endowed by nature with all the faculties to achieve greatness, would be afforded the means and opportunity to pursue their leadership dreams as they saw fit (Brown 2015: 45). It was also in this hope, I believe, that these young South Africans would offer leadership by continuing the struggle for African liberation and renaissance, not as a zero sum game, but in tune with the spirit of a genuinely negotiated and carefully navigated universal recognition of a common humanity informed by the lived realities of all and sundry and not merely as a gesture in tokenism by sterile liberalism. As Raymond Suttner argues in relation to the current student protests in which Mandela is sometimes depicted as a 'sell out' in the compromises he made,

> The settlement of 1994 was not seen as a final settlement of democratic and transformational questions but as creating conditions that would enable those who cherished freedom to move towards fully claiming their rights. It is up to the present generation to ensure that this happens.[5]

This hopeful commitment by Mandela – a flawed hero or not – is worth pursuing as an inclusive nation-building project that targets

South Africans beyond the narrow confines of the middle and privileged classes, or by insisting on selective inclusion flamed by little more than narrow nationalism and autochthony. Such nation-building is best enabled through mutual accommodation and the capacity to forgive without being taken for granted. It is about rising to assume the collective challenge of making it possible for each and every South African to see the wisdom in a declaration by the leadership of a delegation of Afrikaner youth at a meeting with President Thabo Mbeki: 'Yesterday is a foreign country – tomorrow belongs to us!' (Mbeki 1999: xiv). Mbeki, drawing on the statement by the delegation of young Afrikaners to inspire his vision of a new birth of Africa, elaborates:

> They spoke of how our country's transition to democracy had brought them their own freedom; of how their acceptance of themselves as equal citizens with their black compatriots defined apartheid South Africa and its legacy as foreign to themselves; of how South Africa, reborn, constitutes their own heritage (Mbeki 1999: xiv).

Agreeing with Mandela, Mbeki argues that to make yesterday truly a foreign country, requires social movements with a leadership genuinely committed to the inclusiveness needed to bring about a tomorrow that belongs to all, the victors and vanquished of the games of unequal encounters of the past and present.

Mandela has been criticised for not developing a strong social and economic transformation programme during his presidency. Reconciliation as the key trope of the era meant that dispossession and transformation were seldom envisaged. Admittedly, this was unperceived shortcoming from the more optimistic post-apartheid years. But perhaps we may see another vision being pursued by Mandela through his emphasis on leadership and education, especially among the youth. Preoccupied with keeping disaffected youth on the path of moderation, the long term overcoming of the lack of skills and education in a South African black population were distinctive concerns during Mandela's presidency. A short-term prevention of flight of capital could be justified by a long-term strategy of building an educated and skilled South African majority population. But this was and would be an ideal based on being able to canalise resources into the institutional infrastructure that would overcome a half century of apartheid denial of quality education to the black youth of South Africans ((Ramose 2003, 2004, 2010; Jansen 2011). If this is taken to be Mandela's justification of the harness of his name to the Rhodes Foundation, a case could be made to the effect that this was a sacrifice worth making for getting a sort of Marshall Plan for the reskilling and training of the majority of South African people, at a period of investor uncertainty with the radical transition South Africa was undergoing. Granted Mandela's sacrifice, the nation-building envisioned requires sustained political will and economic support above tokenism, lip service and rhetoric. Only such a committed approach would ensure that the sidestepped largely black masses can begin to feel part and parcel of the dignity of being a post-apartheid South African citizen. For the majority of black South Africans to join the bandwagon of those who truly see apartheid South Africa as something of the past and who are eager to celebrate the birth of a new country where all can live, dream and belonging together in peaceful co-existence or conviviality, they would need more than rhetoric and political correctness on their dining tables. With careful political planning and strategic interventions, business – big and small – could contribute creatively towards the form of national integration Mandela subscribed to as a means of harnessing South Africa's wide and varied legacies in the interest of an inclusive, accommodating future where whites and blacks are in tune with the complexity, open-endedness and open-mindedness desired as the building blocks of the new South Africa in the making.

At this point, we may envisage what might have emerged if this had been continued as a sustainable policy. The Mandela- Rhodes connection may have evoked a more elitist idea of education, but the implications in Mandela's speeches were more about how to harness resources for the long-term development of a more responsive and skilful post-apartheid population. This could not come from nowhere after the period of apartheid. Instead the resources were there in the initial policy of welcoming *amakwerekwere* as providers of technical skills, entrepreneurial skills and a means of harnessing long distance business and trade networks to the rest of Africa. The issue being that these were skills that could not come from the white populations of South Africa but depended on re–embedding South African black peoples in to the sustainable business and trading networks of the rest of Africa. Of course, this meant a fast 'catch up' phase to prevent the sense of being overwhelmed by the rest of Africa. This is still the 'big issue'. How to exploit the *amakwerekwere* for the advantage of bringing the majority of black South Africans into not only the informal and other economies of Africa but also to affiliate to the commonalities of cosmology and spirituality.

As Thabo Mbeki puts it, South Africans must rise to the enormous challenge of contributing to 'the recovery of African pride, the confidence in ourselves that we can succeed as well as any other in building a humane and prosperous society' (Mbeki 1999: xx). Such a rebirth of Africanity in South Africa in his opinion, is best achieved by linking up with parallel processes of African renaissance in the rest of the continent, as South Africa cannot afford to act as if it were an island cut off from the rest of Africa. To Mbeki, if the injustices of the past and present must be fought and successfully, South Africans must 'join hands with all other like-minded forces on out continent, convinced that the peoples of Africa share a common destiny, convinced also that people of goodwill throughout the world will join us in the sustained offensive which must result in the new century going down in the history as the African century' (Mbeki 1999: xxi).

With South Africa's baby steps into democracy came steps by the new African National Congress (ANC) government towards realising African Renaissance, in the form of an overt announcement of its intentions to seek reunion with the rest of Africa and to make African Renaissance an agenda (Makgobe 1999; Van Kessel 2001). Vale and Maseko (1998: 271) have pointed out that even before 1994, South Africa's reunification with the rest of Africa had been a significant 'sub-narrative within the processes which led to negotiation over the ending of apartheid'. This sub-narrative was especially pertinent for the ANC, which was readying itself to take over the reins of power in the country. The rest of Africa was, to the ANC, 'an important sphere of strategic relationships that needed to be gently established and maintained with a degree of sensitivity' (Naidu 2004: 207). Part of this sensitivity arose from the compulsion for the ANC to show loyalty towards those African leaders who supported it during the liberation struggle (Naidu 2004; Miller 2004). The ANC's policy documents spoke of the 'fate of democratic South Africa being inextricably bound up with what happens to the rest of the continent' (Naidu 2004: 207). Even at the height of apartheid, South Africa never lost sight of its potential to aspire for a leadership role on the continent, especially in view of its strategic geography vis-à-vis Africa and the rest of the world (Vale and Maseko 1998: 274–276). The ANC, however, had to be cautious about balancing its leadership and world-player aspirations with its bestowed and perceived obligations to South Africans and to the continent.

In 1996, Thabo Mbeki, who was deputy to President Mandela, made his famous 'I am an African' declaration in Parliament at the inauguration of the new South African Constitution. In the speech, he stressed his composite identity as part of all the peoples whose diverse origins, creativity and relationships account for South Africa's very existence.[6] He saw the new Constitution as 'an unequivocal statement that we refuse to accept that our Africanness shall be defined by our race, colour, gender or historical origins' and 'a firm assertion made by ourselves that South Africa belongs to all who live in it, black and white'.[7] This significant and hopeful statement of South Africa's limitless pursuit of inclusiveness was an attempt to accommodate the 'rainbow' ideals of the country's Truth and Reconciliation Commission. It was also a sort of declaration of intention regarding the readiness of the South African state to open up, (re)unite, reawaken and redefine its Africanness in tune with the rest of the continent. As Mbeki continued to invoke the idea of African Renaissance with enthusiasm throughout his own presidential tenure, he raised hope (both in interested South African circles as well as elsewhere on the continent) that African Renaissance was a worthy aspiration (Van Kessel 2001: 48–51).

Mbeki was, of course, not the first to articulate notions of African Renaissance within South Africa, and some would argue, the rest of Africa. Already in 1906, Pixley ka Isaka Seme, founder of the ANC, proclaimed, 'I am an African and I set my pride in my race over and against a hostile public opinion.' This proclamation was delivered at Columbia University in a speech titled 'The

Regeneration of Africa'.[8] Anton Lembede, who was Seme's law partner, founding president of the ANC Youth League and Seme's proclaimed 'ideological heir', also invoked ideas of African Renaissance within South Africa and its politics. Mbeki's conception of African Renaissance – which upholds ideas of the moral reawakening of (dissolute) Africans along with African nationalism – is principally accredited to Anton Lembede's ideas, his expansion of Seme's ideas of African pride and his writings.[9] On the other hand, Mbeki's strong insistence on Africans learning and being conscious of their history and achievements – as a means to revitalise their sense of pride, moral compass and self-confidence – resonates strongly with the articulation of African Renaissance by Cheikh Anta Diop of Senegal (Diop 1996/1952).

The conception and articulation of African Renaissance may not be unique to Mbeki (Van Kessel 2001); however, he certainly played a leading and explicit role in foregrounding African Renaissance within South Africa, to the point of being dubbed 'the Renaissance Man'. Furthermore, foreign policy had, since 1994, ceased to be handled just by the Ministry of Foreign Affairs to become a matter closely linked to the president's office (Vale and Maseko 1998: 284). This point alludes not only to the centrality of Mbeki in discussing South African foreign policy but also to the centrality of understanding how he was perceived, even within the ANC, as the 'architect' of African Renaissance (Vale and Maseko 1998: 272).

Such a renaissance must allow for the open-ended nature of the identities of South African citizens. In his landmark speech to Parliament in 1996, Mbeki proclaimed his Africanness not as excavation, as if there were no present and future informed by a history of multiple encounters. Mbeki's Africanness is a composite reality, one informed by interconnections and the inextricable entanglements that come from sharing the same places, spaces and experiences with others. African identities and cultures are changing and dynamic. African Renaissance requires seeking conviviality and carefully navigating between the popular and the elite, the endogenous and the exogenous in Africa. If being African or pan-African is a permanent work in progress, is there any sense in defining and confining Africa and Africans to the continent of

Africa? And what is there to stop Europeans, Asians and others from claiming their places in the cradle of humankind? There is need to carefully negotiate and navigate the complex contours of an African Renaissance and pan-Africanism that would best serve South Africa and its complexities as a 21st-century democracy. This calls for emphasis on African unity beyond identities confined by geography, primordialism and narrow nationalism, and champions socio-political inclusiveness for all those who willingly claim or are compelled to identify with being 'African'. As a quest for common values as Africans, African Renaissance is an aspirational project towards a continent and world informed by solidarities and identities shaped by a humanity of common predicaments. It is the glue to hold together the dreams and aspirations of Africans divided, among other things, by geography, ethnicity or race, class, gender, age, culture or religion. Forced and voluntary mobility, which has made being African a global and dynamic reality, means African Renaissance as an ideology and an aspiration is realisable anywhere in the world. Hence there should be an effort to conscientise 'Africans' beyond geographical Africa (Nyamnjoh and Shoro 2014).

Seeking inclusiveness, interdependence and conviviality among South Africans and between South Africa and the rest of Africa is a fruitful way forward for South Africa, rather than the current dichotomous tendency where those who want radical change are countered by well-resourced reactionary forces determined to continue the business of maintaining the privileges of the *amakwerekwere* of yesteryear, as evinced by the open letters 'UCT should take a stand against racism' by Graham McIntosh – 'former opposition MP [member of Parliament], alumnus and potential donor' – addressed to Russell Ally, Executive Director of Alumni and Development at UCT. In these letters McIntosh castigates UCT leadership for yielding to the chaos of barbarism at the institution, indicating that he would donate his millions to the institution if only the leadership takes steps to reinstate and maintain the status quo in terms of what is taught and researched.[10] Whether zero-sum games are the answer or in question[11], there is clearly much soul-searching and introspection on the nature, colour and future of South Africa and its universities left to be done

(Ndebele 2007: 165-169; Bhana 2014; Haffajee 2015; MacDonald 2006; Mangcu 2015; Soudien 2010, 2012). The students have merely reminded all and sundry of this unfinished business of transforming South African university campuses into what Ndebele once dreamt of as:

> affirming and humbling places where, over time, people come together to discover and re-discover one another, equal before the quest for knowledge, experience and community. Bodies, minds, conversations, doubts, certitudes, fashions, wealth, poverty, secrets, disclosures and all kinds of histories: they all intersect there, on campus.[12]

With that in mind, there is no better way to conclude this review of the RMF movement than to draw on the wise counsel of Kusi Dlamini, a Rhodes Scholar and member of the University of Pretoria (UP) Council, whom experience has taught to be wary of zero-sum games. He challenges South Africans to seize the opportunity offered by the negotiated removal of Rhodes's statue to begin 'an inclusive and meaningful process of far-reaching socioeconomic transformation that addresses the real issues at the core of students' grievances.' It would be a mistake, he writes, to isolate the student grievances 'from wider societal dissatisfaction with the pace and content of transformation that are perceived to confine the historically disadvantaged to the margins of most sectors of the economy and institutions of power and privilege.' South Africa can and must face up to the imperative of 'a sober and unifying conversation ... to craft an inclusive economy and society.' Such 'a constructive conversation' should aim at producing a 'workable road map to address the aspirations of those who feel excluded and disempowered and the fears of those who feel that transformation would result in their exclusion and disempowerment.' Moreover, those who insist on transformation as a zero-sum game, must reckon with the consequences of non-sustainability of the perpetual, irrational and inexcusable marginalisation of the majority.[13]

Dlamini argues that 'current and future generations have an obligation to normalise power relations skewed on a narrow racial basis.' There is need to exorcise in unifying ways the visible and

196

invisible colonial and apartheid statues and monuments that currently 'litter' most of South Africa, but this can only be achieved in a spirit that builds on 'a continuum from the 1994 national unity and reconciliation project of building the new from the old and ensuring that South Africans find a tangible sense of common purpose that unifies and strengthens' South Africa as an accommodating place and space. In this project of forging a common future steeped in mutual recognition and respect for a common humanity, 'tribalising and racializing responses... are unhelpful and divisive'.[14] Dlamini refuses to embrace a zero-sum attitude even when it comes to the much demonised Sir Cecil John Rhodes, agreeing with those who, like columnist Simon Lincoln Reader, have argued that a monument, however imbued with symbolism, cannot 'capture everything wrong with a country', and that Rhodes, apart from being 'a product of his environment, seduced by the narrative of seemingly divine Empire', could hardly be described as unique in his propensity for dictatorship and pathological motivation to acquire personal wealth by violent means of dispossession.[15]

Dlamini writes:

> As a Rhodes Scholar who benefited from Cecil John Rhodes's money, which paid for my Oxford education, I feel the debate around his statue should provide a golden opportunity for us to engage seriously in a vision and values debate about the kind of South Africa we want.
>
> Rhodes Scholars like Bram Fischer and Arthur Chaskalson returned from Oxford to play a meaningful role in the Struggle and as lawyers for Nelson Mandela and his comrades in their treason trial.
>
> Other Rhodes Scholars, like Julian Ogilvie-Thompson, the former chief executive of Anglo American, Jacko Maree, former chief executive of Standard Bank, and Loyiso Nongxa, former Wits University vice-chancellor, have played key and helpful roles in business and academia.
>
> My generation of Rhodes Scholars were and are fully committed to meaningful transformation of the economy and society in ways that build, unite and strengthen South Africa as a great and winning nation. When I was the president of the Rhodes Scholars Southern Africa Forum at Oxford, we used to fund many Rhodes Scholars from different parts of the world to

do charity and community development work in impoverished parts of South Africa.

We were determined to spread the awareness to the global Rhodes Scholar community that Rhodes's money came from southern Africa and that giving back to southern Africa was the right thing to do although it was not an obligation that scholars had to sign up to.

All this does not change who Rhodes was, what he stood for or the racial oppression and exploitation he unleashed on black people.

What I think it demonstrates is that it is possible to use certain aspects of his legacy, such as the scholarship, to do good by advancing the socioeconomic transformation project to build an inclusive and empowering South Africa for all – as indeed we can and must.[16]

Paradoxical as it might seem, the Rhodes Scholarship programme, is likely to continue to be relevant in a 'transformed' South African higher education landscape as government and universities explore ways of minimising the cost of higher education, especially for poor black students. Dubbed #FeesMustFall on twitter, the protesting students made a point of reiterating that education is a human right, insisting on its ultimate outcome of education as liberation.[17] To date, despite repeated rhetoric by ANC politicians since the Mandela presidency, the South African government has not offered free education, notwithstanding insistence by the South African Students Congress that 'the only way we can protect the democracy that was won by our grandparents and parents, is by arming the youth with quality education'.[18] Free education, especially at the level of the university, may not be impossible to contemplate, but it is likely to be considered as unjust by those with the power, wealth and privilege to make it possible. According to UCT philosophy major, George Hull, while making all students pay fees upfront maybe unfair, free higher education would prevent the employment of well-trained doctors, lawyers, teachers, accountants, managers, engineers, journalists and civil servants on university campuses.[19] Columnist, Helen Walne, echoes this claim, stating that student fees are needed 'to pay for quality academics, cutting-edge systems and top libraries'. She insists that those who can afford to pay full fees should, while those who cannot should be subsidised by the state.[20]

What students should be fighting for, some commentators insist, is 'adequate' and 'equal' education, not free. The idea that one has to work and pay for, in only to be seen to have earned one's education, is particularly strong among the descendants of the *amakwerekwere* of yesteryear, those with the added advantage of having benefitted, collectively, from racialized opportunities privileges and protection enshrined and gifted them by apartheid. As for the majority black students, most of whom may only have inherited the stubborn wounds of collective dispossession and debasement, they looked to Minister of Higher Education Blade Nzimande to intervene and reassure them that it was still possible to hope for a descent higher education as a poor black student in the purportedly new South Africa. They were disappointed when the minister was not categorically reassuring, some going to the point of demanding that he be fired.[21] The #FeesMustFall movement erupted into a series of protests with an initial goal of preventing the ten per cent fee increase and improving the student agenda.[22]

If South Africa cannot afford free education for all as economics professor Steve Koch of the University of Pretoria argues[23], how can it afford to distance itself from the Rhodes Scholarship programme by throwing the baby out with the bathwater of Rhodes's excesses? If black South African students claiming the status of bona fide sons and daughters of the soil or that of born free must rise and claim their rights and entitlement to education and related aspirations guaranteed in the South African constitution, they would have to be creative, strategic and visionary in how they claim and articulate the imperatives of decolonisation, transformation and inclusiveness. Zero sum games, instinctively attractive as they often are in abstraction and for those who believed themselves divinely pre-ordained to win eternally, are hardly the answer for the majority victims of ambitions of dominance, those who merely want the space to be able to get by, having something to hang onto and to hand down to the next generation, so that the struggle against dominance, however defined or articulated, might continue.

It would appear, given the recent Fees Must Fall protests that followed closely at the heels of the Rhodes Must Fall protests which brought down the Rhodes statue, that Rhodes (and white monopoly capital and white privilege by extension) may not have said the last word yet on the future of South Africa generally, and that of higher education in particular. But it would be wrong for those who oversee Rhodes's legacy and protect the interests of white monopoly capital, to see in this an opportunity to celebrate the attitude of business as usual. Rather, it would benefit them more and long term, if they were to take seriously the current proliferation of movements for decolonisation, transformation and inclusiveness as a red flag or a red card, urging them to accelerate and accommodate or forever perish in the violent flames of burning rage.

In October 2015 a proposed increase of student fees by between 10 per cent and 12 per cent for the 2016 academic year enraged students, as many believed that the fee increase would 'prevent poor black youths from accessing education'.[24] Sparked by outrage, students initiated the #FeesMustFall protest on several universities across the country, including in Pretoria, Johannesburg, Durban, Cape Town, Port Elizabeth, Potchefstroom, Grahamstown and Stellenbosch. There was an overwhelming perception among students and even among ANC youth-league members that Minister Nzimande, had failed students. His declaration that 'although free education for all university students would be the ideal, it is economically unfeasible right now',[25] did not go down well with especially black students.

The '#FeesMustFall' protests caught on like wildfire, resonating with students across the country, and attracting international support and solidarity from university students globally.[26] A *Mail and Guardian* collection of 'FeesMustFall posters that made us sit up and pay attention' gives a sense of how some of the students articulated their concerns.[27] These protests were evidence not only of well-structured (even if spontaneous and lacking in a central coordinating leadership beyond the party political affiliations of the individual members of the different SRCs involved) student movements countrywide, but also of repeated statements by leaders of the RMF movement that bringing down the statue was just the beginning of a long list of items on their transformation menu, including the right to free education promised to them in the constitution and repeatedly reiterated by the ANC leadership, including the late Nelson Mandela.

The protests acknowledged the need for access to various opportunities that would improve the lives of blacks and non-privileged students and outsourced workers[28] studying and working in universities across the country. The protests, furthermore, sought to address 'the dissolution of structural racism and disenfranchisement' suffered by many black students on a daily basis.[29] Students, academics and workers participated in the protests, taking a stand against various institutions and the systems that perpetuate malignant poverty and compound inherited inequalities.[30] Many a protester blamed the activists of yesteryear for compromises that only perpetrated the injustices afflicting the present generation. In the words of one,

> it was the 1980s generation who was to blame for the current state of affairs, by our betrayal of the Struggle, because we settled with the apartheid order and did not stay true to our ideals of creating a society in which education was a right and not a privilege.[31]

Seen in these terms, the protests were aimed at rewriting, by the victims, the history of unequal encounters between the *amakwerekwere* of yesteryears and those who felt dispossessed and victimised in the course of their adventures and treasure-hunts.

In solidarity and a single-minded focus on liberation, protesters used social media as a platform to voice their concerns.[32] They also engaged in 'marching, singing, occupying [university and government spaces] and rebelling against the hateful policies and processes that continue to exclude non-white and non-privileged youth from so many institutions of higher learning in the country'.[33] Though the majority of protesters were black, there were white protesters as well. In many ways, the Fees Must Fall protest found more traction with whites than did the Rhodes Must Fall and the End Outsourcing protests. Could it be that whites saw the issue of fees as a matter of class, while Rhodes was more a question of race and outsourcing a way of life? But the intersection of class and race in South Africa seldom hides for long. Thought and action are instinctively black and white in South Africa. This was true of the Fees Must Fall protests as well, where participating whites, to qualify to sing the song of black pain, were expected to acknowledge their privilege as a white collective in 'the context of racism – specifically, the day-to-day, violent, structural anti-black legacy of colonialism and apartheid, obscured today by the rhetoric of the rainbow nation'.[34]

With the moral support of many staff members across universities, protesting students pursued their demands. Occasionally, actions led to violence, and the violence risked a loss in legitimacy in the eyes of the largely supportive public and mainstream media. However, the violence was not always by the protesting students, as both the police and non-student opportunistic agent provocateurs were part of the action. When protests led students in Cape Town to Parliament, for example, they were met by riot police who used stun grenades, riot shields and batons and inflicted bodily harm by choking and wrestling some protesters to the ground[35]. At least two dozen were arrested, facing charges of trespassing and public violence.[36] While students attempted a non-violent protest, officers 'vacillated between acting out the blunt impetus of a violence they had initiated and mitigating its effect'.[37] Most notable was the stark contrast of treatment between black and white protesters, where white protesters could move among the officers unimpeded unlike black protesters who were physically hindered. This was a not so subtle reminder of 'the reality of a system that privileges white bodies as it does violence to black bodies'.[38] Other instances of violence include the day students marched to the Union Buildings to deliver a memorandum to President Jacob Zuma. It was reported that some of the violence may have been by agent provocateurs who had infiltrated the student ranks.[39]

In addition to the occasional violence resulting from the protests, there was a general sense of uncertainty and tension felt in the country, particularly on campus environments where students had no clear direction of how these protests would affect their academic futures and educational livelihoods. While active protesters fought to have their demands met, students in the background had to come to terms with the potential loss of loans and bursaries, the threat of academic exclusion based on academic performance which had been disrupted during the protests and the potential loss of private accommodation. There was also concern that students would be unable to complete their courses and sit their final examinations.[40] The suspension of classes was a crucial element during the protests. Tshwane University of Technology (TUT) students, for example, blocked entrance and exit points of campus, making the suspension of classes inevitable.[41] As campuses were closed during the protests, final examination dates were reset to accommodate the protesting students, though the disruption was still widely felt. Here too, it was suggested that some of the hardliners may have been outsiders fronting as students. The atmosphere of protest often made it difficult to separate the students from the non-students. Eventually, students were able to resume courses and sit examinations, more successfully in some cases than in others. Gradually, the campus environment returned to a functioning state, more or less. In general, though by no means easy, many a university management sought to accommodate as much as they could the shopping list of demands, even when this kept shifting.[42]

By and large, when the protests erupted, universities and government set about desperately seeking solutions. The first action was an emergency meeting of university leaders nationwide in Cape Town on Tuesday 20 October 2015 with Minister Nzimande. Students SRCs were represented at the meeting, at the end of which an agreement was reached to cap the fees increase at 6 per cent for 2016.

The striking students rejected the agreement, insisting on zero per cent increase. On Wednesday 21 October, universities nationwide were grounded by student action, the highlight of which being, as mentioned above, the mobilising of the police to disperse with violent force a group of UCT and Cape Peninsular University of Technology (CPUT) students who descended on the Parliament building in Cape Town, requesting to be addressed by Minister Nzimande.[43] When the student protests persisted and intensified, President Zuma organised an emergency meeting at the Union Buildings with vice-chancellors, chairs of university councils and student representatives on Friday 23 October, at the end of which they resolved in favour of 'a zero increase of university fees in 2016.' A task team to address a package of important related issues was also agreed upon. Among the issues the team would follow up on were demands for free education, the need to address institutional racism in universities, the question of the extent of institutional autonomy for universities, and the challenge of transformation of curricula and higher education in South Africa. 'Government understands the difficulty faced by students from poor households and urges all affected to allow the process to unfold to find long term solutions in order to ensure access to education by our students', President Zuma urged.[44]

Some accounts have commented critically on the protests' achievements and shortcomings, insisting as well on the much deeper structural inequalities and challenges at South African universities and the wider society that needs urgent attention.[45] Bemoaning the inability by students to follow in Steve Biko's footsteps and 'harness anger and channel it into powerful protest gestures that exclude violence and thuggery'[46], Tinyiko Maluleke believes that whatever victories students have achieved in the protests have come not because of but despite the leadership of the SRCs of the various universities. As he puts it:

> Consciously or unconsciously, SRCs have, rightly or wrongly, been seen by many students as part of the new establishment comprising the higher education ministry, university councils, university management and academia at large. Often caught between the competing demands of their political principals, a divided student body and university authorities, many SRCs have been paralysed.
>
> The party-political nature of SRCs and their elections has not only divided the student body but may also be a contributing factor in the low voter turnout in the majority of SRC elections, which hovers between 9% and 15% in most cases.
>
> With such encumbered SRC structures, it means student grievances, bottled up for many years, have had to find other channels of expression.[47]

Maluleke calls on students to be well equipped and well informed by demonstrating a 'firm grasp of the knowledge base, vision and strategies of past generations of student leaders', and especially by forging unity across narrow party political loyalties. He warns that the student leadership can ill-afford to yield to the carrots of diversion and business as usual that are most likely to be dangled before some of them by power and privilege reluctant to make concessions.[48]

On his part, Paul Kaseke makes a case for student leaders to 'be elected on merit, not party affiliation', arguing that the momentum and solidarity generated by the student protests were soon dissipated once the party political considerations of the various student leaders were prioritised over and above the broader interests and concerns of the student body. Kaseke's point is buttressed by the situation at UWC, where students continued the protests despite the announcement of zero fee increment by President Zuma, calling on the university to write-off student debts worth more than R270-million[49], and resorting to violence and physical confrontation to make their case.[50]

In February 2016, violent protests again erupted in some universities, including UCT, the University of the Free State (UFS) and the North West University (NWU).[51] In an article title 'UWC caught between a rock and a hard place', Thulani Gqirana bemoans the 'demands that lack legitimacy' as well as 'a student leadership not elected through a democratic process', and 'who lack negotiation experience'.[52] As Giovanni Poggi puts it, 'compromise and conciliation are not on the agenda', and the distrust of established authority, however legitimate, cannot serve to suggest that a future where South Africans are permanently caught between reform and violent revolution is a *sina qua non*.[53]

To John Higgins, Professor of Literature at UCT, there is a danger that what the #Fees Must Fall protest movement may have gained in speed and reach through its use of a hashtag, it may have lost in depth. Real change to him consists in attending to the substantive systemic problems plaguing higher education in South Africa since 1994, when universities lost their elite status to the imperative of mass production of graduates in a context of dwindling state support funding.[54]

The sort of negotiated disposition of mutual accommodation proposed by Dlamini and echoed by other commentators above and elsewhere was perhaps what President Jacob Zuma was recommending when, speaking at the 22nd anniversary of the assassination of Chris Hani in Johannesburg. He called on angry and frustrated black South African youth to be more tolerant of

205

colonial and racist symbols in recognition of the Bill of Rights, which proclaims that South Africa belongs to all those who live in it, and should commit to building a new and inclusive heritage in mutual recognition and respect. He cited a long list of liberation heroes who had been honoured by having public places and institutions named after them, and others to whom monuments and statues had been constructed to promote a new landscape benefiting the democratic pretensions of the new South Africa. He also elaborated on heritage sites built or commissioned by the ANC government. 'We are aware of the frustration of our people when it comes to colonial and racist figures. It is true that transformation with architecture is not happening fast enough, but destroying the figures is not the solution. We need to observe the law in this regard.' He added that although colonial symbols were not the most welcome sights, they formed an important part of South African history which could not be obliterated, however painful: 'When you read a history book and you come across a painful page, you do not just rip it out.'[55]

In this regard, the Nigerian poet and novelist Ben Okri had the following words of wisdom when he delivered the 13th annual Steve Biko Memorial Lecture held in the Jameson Hall at UCT on 12 September 2012[56]:

When a people overcome the impossible, they achieve eventually a kind of evolutionary shift and epistemological break. They realise, eventually, deep in their souls something powerful about their will: they are never quite the same people again. They change subtly something in their DNA. They also experience a state of unreality.

History is like a nightmare we wake up from after a struggle and blink in stupefaction at the strangeness of daylight. With awakening a great energy is freed; a new question is posed: the nightmare is over but what do we do with the day? We do not have enough psychologists of history. Everyone seems to treat history as if our reaction to it should be logical. The people have emerged from a mutual nightmare, what should they do upon awakening? What should anyone do after a long trauma? What can anyone do?

Nations too, like individuals, need to heal. And healing takes several forms. For some, healing is probing the wounds, seeking causes, pursuing redress. For others, healing is dreaming, it is an active vision during which time a future is dreamed of, shaped and put into place. For them healing is an opportunity to transform

206

themselves out of all that suffering, all that trauma, and the heroic effort of all that overcoming. The unfortunate thing about history is that it gives us no rest, no holidays. There are no pauses; we go from struggle to struggle. The struggle to overcome and then the struggle to live, to grow, to realise the potential seeded in our bones. We go from tearing down the unacceptable to building the desirable without much of a break in the dance.

But how long does this magic period last, the period of raised consciousness when a people realise that the surging through them of all the best energies of the human spirit? When they have effected a profound change in their destiny and feel the euphoria of overcoming? How long does it last, this sense of having climbed a mountain-top against all the odds and gazing back down over the journey accomplished and feeling for a long historical moment the sense that with the will power and the vision clear, anything is possible?[57]

South Africa is indeed twenty one years into the morning after a nightmare of historic proportions. What does it do with the day now that the nightmare is over? And how does it take along those for whom the nightmare is yet to end? Much as accommodation and inclusiveness are the clarion call of sanity with great promise for the future of South Africa, for existing colonial statues and monuments to signify anything but oppression and dispossession, they would have to be re-articulated, recalibrated and reconfigured into multicultural symbols of reconciliation. This calls for humility and alertness to the sensitivities and sensibilities of the various shades of the imagined dream of a rainbow nation. It may be up to every South African to be the change for which they aspire.[58] However, that change can come about only if whites and whiteness as epitomes of privilege and supremacy in South Africa move from quibbles and rhetoric to substantive gestures of inclusivity through significant recirculation of the wealth and resources brought their way by the injustices and inequalities propagated under colonialism and apartheid of which Rhodes and his contemporaries were forerunners. The case for restitution and reparations or distribution has never been more urgent.

Those who harness their intellect, art, skills, effort and time to foster greater social and cultural integration with selflessness and commitment to a common humanity, and who are recognised and encouraged for doing so, point to a future that is neither trapped in delusions of superiority nor in the celebration of victimhood. However, the failure to enforce greater integration beyond elite circles combines with ignorance and arrogance to guarantee continuation for racism and prejudices. Apartheid may have died officially, but slow socio-economic transformation and slow reconfiguration of attitudes, beliefs and relationships in favour of greater mutual recognition and accommodation have meant its continued reproduction in less obvious and more insidious ways.

Notes

[1] See http://mg.co.za/article/2015-03-26-rhodesmustfall-protest-spreads-to-other-campuses, accessed 4 October 2015.

[2] See http://mg.co.za/article/2015-03-26-rhodesmustfall-protest-spreads-to-other-campuses, accessed 4 October 2015.

[3] See http://www.rhodeshouse.ox.ac.uk/the-mandela-rhodes-foundation, accessed 5 December 2015.

[4] See http://www.rhodeshouse.ox.ac.uk/nelson-mandelas-partnership-with-the-rhodes-trust, accessed 5 December 2015.

[5] See Raymond Suttner, http://www.dailymaverick.co.za/article/2016-03-08-op-ed-did-mandela-sell-out-the-struggle-for-freedom/#.VuPlc3rCAdw, accessed 12 March 2016.

[6] See 'I am an African' – Thabo Mbeki's speech at the adoption of The Republic of South Africa Constitution Bill, 8 May 1996, Cape Town. http://www.anc.org.za/show.php?id=4322, accessed 19 July 2013.

[7] See 'I am an African' – Thabo Mbeki's speech at the adoption of The Republic of South Africa Constitution Bill, 8 May 1996, Cape Town. http://www.anc.org.za/show.php?id=4322, accessed 19 July 2013.

[8] The speech and some of the details of Seme's life can be found on South African History Online (SAHO). See http://www.sahistory.org.za, accessed 19 July 2013.

[9] Gevisser M, The Thabo Mbeki story: The chief, *Sunday Times*, 20 June 1999. http://www.armsdeal-po.co.za/special_items/profiles/mbeki_chief.html, accessed 8 July 2013.

[10] McIntosh is clearly upset by the concessions made by the leadership to the RMF protesters. His letters eventually elicited a response from Russell Ally, claiming that among other things, UCT is not for sale. For one of Graham McIntosh's letters,

see http://www.politicsweb.co.za/documents/uct-should-take-a-stand-against-racism--graham-mci, accessed 5 October 2015; and for the response on behalf of UCT by Russell Ally, see http://politicsweb.co.za/news-and-analysis/uct-is-not-for-sale--dr-russell-ally, accessed 5 October 2015.

[11] See John Laband's detailed analysis titled 'Rhodes Must Fall: Unleashing the racist demon', http://www.politicsweb.co.za/news-and-analysis/rhodes-must-fall-unleashing-the-racist-demon?utm_source=Politicsweb+Daily+Headlines&utm_campaign=140c62bedf-DHN_Sept_15_2015&utm_medium=email&utm_term=0_a86f25db99-140c62bedf-140192113, accessed 5 October 2015.

[12] Njabulo Ndebele, 'Reflections on Rhodes: A story of time', http://www.uct.ac.za/dailynews/?id=9038, accessed 6 October 2015.

[13] Simon Lincoln Reader, 'One monument cannot capture all country's ills', http://www.bdlive.co.za/opinion/columnists/2015/03/27/one-monument-cannot-capture-all-countrys-ills, accessed 3 October 2015.

[14] Kusi Dlamini, 'Rhodes Scholars play a vital role in SA', http://www.iol.co.za/sundayindependent/rhodes-scholars-play-a-vital-role-in-sa-1.1843802#.VfWkSJce4TZ, accessed 3 October 2015.

[15] Simon Lincoln Reader, 'One monument cannot capture all country's ills', http://www.bdlive.co.za/opinion/columnists/2015/03/27/one-monument-cannot-capture-all-countrys-ills, accessed 3 October 2015.

[16] Kusi Dlamini, 'Rhodes Scholars play a vital role in SA', http://www.iol.co.za/sundayindependent/rhodes-scholars-play-a-vital-role-in-sa-1.1843802#.VfWkSJce4TZ, accessed 3 October 2015.

[17] Katlego Disemelo, http://mg.co.za/article/2015-10-29-student-protests-are-about-much-more-than-just-feesmustfall, accessed 29 October 2015.

[18] Zamokuhle Manqele, http://www.iol.co.za/dailynews/opinion/students-rewriting-history-1.1937213, accessed 29 October 2015.

[19] George Hull, http://mg.co.za/article/2015-10-28-free-university-education-is-not-the-route-to-social-justice, accessed 29 October 2015.

[20] Helen Walne, http://www.iol.co.za/capeargus/not-everyone-s-education-can-be-free-1.1936704#.VjI8iise4TY, accessed 29 October 2015.

[21] Qaanitha Hunter & Mmanaledi Mataboge, http://mg.co.za/article/2015-10-22-is-blade-safe-from-ancs-knives, accessed 29 October 2015.

[22] Lizeka Tandwa, http://mg.co.za/article/2015-10-27-wits-management-reaches-an-agreement-with-src, accessed 29 October 2015.

[23] Steve Koch, http://theconversation.com/how-south-africa-could-fund-steeper-higher-education-costs-50539, accessed 19 November 2015.

[24] See Ludovica Laccino, http://www.ibtimes.co.uk/south-africa-fees-must-fall-protests-will-continue-jacob-zuma-meet-students-1525137, accessed 29 October 2015.
[25] See George Hull, http://mg.co.za/article/2015-10-28-free-university-education-is-not-the-route-to-social-justice, accessed 29 October 2015.
[26] For details, see for example, http://www.timeslive.co.za/local/2015/10/19/Rhodes-shuts-down-as-students-blockade-entrances; http://www.timeslive.co.za/sundaytimes/stnews/2015/10/19/UCT-appeals-for-calm-ahead-of-Tuesday%E2%80%99s-fees-protest; http://mg.co.za/article/2015-10-19-rhodesmipmustfall-brings-rhodes-university-to-a-standstill, accessed 20 October 2015.
[27] See http://mg.co.za/multimedia/2015-10-28-the-feesmustfall-posters-that-made-us-sit-up-and-pay-attention, accessed 29 October 2015.

I have taken time to transcribe what the posters bore:

1. Education is not just for the elite. #Fuckclassism; 2. UJ students want 0% fee increase; 3. #occupy Luthuli house – Daddy, please don't shoot! We are coming home, we just want to LEARN!!!; 4. Fees must be reduced to a figure Zuma can read. Fall – TUKS rise; 5. We are not asking for much!! Just a 0.00% increase! That's all!! #UJSHUTDOWN; 6. Oscar is walking free but students are being arrested by fees!!; 7. #Asijiki; 8. I refuse to end up like my president #feesmustfall; 9. The formerly oppressed has now become the oppressor #Apartheid Tactics #Fees_Must_Fall; 10. Actually, I'm worth it!! We are worth it!! #FeesMustFall; 11. We are students, not customers; 12. Always remember that this university belongs to us; 13.Free education in our lifetime; 14. #ANCMustFall Comrades with double standards and hypocrisy; 15. Students are SA's future; 16. Run Habib run; 17. Habib + Council + Blade = No balls; 18. #WitsMustFall; 19. Open Access = No (Zero!) financial exclusion!; 20. Education is not a privilege; 21. Blade! Come to the party!; 22. Chris Hani (the rest is not clear); 23. We are the ones we have been waiting for; 24. What does our future hold if some of our brightest minds are excluded from a university education?; 25. 6 uthi awunyi perhaps?; 26. Say no to fee increases; 27. 50% increase Wo o nye perhaps? #Feesmustfall; 28. My mom is too single for these fees #Uprising; 29. Single mothers pay fees!; 30. Moloko does not have enough sugar daddies; 31. Ons wil swat; 32. Julle steel ons geld!; 33. Joining youths of 1976 in fight for change #FeesMustFall; 34. Liphi legundane elidakiwe (image of gun and 6%); 35. All I ever did wrong was be black; 36. Stop misallocating funds Blade – Put the money where the minds are; 37. A loan is not free education; 38. Too black to pay your 6% #Uprising; 39. 0% increase. Phansi ngama capitalist TUKS fees must fall; 40. TUKS fees must fall #Uprising; 41.What a

time to be a student #Uprising #FeesMustFall; 42. Straight out of underprivileged #Uprising #FeesMustFall; 43. #EducationIsNotACrime #NotACrime; 44. TUKS of Niks; 45. Make History; 46. Blade what's good?
[28] It could be argued that the #Endoutsourcing campaign is exemplary of demands for transformation at all levels since workers tend to be of lower class than the vast majority of students.
[29] Katlego Disemelo, http://mg.co.za/article/2015-10-29-student-protests-are-about-much-more-than-just-feesmustfall, accessed 29 October 2015.
[30] Phaphama Dulwana, http://thoughtleader.co.za/readerblog/2015/10/28/witsonfire-student-divisions-must-fall, accessed 29 October 2015.
[31] Zenariah Barends, http://www.iol.co.za/capeargus/activists-must-support-student-struggles-1.1937296#.VjI66ise4TY, accessed 29 October 2015.
[32] Ludovica, Laccion, http://www.ibtimes.co.uk/south-africa-fees-must-fall-protests-will-continue-jacob-zuma-meet-students-1525137, accessed 29 October 2015.
[33] Katlego Disemelo, http://mg.co.za/article/2015-10-29-student-protests-are-about-much-more-than-just-feesmustfall, accessed 29 October 2015.
[34] Timothy Wolff-Piggott, http://mg.co.za/article/2015-10-27-stepping-up-and-forward-as-a-white-student-was-imperative, accessed 29 October 2015.
[35] Timothy Wolff-Piggott, http://mg.co.za/article/2015-10-27-stepping-up-and-forward-as-a-white-student-was-imperative, accessed 29 October 2015.
[36] Qaanitha Hunter & Mmanaledi Mataboge, http://mg.co.za/article/2015-10-22-is-blade-safe-from-ancs-knives, accessed 29 October 2015.
[37] Timothy Wolff-Piggott, http://mg.co.za/article/2015-10-27-stepping-up-and-forward-as-a-white-student-was-imperative, accessed 29 October 2015.
[38] Timothy Wolff-Piggott, http://mg.co.za/article/2015-10-27-stepping-up-and-forward-as-a-white-student-was-imperative, accessed 29 October 2015.
[39] See Bongani Nkosi, http://mg.co.za/article/2015-10-23-sas-students-take-on-union-buildings, accessed 3 March 2016.
[40] Phaphama Dulwana, http://thoughtleader.co.za/readerblog/2015/10/28/witsonfire-student-divisions-must-fall, accessed 29 October 2015.
[41]Bongani Nkosi, http://mg.co.za/article/2015-10-26-tut-suspends-classes-as-students-continue-protest, accessed 29 October 2015.

[42] See Robert Morrell, http://www.dailymaverick.co.za/article/2015-11-11-op-ed-treasure-or-curse-south-africas-university-vice-chancellors/#.VtfIn-bCBV8, accessed 3 March 2016.

[43] See https://www.enca.com/south-africa/live-stun-grenades-chaos-stairs-parliament-feesmustfall, accessed 29 February 2016. Students were further incensed by Minister Nzimande's joke in bad taste that if students did not agree with the settlement, then 'StudentsMustFall', see http://www.news24.com/Live/SouthAfrica/News/WATCH-Blade-Nzimande-says-Students-must-fall-and-laughs-20151022, accessed 29 February 2016.

[44] See http://www.scribd.com/doc/286630723/President-Zuma-no-fee-increase, accessed 23 October 2015.

[45] See Vito Laterza and Ayanda Manqoyi, http://www.dailymaverick.co.za/article/2015-11-06-looking-for-leaders-student-protests-and-the-future-of-south-african-democracy/#.VkiN67-3ud8, accessed 15 November 2015; and David Dickinson, http://theconversation.com/fee-protests-point-to-a-much-deeper-problem-at-south-african-universities-49456, accessed 16 November 2015.

[46] See Tinyiko Maluleke, http://mg.co.za/article/2015-10-03-we-should-all-follow-bikos-teachings, accessed 25 February 2016.

[47] See Tinyiko Maluleke, http://mg.co.za/article/2016-01-28-current-heat-is-forging-a-new-university/, accessed 17 February 2016.

[48] See Tinyiko Maluleke, http://www.iol.co.za/sundayindependent/best-embrace-student-protests-1931741, accessed 25 February 2016.

[49] Mounting Student debts are a serious and legitimate concern. According to Belinda Bozzolli, spokesperson on higher education and training for the Democratic Alliance (DA), 'Students owe universities R4-billion in debt' and 'Many of them have actually finished their degrees, but can't graduate because they owe so much money. That debt needs to be dealt with by government in some way or another.' See Bongani Nkosi, 'Will #FeesStillFall?', *Mail & Guardian*, December 11-17, 2015.

[50] See http://theconversation.com/why-student-leaders-should-be-elected-on-merit-not-party-affiliation-49549, accessed 17 November 2015.

[51] See Robert Morrell, http://www.dailymaverick.co.za/article/2016-02-22-op-ed-the-burning-issue-of-campus-violence/#.VtGXuubCBV9, accessed 26 February 2016; and see also, Pontsho Pilane, http://mg.co.za/article/2016-02-25-protest-politics-and-prayers-at-south-africas-universities, accessed 27 February 2016; Vumani Mkhize, 'NW University closed indefinitely after burning of Science Centre', http://ewn.co.za/Media/2016/02/25/Education-goes-up-in-flames-at-North-West-University, accessed 28 February 2016;

Reinart Toerien, #UFS students: 'Decolonise our university', http://ewn.co.za/Media/2016/02/24/Issues-of-transformation-and-wages-stir-tensions-at-UFS, accessed 28 February 2016;

Reinart Toerien, '#UFS: Tensions soar, 21 students arrested', http://ewn.co.za/Media/2016/02/26/At-least-21-students-arrested-as-protest-tensions-sore-at-the-University-of-the-Free-State, accessed 28 February 2016.

[52] See http://mg.co.za/article/2015-11-17-uwc-caught-between-a-rock-and-a-hard-place, accessed 17 October 2015.

[53] See http://theconversation.com/student-protests-in-south-africa-have-pitted-reform-against-revolution-50604, accessed 19 November 2015.

[54] See http://theconversation.com/student-protesters-must-move-beyond-hashtags-to-real-change-51138?, accessed 28 November 2015.

[55] See http://www.news24.com/Archives/City-Press/Zuma-tackles-colonial-statues-xenophobic-attacks-20150429, accessed 6 October 2015. For the full video of the event, see https://www.youtube.com/watch?v=draGELk8grU, accessed 6 October 2015.

[56] See https://www.youtube.com/watch?v=uhre8OP7Rkw, accessed 4 December 2015.

[57] See Ben Okri, http://sbeta.iol.co.za/capetimes/full-speech-ben-okri-honours-biko-1382746, accessed 4 November 2015.

[58] See Kat Edmonson, 'Be the Change (Official Music Video)', https://www.youtube.com/watch?v=nrv3hteHgII, accessed 28 October 2015.

Chapter 6

Pure Fiction:
What I Almost Had in Common with Rhodes[1]

A firm believer in empire, Rhodes is reported to have 'read and re-read the million and a half words of Gibbon's Decline and Fall of the Roman Empire before he was twenty' (Brown 2015: 60). Of the British, Rhodes declared: 'I desire to act for the benefit of those who, I think, are the greatest people the world has ever seen, but whose fault is that they do not know their own strength and their greatness and their destiny'(Brown 2015: 59). As an imperial evangelist, his preying gaze was firmly on Africa, from Cape to Cairo, believing that 'Africa was ripe for 'civilised' occupation, and that this belief was shared both by his Queen and his God' (Brown 2015: 46). His commitment to empire-building with missionary zeal and evangelistic fervour was not in doubt, and 'no one was able to stand up to Rhodes's ferocious evangelism' when this really got going. Rhodes not only believed that his imperialism was divinely ordained, he associated the relative ease with which he came by his diamonds and gold in abundance to 'manna from heaven' that would enable him to pursue his dream of enhancing and protecting the British empire (Brown 2015: 46).

In his imperial eyes, Rhodes believed he was serving God's cause in honour of the chosen country, Britain, and the finest race in the world, the British. Instead of simply handing his enormous wealth to Queen Victoria and the government of the day more directly invested in imperial power, Rhodes, convinced of his Godlikeness, would not settle or any intermediary between him and God. He felt personally preordained to hunt Africa down like a pheasant and grab it by the scruff of its neck as an imperial trophy. Guided by his own bible – *The Confession of Faith* – written by none other than himself[2], Rhodes 'established his own church with its own dogma, and with disciplines modelled on those of one-time-knight, mystic, missionary and ascetic, Ignatius Loyola', who founded the Society of Jesus in 1540 (Brown 2015: 47; see also Baker 1934: 142-143). The parallels between the Society of Jesus

215

membered by Jesuits, and the Secret Society established by Rhodes are telling. According to Brown:

> As Rhodes defended his actions against 'barbarians' by insisting he was bringing 'civilised standards', the Jesuits justified their activity on the basis of being part of the Church Militant, fighting to establish God's kingdom on earth. The Jesuits are today active in 112 nations on six continents, specialising in education, research and missionary work, paralleling Rhodes's Society in many ways.
>
> The Jesuits proselytised in accordance with their own rules in order to meet their desired ends. The rules, which Rhodes effectively copied, allowed Jesuits the authority to use whatever means was necessary to accomplish their tasks. This placed them above the state, and the laws of the state. They suppressed several heathen tribes, particularly in South America, just as Rhodes took military action to suppress uprising by the Matabele and the Shona, even though his only writ was a disputed mining charter (Brown 2015: 47).

Like a black, African sweet-footed *makwerekwere* with ambitions of dominance of my own, I wish I had Sir Cecil John Rhodes's capacity to turn dreams into diamonds and gold with callous indifference towards those I crush on my way to fortune and fame. No one has the monopoly on violence and violation in an interconnected world in which the only currency of visibility of any kind that matters is the zero-sum game. Unfortunately, I have neither the influence nor the technology to power my ambitions to extravagant fruition the way Rhodes did, and the way his progeny continue to. I am stuck with my imagination and my fantasies of a life in which I excel at conversion instead of conversation. An appeal to privilege conversation over conversion is the Bible of the weak and humbled, the considerate and the contemplative. Like the late Nigerian writer Amos Tutuola – author of *The Palm-Wine Drinkard* and *My Life in the Bush of Ghosts* –, I invite you to join me in my fantasy world, and to explore with me my imagined life as a powerful converter in the image of a zealous missionary of the same megalomaniac proportions as Rhodes. In this scenario, the only difference between Rhodes and me is that he was thoroughly white, and I am black through and through – the very heart of darkness, if ever there was one. Feel free to label my fantasy *Ambitions of Dominance in the Heart of Darkness* if you please.

In any case, I would like you, in the manner of the earthly seven-year-old boy in Tutuola's *My Life in the Bush of Ghosts*, to vanish into the bush of ghosts under the baobab tree of my imagination.

* * *

I come from a long ancestry of missionaries, dating back to my great, great, great grandfather. The family tradition and commitment to evangelism has been unshakable for centuries. Our mission is conversion. And there is a lot out there to convert. Since the days of my ancestors, we have waged war against paganism, and have beamed the torchlight of Christian civilisation into the dark zones of the world, spreading the Word of the *One True God*, winning and baptising converts, and inviting those who have seen the light and come to believe to say farewell to heathen ways and practices. We sought to exorcise the forces of darkness in those we converted. In particular, we did more than frown on the influence of witchdoctors and fetish priests. We systematically destroyed their totems, shrines and objects of practice. We actively discouraged polygamy and promiscuity. Where for generations the people we encountered had known nothing of chastity, their lives dominated by animal passions from time immemorial, we sought to instil self-discipline.

It was not always easy to achieve self-control, especially among those for whom immorality was like a village sport, or those for whom dishonesty, untruthfulness and a myriad of other vices were second nature. Those given to violent emotions and sudden outbursts of excitement were particularly taxing, challenging us beyond measure. Our patience was often stretched to the limit, especially by encounters with people of extremely shallow nature – those whose reasoning faculties seemed to be on a permanent leave of absence. In church people were sometimes present only as bodies. My grandfather had a favourite story he often told to illustrate this. One day he was preaching to a full congregation: 'The Lord be with you' he said. 'And also with you' the congregation chanted. 'There is something wrong with this microphone', he continued. 'And also with you', they replied. Absent-mindedness was the congregants' stock-in-trade. Their sheepishness sometimes made us doubt the extent to which they were guided by reason and logic. Not only did we sense a lack of responsibility among them, but we also had the feeling we were dealing with adults trapped irredeemably in childhood. The temptation and tendency to relapse into their sinfulness of origin loomed large with such propensity to be infantile. In those situations, how could we afford to relent or to yield to the temptation to rest on our laurels?

It is therefore hardly surprising that in addition to converting our pagans into Christians worthy of the Grace of God, we ordained ourselves with the responsibility of educating them. They needed cultivation – body, mind and soul. We could not consider our mission accomplished simply by converting souls. That would have been most irresponsible of us. We also had to save lives by taming bodies into civilised containers of the Holy Spirit and the sanctioned words and longings of God's chosen messengers in the accursed native soils into which we ventured. Of course, we had to teach our converts to read the Bible, but to limit teaching to reading the Holy Scripture was to limit our influence and power over the forces of darkness. If the ways of the simple-minded, unsophisticated pagans we converted were steeped in magic and witchcraft that made them imagine all sorts of evil and harmful influences by invisible malevolent powers and spirits, then we needed to do more than teach them how to read the Word. We had to teach them how to develop the spirit of rational thought and civilised behaviour. We had to infuse in them the power of discipline over the longings of the flesh in which they were trapped.

Blinded by our determination to convert everything unfamiliar, we did not imagine then that the firm belief in the invisible, espoused by some of those we encountered and sought to convert, could connect us more closely with an idea of God as complex, omniscient, omnipotent and omnipresent. The idea of God as a present absence and an absent presence is not that dissimilar to the belief in witchcraft and magic that lends itself to a world of infinite possibilities – a world of presence in simultaneous multiplicities and eternal powers to redefine reality. This was a world in which time and space were not allowed to stand in the way of the truth. It was a world that we would understand a great deal better only much later with the advent of new information and communication technologies (ICTs) such as the internet, the cell phone and the smartphone, along with their magic and witchcraft of instant availability and reachability, as well as their propensity to facilitate narcissism, self-indulgence and the keeping up of appearances.

Similarly, the pagans' sense of collectivism and interdependence – called *ubuntu* by some of them – could have benefited our marked individualism (or should I say *freedom without responsibility*) had we privileged conversation over conversion. Instead, we insisted that these communities were buried in a long, dark night and desperately needed awakening by the warmth of the sunlight of our religion and civilisation. We were on a converting civilising mission. So we toiled day and night to make daybreak possible in the regions where we implanted ourselves, and to chase away their shadows. Joy was ours in abundance as we watched our converts awaken like sleeping flowers at the call of dawn. Whatever the obstacles and detours in our mission, we were certain of having the last laugh.

We knew that paganism, fetishism and the dark ways of those we encountered and converted could not withstand the full impact of the education and civilisation from which we hailed and drew inspiration. We were determined to flood the abyss of darkness with eternal light. So we extolled the value of mission education, with emphasis on practical skills. We set up training institutions – schools to train converts for a higher calling, domestic work centres to keep women and girls busy, and vocational workshops for men and boys to acquire skills (as printers, weavers, carpenters, blacksmiths, agriculturists, gardeners and domestic servants, for example) that would keep them away from the devil and his workshop for idle hands. We were bent on promoting not only a change of heart through baptism, repentance and remission of sins, but also a change of mind and manner of life by pointing to and actively seeking to instil the desire in our converts for the modern ways of life we championed. We were determined to inebriate them with the Word of God and the ways of the man of God. We needed more than Christians in name. To learn to recite the Bible is not evidence of understanding and living in accordance with the Gospel. We needed conviction and enthusiasm from the flock.

And because we were unlike God in his capacity for presence in simultaneous multiplicity – as the magic and witchcraft of the internet, cell phones, smartphones and the interconnections made possible by social media existed then only in the form of the pagan witchcraft and magic which we virulently denounced – we had to strive to make converters of those we had converted, so as our foot soldiers they could take to others the Gospel that had changed their hearts and transformed their lives. We invited them to embrace the missionary spirit, and to propagate our message of salvation far and wide. In some instances it didn't take long for converts to exude evangelism and religious fervour in a manner we could hardly have fathomed when we first embarked on what looked like then as mission impossible. Thanks to our devotion to conversion, preaching the word of God is no longer our preserve. Converts taking the Gospel to remote areas on evangelistic tours, operate as veritable missionaries in their own right. What more evidence do we need to prove that our converts show promise of steady and remarkable development under good tutelage?

By promoting the conversion of souls and the transformation of bodies and ways alike, we succeeded in freeing many a heathen people from the terrible wastage of human life to which they had been subjected prior to the civilising mission of our evangelism. We taught them how to free themselves from superstitious beliefs in magic and witchcraft, human sacrifices, cannibalism, primitive desires and many other cruelties for which they were notorious, and because of which they struck us as underdeveloped and starved of enlightenment. While we resisted thinking of our converts as inferior, truth be told, it was nonetheless our experience that training them was often a slow and tedious process, and understandably so, as it takes much effort to domesticate the wild, to transform the raw, to civilise the primitive, to savage savagery.

Detours and cul-de-sacs notwithstanding, our long and dangerous journeys of conversion into various interiors paid off, quite handsomely. Our labours were rewarded with measures of great success. We converted the lowly, but we converted kings as well.

My grandfather carried our zeal for evangelism to the point of zealotry. He was determined to convert everyone he came across, forcefully if necessary. Totally committed to the God we worshipped, he deftly sought to make our God the one and only God in the world. He could literally flog his flock into compliance. He travelled into distant remote villages, where for months, day and night, he would go about like a veritable lone ranger, converting souls and whipping all and sundry into compliance or ludicrous defensiveness. He even took conversion to another level. Animals, rivers, forests, minerals, rocks and everything his good Lord had made – be these animate or inanimate, visible or invisible – caught the attention of his zeal to convert. On Good Friday, he could even convert beef into fish just by prayerfully sprinkling water and renaming it, in tune with the biblical turning of water into wine by Jesus Christ at Canaan.

One evening, after a particularly fulfilling day of conversion, he was returning home in anticipation of his dinner, prepared as usual by his favourite catechist, who doubled as a cook – my grandfather used to adore Irish potatoes served as French fries with a Spanish omelette, complete with a glass of Italian wine – when he came face to face with a lion. The lion looked even more famished than he. Caught completely off guard, the only thing the great converter could do was turn to the God he had served so well. 'Lord, Heavenly Father, inspire upon this lion the sentiments of a Christian', he invoked. Immediately, the lion knelt down and started praying: 'Lord, God, bless this meal which I am about to receive and grant to everyone his fair share of a missionary.'

You can well imagine how horrified I was when I learnt of the fate of my grandfather – a compulsive converter converted into a meal by one of his converts. Had he survived the deadly encounter, he would probably have named the lion 'Cecil', and considered it one more trophy in his hunt for desperate souls.

I concluded that, as a family, our lion's share of ferocious evangelical zeal had met its Waterloo. I decided to turn my back once and for all on evangelism and dogma. I had had enough of overbearing prescriptiveness and pontification. I wanted something categorically different. I longed for an environment and a practice in which I would not be too full of myself and our family traditions, a place and space where I could seek and entertain genuine curiosities and the freedom of conversation about the world and the relationships it made possible, without, a priori, claiming papal infallibility, even though I was named *Francis*, after Francis of Assisi, who inspired Ignatius Loyola, creator of the Society of Jesus in 1540. Those who knew me pointed me in the direction of the *university*. But not just any university – they insisted on a *secular* university. So to a secular university I went, carefully turning a blind eye on the Jesuit and other missionary universities that had moulded dogmatic nightmares like my grandfather.

Guess what I found in the seclusion of the secular university campus? I found that labels can be deceptive, and that to name differently did not necessarily imply a different reality. God does indeed work in mysterious ways. He is indeed present in simultaneous multiplicities. Not only are universities created in the image of God, they reproduce and celebrate celestial and ecclesiastical orders and hierarchies.[3] There is a hierarchy of disciplines and disciples. Popes and ayatollahs proliferate in purportedly secular academic robes, along with their cardinals, archbishops, bishops, high priests and gurus. Universities have catechists, mass servants and the lay congregation, as well as the Lord's Prayer, credos, rosaries and hymnals. Praise singing, devotion and recitals are the order of the day. Indoctrination and baptism are rites of passage. Questioning can be a serious offence even as the rhetoric privileges conversations and critical engagement over conversion. Academic heavens exist for chosen gods, and hell is there for Lucifer and his subversives. Limbos serve as waiting rooms or transit zones for imprisonment or salvation for life. I was amazed by the extent to which secularism served as a smokescreen for all sorts of fundamentalisms and denial of the prevalence of blind faith. Not only had my grandfather somehow been smuggled into and buried at the Secular University, but like the Prince of Darkness, he had risen again.

I am particularly interested in the disciplines taught at the secular universities. I want to understand their relative positions of strength and precariousness, and how they attempt to cope with their various degrees of prominence and marginality, both within themselves as disciplines and at the hands of other academics. In pursuing this interest I have no answers, only a catalogue of ever-surging questions. What, for example, does the feeling of powerlessness vis-à-vis others generate in practitioners of particular disciplines? I have heard that the intolerance, dictatorship, dogma or evangelism of an underling or a residue is often more devastating than that of the overlord, master or superior. How applicable could this claim be to the social sciences and humanities and to how these relate to superior and inferior others on the hierarchies of credibility within and outside the university?[4] How would any such discipline in the humanities and social sciences – considered and treated as marginal in many a university in Africa and indeed globally – relate to the impulse to convert rather than seeking to understand a world of interconnections and relationships informed by global and local hierarchies, and shaped by factors such as race, place, class, gender and age, to name only a few? If a marginal discipline were to feel particularly drawn to being relevant to the emancipation of souls forgotten by the politically and economically powerful at local and global levels, how would it provide for balancing this mission with the need to pay ever more attention to rigorous contemplation of knowledge-production practices as evidence of the academic legitimacy of the discipline? In other words, how satisfactorily does any discipline in the humanities and social sciences distinguish between their academic practices on the one hand and their engaged or public interventions on the other? These are some of the questions worth considering in any serious endeavour to transform resilient colonial education in Africa. How I wish I had the fundamentalist zeal, influence and technology of a Cecil John Rhodes to be ruthlessly single-minded and visionary in this regard! I may be *makwerekwere* like him, but do I have what it takes to be a Sir Cecil John Rhodes? Not yet!

* * *

My delirious and extravagant fantasies of dominance, competing with my grandfather's (see also Walker 1911) and aspiring to be like Rhodes's (Brown 2015), are ill-placed, given what I know about zero-sum or winner-takes-all games. As is evident from the legitimate clamours for transformation discussed above, black pain matters and should matter, and all one-dimensional claims to hybridity as a way of life must be critically interrogated for evidence of what they are deployed to mask. For every pain to matter, there is need to explore and provide for a dispensation that truly accommodates the pain of all, regardless of the hierarchies that might seek to legitimate such pain. If we liken each and every person in South Africa, irrespective of background, origin or status, to porcupines brought together by mobility and the quest for fulfilment – a legitimate attribute of being human – every interaction or attempt at sociality of any kind makes us aware of our quills and imposes the imperative of all and sundry keeping their quills in check if we are to get along (Lategan 2015). All being equal, we would each prefer, just like Rhodes and my fantasy self, to dominate the rest of the world with our whims and caprices, spanning out our quills to protect us against even the most warm-hearted of neighbours or strangers. Armed with our defensive quills, we would love to create protective barriers, reasserting our cherished notions of the autonomous self and distancing ourselves from encumbering others.

Yet, as the transformation-related protests have made and continue to make abundantly clear, every daily experience of the tensions and dangers of quills is a subtle call to recognise that however complete we may aspire to be or to feel when we have a purported victory to celebrate, we are, at the end of the day, always better off as interdependent and inclusive beings. It is in the interest of porcupines, whatever the size and length of their quills, to cultivate conviviality. Sooner or later, given the ever-changing challenges of life, a porcupine is bound to realise that not every problem it encounters requires its longest or shortest quill to solve. Once the illusion of completeness is mitigated by the reality that however much we accumulate, there will always be something that escapes our repertoire the need to create space for one another to get by begins to be considered seriously. The porcupines start to see and relate to one another as 'intimate strangers' in their incompleteness and even the idea of hybridity seems to be a zero-sum game – in the sense of those perceived to be inferior making an effort to be like their supposed superiors by shopping up for cultural values to enhance their circumstance. This demonstrates the prickly paradoxes of intimacy and mutuality.

If Rhodes and my fantasy self are to borrow from porcupines compelled to get along despite themselves, then we would have to take seriously an idea of conviviality that rests on the nuances inscribed and imbibed in everyday relations by individuals and communities at micro and macro levels, within and between societies big or small. We would have to cultivate and sustain accommodating and interdependent styles of relating, of sociability and communality, through careful and innovative negotiation of the constructive and destructive dimensions of being human. Such a style of relating has little room for neat dichotomies emphasising distinct places and spaces for different social categories and hierarchies. Like porcupines compelled to huddle together to keep warm in winter, we can ill-afford to insist on rising above the messiness of everyday realities. Nor can we insist that those realities simply do not apply to us, that we are the exception. If everyone is a real or potential *makwerekwere*, liable to being compelled to share spaces and places as intimate strangers in a world of flexible mobility where no one enjoys a monopoly on quills, it is incumbent on us to seek to understand histories and imbue with new meaning often taken-for-granted notions, categories and terms that license inclusion and exclusion, such as citizenship and nationality, insider and outsider, us and them, family and stranger, intimacy and distance.

Notes

[1] I was awarded a three months visiting research fellowship to Saint Anthony's College Oxford England, by the Rhodes Chair Committee for Race Relations and African Studies, from October – December 1997. While at Oxford, I worked on '*Politics, Witchcraft and the Occult in Cameroon*', a study that touched on orders such as Freemasonry and Rosicrucianism, both very popular with African political leaders. In his empire-building and private life, Rhodes invested obsessively in secrecy and loyalty, to the point of founding a secret society of his own, modelled on the Jesuit Society of Jesus (Brown 2015). According to Robin Brown, 'For a brief period at Oxford, Rhodes was a Freemason, and his Groote Schuur library shelves held many books on topics such as the Rosicrucians and

225

Annie Besant's Theosophical Society. One such book dealt with the Hermetic Order of the Golden Dawn, a closed society similar to Rhodes's own Secret Society' (Brown 2015: 110; see also Flint 1974: 28-33).

[2] See John Flint (1974: 248-252), for a full reproduction Rhodes's 'Confession of Faith' of 1877.

[3] Indeed, as Joel Carpenter, Director of the Nagel Institute for the Study of World Christianity at Calvin College in Grand Rapids, Michigan, USA, observed when I shared with him an earlier draft of this section of the book, along with an article by Bradley W. Bateman titled 'The Evangelical Roots of American Economics', http://www.theatlantic.com/author/bradley-bateman/, accessed 20 February 2016, apparently secular universities in the USA for example, have far more in common with Christian social concerns than meets the eye. This is especially true of modern social sciences, whose roots are to be traced to earlier Christian social concerns. Carpenter's email to me dated 21 February read:

> Many thanks, Francis. This is an excellent summary of the oft-forgotten roots of the modern social sciences in American universities: they were very much seen as handmaidens of Christian social concern. The inaugural department of sociology at the University of Chicago in the late nineteenth century was called the 'department of Christian sociology.' Sociologists, historians and economists, especially R.T. Ely of Wisconsin noted here, were frequent contributors to church conferences on social mission.
>
> There have been some really remarkable historical works that document the rise of the modern social sciences in the U.S., and inevitably, they have to deal somehow with their secularization. One of the best summaries across all fields—natural and social sciences and humanities—is Jon H. Roberts and James Turner, *The Sacred and the Secular University* (Princeton, 2000). A good case study on evangelical Protestants' role is Louise L. Stevenson, *Scholarly Means to Evangelical Ends: The New Haven Scholars and the Transformation of Higher Learning in America, 1830-1890* (Johns Hopkins, 1986).
>
> There is another powerful overview of the whole secularization process in the American universities which deals with the issue from a somewhat different vantage point than Turner and Roberts, who look at the trends within the disciplines. This other study looks more from the vantage point of university leadership and changes in overall policy and orientation: George M. Marsden, *The Soul of the American University: From Protestant Establishment to Established Nonbelief* (OUP 1994). Marsden makes a point very similar to yours, to the effect that the

main narrative is not from church domination to secular freedom. The main story is the shift from one establishment and orthodoxy to another.

George, like me, comes from studying the history of Christianity in America. He taught at Calvin for many years, then a few years at Duke, and a long period, up to retirement, at the University of Notre Dame. He moved back to Grand Rapids in retirement, but continues to be active in American intellectual history. His latest book is *The Twilight of the American Enlightenment: The 1950s and the Crisis of Liberal Belief* (NY: Basic Books, 2014). If you ever would like to get in touch with him, just let me know (see also Carpenter 1998).

[4] See John Higgins (2013) for a discussion of the possibilities of and challenges to academic freedom in post-apartheid South Africa. Writing on the ferment in post-apartheid South African higher education, and the 'state of urgency' that characterizes the current 'tumultuous moment', Higgins and Peter Vale lament the global and local pressures exerted on 'the possibilities and potentials for humanist study and critical reflection'. They regret the combined negative effects on the humanities of the persistence of past injustices and inequalities on the one hand, and 'the dictates of a national higher education policy cloned from a global template indifferent or even hostile to the humanities and the qualitative social sciences' on the other (Higgins and Vale 2016: 3). See also Premesh Lalu's stinging critique of the manner in which the South African government overly privileges the natural and laboratory sciences to the detriment of the humanities in its allocation of research funds through a competitive system of appointment of research chairs administered by the National Research Foundation. http://mg.co.za/article/2012-02-24-still-searching-for-the-human, accessed 14 February 2014.

Chapter 7

Conclusion:
We Are All *Amakwerekwere*

If mobility is at the very heart of being human and being social, and if contemporary South Africa has come about thanks to the human mobilities, however unequal, of yesteryear, then what do current questionings of particular categories of mobility – that of white South Africans (the *amakwerekwere*, *Uitlanders* or European colonisers of yesteryear) and that of blacks from Africa north of the Limpopo (present-day *amakwerekwere* in the eyes of present-day sons and daughters of the native soil) – tell us about claiming and denying belonging as a mobilising force, a form of strategic essentialism and in historical perspective? If boundaries (physical, social, cultural, psychological and otherwise) are made, contested, unmade and remade through human mobility, action, and interaction, how do we interpret the violence of Rhodes Must Fall and that targeted at black immigrants – be it xenophobia or Afrophobia? What does the insistence by black South Africans (in the academy and suburbs as well as in townships, informal settlements and crowded city centres) claiming the bona fide status of sons and daughters of the native soil, on lighting their cigarette from both ends imply?

I argue that bounded notions of citizenship and problematic representations of African mobility by Rhodes and his fellow *amakwerekwere* of European origin of yesteryear (representations unfortunately uncritically reproduced by so-called independent African nation-states) are at the heart of current articulations of citizenship and belonging as a zero sum game in South Africa and throughout the African continent. The situation, as we have seen in the case of South Africa, is only compounded by an uncritical commitment to whitening up that characterises blacks caught betwixt and between interconnecting global and local hierarchies of being human and distinguishing oneself through social cultivation, the apex of which whites and the West are assumed to embody. We

229

have seen how South-Africanness is claimed and denied with expediency since the days of Rhodes, when citizenship was largely confined to white *amakwerekwere*, who fought among themselves to establish ultimate supremacy. While all present-day claims and denials to being South African may be founded, not every claim is informed by the same considerations. If being and becoming South African were compared to shopping at a supermarket (be it Shoprite, Pick n Pay, Checkers, Woolworths, or other), one could argue that some are flexible in what they put into their shopping baskets while some are picky, even as others are reduced to window or spaza shopping because of their modest purchasing power. And some have expired products thrust down their consumer palates.

Citizenship can be a very nebulous concept. The idea of a citizen as an autonomous, rights-bearing individual who enjoys total freedom of rational choice in a legal and political sense, and who is answerable to none other than the constitution as supreme law of the land protected by a minimalist enabler-state, sits uncomfortably in the context of Africa caught in the web of corrupted cultural traditions and a blighted modernity. To insist deftly that there are no intermediary solidarities and loyalties between the individual and the state (except those arrived at through freedom of association guaranteed by the right to subscribe and unsubscribe in tune with the whims and caprices of each individual member), or to ignore such loyalties (which are determined not always by choice but often by blood) where their existence is recognised and actively reproduced by those who share them, is to force Africans to live a lie or to live in chains in the name of freedom.

When such insistence is made by scholars, it is tantamount to privileging a prescriptive scholarship of sterility and teleology with little bearing on the lived experiences of the supposed citizens studied, as the impression is given that the shelf life of concepts is more important than their analytical relevance and empirical grounding. Yet, often isolated from the rights and privileges of the included or of those who 'belong', 'outsiders' tend to mediate barriers, borders and boundaries in fluid and dynamic ways, producing identities that run across cultures, languages, spaces and places in cities and national contexts (Nyamnjoh 2006). The efforts and processes they engineer as 'composite' or 'frontier' identities (Kopytoff 1987, Nyamnjoh 2015b) often escape scholarship that uncritically reproduces taken-for-granted dichotomies and bounded notions of being and belonging. Not to recognise such extensions to the conceptualisation of citizenship made possible by ordinary Africans immersed in popular traditions of meaning-making, would be contrary to the very affirmation of autonomy of thought and representation accorded citizens (regardless of class or status) in principle. However schooled in Western modernity the state elite may be, to label and dismiss as a contradiction to citizenship all that is counter to their Western-inspired templates, is to belie the very claim that their project is predicated on the principle of freedom of choice. It makes little sense to employ free-floating, untested assumptions about citizenship in the study of Africa, where people, in their lived realities, have little room for neat dichotomies, even when their pronouncements or discourses might sometimes suggest otherwise. If the test of our theoretical puddings must come from the practical eating, this is as true of citizenship studies as it is of every other facet of being and living in Africa.

A nuanced understanding of citizenship would not shying away from the complexity of being African but rather embrace it. Identities on the continent, like identities elsewhere, are permanent works in progress. Stereotypical evolutionism aside, human beings everywhere are complex and intricate, and identities the result of processes of becoming, best understood as flexible, fluid and full of ellipses – unfinished and unfinishable stories in sociality and civility. Being and becoming citizens as works in progress requires open-mindedness and open-endedness in encounters and the relationships they engender, reproduce or contest. Particular contexts challenge us in particular ways to raise or lower the bar of acceptability and tolerability in claims and denial of citizenship. It is through recognition of Africans' capacity to act on others as well as to bear the actions of others in time and space that an appropriate citizenship actualises. Such a citizenship is far from possible in contexts where the myth of self-cultivation, self-activation and self-management is uncritically internalised and reproduced with effortless abundance like an easily counterfeited devalued currency.

231

Citizens are not citizens in abstraction, but through binding relationships and social action.

The future of citizenship in Africa and globally lies in recognising and providing for the truism that rights articulated in abstraction and without obligations do not amount to much. Throughout the world civic citizenship is facing hard times, as multitudes (ranging from women's movements to diasporas through youth movements and cultural communities big and small) clamour for inclusion by challenging the myopia implicit in the conservative juridical-political rhetoric and practices of nation-states. In Africa, social-media-driven youth movements (such as North Africa's Arab Spring and South Africa's RMF) are involved in renegotiating the exclusionary bases of citizenship that have fuelled conflicts over belonging and representation (Honwana 2012, 2013; Weddady and Ahmari 2012; Branch and Mampilly 2015). Women's movements are equally active throughout the continent, challenging the indicators of citizenship narrowly informed by the privileged biases of Western and African masculinities (Tripp et al. 2008; Amony and Baines 2015)

There is a clear need to reconceptualise citizenship in ways that create political, cultural, social and economic space for excluded nationals and non-nationals alike both, as individuals and collectivities. Such inclusion is best guaranteed by a *flexible citizenship* (Ong 1999; Nyamnjoh 2007b; Isin 2012) unbounded by race, ethnicity, class, gender or geography, and that is both conscious and critical of hierarchies that make a mockery of the juridical-political regime of citizenship provided by the coercive illusion of the nation-state. In this fluid and open-ended idea of citizenship, space should be created for its articulation at different levels, from the most global to the most local or autochthonous, from the ethnic to the civic, and from the individual to the collective. Just as cultural, economic and social citizenships are as valid as juridical-political citizenship, so collective, group or community citizenship is as valid as individual citizenship, and is to be claimed at every level, from the small-scale local level to the mega-scale global level. The ideas of corporate, digital, electronic, cyber, global, itinerant and related claims to citizenship are easily understandable and accommodated under the framework of flexible citizenship. The emphasis should be on the freedom of individuals and communities to negotiate inclusion, to opt out, and opt in with total flexibility and reversibility of belonging in consonance with their realities as repertoires, melting pots, mosaics or straddlers of various identity margins.

Society not being a monolith whatever the ambitions of some in this regard, citizenship as recognition of and representation for pluralism and diversity requires a delicate balancing of tensions between competing and often conflicting interests, aspirations and truths. The more intricate the constellations of interests are, the greater the divergences in claims of citizenship, and the more imperative a case for a negotiated, accommodating consensus. Depending on the society in question and the disposition for mutual accommodation of its members, the interests are shaped by real or imagined identity or boundary markers. Articulated either as cast in stone or as lines drawn on beach sand, such markers may include the race or ethnicity, place or geography, class or status, gender or sexuality, generation or age of the individuals or groups competing for civil spaces and opportunities to activate and cultivate themselves to realise, inter alia, their political, social and economic dreams and aspirations. Such factors are the basis on which privileges are claimed and contested, sought and maintained. Within a given social context, the fulfilment of citizenship is dependent on the relative advantage or disadvantage of each social category in relation to others in the interplay of hierarchies engineered by all or some of these factors and more. The interplays in turn result in hierarchies of interests legitimated by the relationships and power dynamics between the social actors compartmentalised by these same factors. Histories and processes of encounters among social categories and between societies are critical for understanding the changing configurations of citizenship.

The above understanding of citizens and citizenship is a particularly relevant framework for Africa, in view of the phenomenal challenges facing current postcolonial attempts at crafting a common political and legal citizenship. In recognition of

233

these challenges and tensions Mahmood Mamdani, in *Citizen and Subject* (1996), invites us to recognise the bifurcated nature of citizenship in Africa by distinguishing between 'ethnic' and 'civic' citizenship. Overt tensions and conflicts within and between states speak of the unfinished and sometimes unstarted business of nation building around a shared or consensual set of core values. In many a situation, the state remains an extravagant irrelevance, with hardly any significant legitimacy beyond the handful of elite in power. Popular forms of citizenship and legitimacy with much longer histories of practice, relevance and suffrage are more likely to be expressed along lines of indigenous and endogenous forms of social organisation and government than along lines of political parties or of civil society organisations of voluntary membership that came with European colonialism or mimic present-day Western associations. Given the very recent colonial past of the continent, and in view of the overwhelming grip of Western modernity on postcolonial state-making, the challenges facing citizenship projects in Africa are particularly daunting.

In postcolonial Africa, where social action unfolds within a framework of interconnecting global and local hierarchies, communities large and small have both accepted and contested arbitrary colonial and postcolonial administrative boundaries and the dynamics of dispossession. In the South African context where student protests are acting to reclaim social justice in their universities as well as in the wider society, Robert Morrell observes that:

> People who stand against social justice are often those who seek to protect self-interest, and believe that the best way of doing this is to resist claims for social justice. They defend narrow, sectarian interests, and they ignore the obvious benefit that regimes of social justice bestow broadly.[1]

Perhaps in recognition of this truism, social movements and associations (voluntary and otherwise) concerned with the struggles for freedom and social justice of marginalised social categories and identities have proliferated across Africa, sometimes with the assistance of alternative and social media. Failing to achieve the idealised 'nation state' form and being relatively weak vis-à-vis global forces, African states have often sought to capitalise on the contradictory and complementary dimensions of civic, ethnic, and cultural citizenships. In this context, being a citizen in ethnic or cultural terms is much more than merely claiming to be or being regarded as an autochthon or an authentic son or daughter of a native soil. Under colonial and apartheid regimes, when technologies of dominance were perfected with policies and practices of divide-and-rule, to be called 'indigenous', 'autochthonous' or 'native' was first to create and impose a proliferation of those very same essentialised identities circumscribed by arbitrary physical and cultural geographies, which were mapped onto the psychological geographies of the oppressed (and oppressors) in such a successful manner that we still struggle with them today. Second, it was to make possible distinctions not only between colonised 'native' and colonising Europeans but also between 'native citizens' and 'native settlers' among ethnic communities within the same colony. Finally, to be 'native' was to be primitive with 'nothing but bush' to show[2], and therefore a perfect justification for the colonial *mission civilisatrice*, and for dispossession and confinement to officially designated tribal territories, homelands or bantustans, often in callous disregard of the histories of relationships and interconnections forged with excluded others, or of the differences and tensions even among the included.

Overall, being an ethnic citizen was for the majority colonised 'native' population to be shunted to the margins. These dynamics of classification and rule conceived of the 'natives' through frozen ideas of culture and imagined traditions, therefore to be governed by what Mamdani (1996) has termed 'decentralised despotisms', in rural areas; while the town and city were reserved for the minority colonial-settler population and their purportedly 'modernising', 'cultured' and 'detribalised' African servants and support staff. Today, towns and cities are still instinctively perceived as the places and spaces well suited for civic citizens, while rural areas and villages are the reserve and preserve of ethnic citizens and ethnic strangers who are confined or subjected to the diktats of culture and tradition under chiefly authority. Few, even among critical-minded scholars, are ready to entertain the notion that Africans are active agents, busying themselves with domesticating imported ideas of citizenship by bringing them into conversation with endogenous ideas of citizenship, some of which pre-date the continent's subjection to the whims and caprices of European ambitions of dominance.

If the negative colonial and apartheid history of ethnic or cultural citizenship continues to shape the highly critical stance of African intellectuals and nationalists towards all claims of autochthony, it has also, quite paradoxically, tended to render invisible the everyday reality of postcolonial Africans (including those same intellectuals and nationalists) who straddle civic, ethnic and cultural citizenships, on the one hand, and multiple global and local cosmopolitan identities, on the other. The baby of ethnic and cultural citizenship does not have to be thrown out with the bathwater of colonialism and apartheid.

Amid growing uncertainties and the questioning of the inadequacies of civic citizenship and its illusions of autonomy, rigid and highly exclusionary affirmations of being indigenous have become obsessive among majority and minority communities alike within various states in Africa. An outcome is covert or overt confrontation and conflict over territoriality and access to power and resources. The logic of ever-diminishing circles of inclusion dictates that the next foreigner, stranger, *Uitlander, makwerekwere* or Rhodes is always one layer below the obvious one.

South Africa, where xenophobic eruptions against migrants from elsewhere in Africa are commonplace, offers excellent illustrations of this obsession both in a song by popular Zulu musician, Mbongeni Ngema[3], released in May 2002 and in a Nando's[4] – a popular chicken fast food chain of restaurants – diversity advert released in June 2012. Titled AmaNdiya, Ngema's controversial song claims to 'begin a constructive discussion that would lead to a true reconciliation between Indians and Africans', (Nyamnjoh 2006: 56–63) and accuses South African Indians of opportunism and of enriching themselves to the detriment of blacks. In the song Ngema goes on to say that if Indians are to be

236

taken seriously as belonging to South Africa, they must display greater patriotism and stop straddling continents. Implied in his song is that Indians risk losing their South African citizenship should they refuse to change their ways – an implication compounded by recent allegations against the Gupta family and their claim that they are the victims of xenophobia.[5] And if and when Indians disappear from this bizarre nativity game of exclusionary violence and South Africa's problems are still unsolved, the next outsider group is just a layer below.

This regressive logic and the scapegoating of perceived outsiders are also well captured by the Nando's diversity advert. The advert articulates an idea of identity and belonging that is both conscious and cognisant of the histories of mobilities of peoples that have made South Africa possible. The ad starts with black Africans illegally crossing a barbed-wire border fence into South Africa. Each time the voice-over calls out a name, the group of people who represent that particular identity are transformed into a cloud of smoke, as follows:

> You know what is wrong with South Africa: all you foreigners. You must all go back to where you came from – you Cameroonians, Congolese, Pakistanis, Somalis, Ghanaians and Kenyans. And of course you Nigerians and you Europeans. Let's not forget you Indians and Chinese. Even you Afrikaners. Back to Swaziland you Swazis, Lesotho you Sothos, Vendas, Zulus, everybody.

In the end, only one person is left standing, a San man who, armed with a bow and arrow and ready to explore the wilderness, confronts the voiceover with these words: 'I'm not going anywhere. You found us here.' The ad concludes with the voiceover saying: 'Real South Africans love diversity. That's why we have introduced two more items: new peri-crusted wings and delicious trinchado and chips.'

The declaration by the San man in the Nando's diversity add echoes the following statement by Herbert Baker, Rhodes's architect:

> It is too often forgotten that the Bantu races had but little more title to their settlements in South Africa than had the Europeans. They held

237

their possessions by conquest and the extermination of the Hottentots and other indigenous tribes. And the migrations of the conquering Bantu met and clashed in inevitable conflict with the northward movement of the voortrekkers and settlers (Baker 1934: 96).

To my mind, the Nando's ad, far from promoting xenophobia, challenges narrow and parochial identities, or ideas of being and belonging as a zero-sum game that denies the reality of mobility as a normal way of being human, or tends to privilege the mobility of some to the detriment of that of others. This is especially significant in a South African context that has historically – that is, since the Dutch first landed in the Cape in 1652 – privileged immigration by whites while expecting non-whites, blacks in particular, to stay in their ethnic ('tribal') homelands or confines or their own countries until they are needed as devalued labour in mines and elsewhere (Peberdy 2009; Klaaren 2011). The ad plays with exclusionary obsessions by demonstrating the absurdity of ever-regressive logics and ever-diminishing circles of being South African in a world (and indeed a South African history) characterised by the flexible mobility of people, even if not always on their own terms, as was all too often the case with the black population. It invites us to contemplate what it is to be South African, if every colour of the country's current rainbow configuration must go back to its Bethlehem and be counted.

If belonging is articulated in rigid exclusionary terms and with scant regard to histories of constitution of human settlements, where everyone however mobile, is considered to belong to a particular homeland somewhere else, a never-ending spiral into bedlam, a place they cannot outgrow and which they must belong to regardless of where they were born or where they live and work, then South Africa can only belong to one group of people, those who were there before everyone else –the San. Although few want to identify with them, – given the obsession with a civilisation that entails a never ending spiral of whitening up and in view of their presumed lowly position in the hierarchy of humanity inspired by such a unilinear index of being modern, – the San know only too well that they are the unassuming bona fide sons and daughters of South Africa's soil and its resources – the only authentic South

Africans, if the zero sum game of exclusionary articulations of belonging were to be taken to its logical conclusion. Yet the San have been overly generous and accommodating, even when the strangers to whom they have reached out have tended to dispossess and debase them. Both the Nando's ad and Ngema's song demonstrate that citizenship is negotiated from an unfolding history of encounters among different peoples and ideas, and among a diversity of interests and aspirations.

As much as we would like those we encounter in our nimble-footed *amakwerekwere* adventures to be accommodating, we cannot afford to delude ourselves that we would continue to get away with imposing a world order narrowly construed around and confined to our sensibilities and insensitivities to others, however defined. Not even Cecil Rhodes, with all the power, wealth and ruthlessness at his disposal, found this an easy option, as was made abundantly clear by his calamitous Jameson-precipitated raid of the Boer Republic of the Transvaal. Even the fact that Rhodesia was reconverted into Zimbabwe at the earliest opportunity by sons and daughters of the native soil whom he had debased, vandalised and dispossessed with impunity and reckless abandon is another indication that power is not a permanent attribute of even the rich and privileged dictators of the world, and that whitening up can yield results in which black and whites trade places in the game of social visibility, distinction and prestige.

As Steve Biko (2004 [1978]; Pityana et al. 1991; Malusi and Mphumlwana 1996; Mngxitama et al. 2008a; Mangcu 2012; Hook 2014) and Robert Sobukwe (Pogrund 2015 [1990]), both leading intellectual crusaders for black liberation in South Africa, repeatedly emphasised in their day – sentiments echoed by political and moral authorities such as Nelson Mandela (Mandela 1995, 2010; Asmal et al. 2004) and Archbishop Desmond Tutu (Tutu 1999, 2004; Sparks and Tutu 2011) – it is important to be driven in principle and practice by a resolute and non-negotiable commitment to a common humanity not subjected to such determinisms as race, class, gender, culture, religion, education, age, place or space. This calls for commitment to fairness, justice and selflessness in the interest of the convivial world craved by all and sundry. Since

239

claims of autochthony and *makwerekwereness* are relational, it behoves us to articulate any such thoughts with an understanding of the intricacies involved and the histories of interconnection that have privileged certain forms of mobility over others. The context in which power and privilege are claimed and denied matters. But even more important is how to provide for the edification of a common humanity in how we seek inclusiveness. It takes moral courage and humility to seek freedom not only for oneself, but also for those who have made that freedom elusive at every opportunity.

This is the spirit of Ubuntu, which Nelson Mandela – a son of the native soil who competes favourably with Cecil Rhodes in terms of what Tinyiko Maluleke has termed 'the global rain of ... books, articles and artefacts' which his name continues to inspire, and in how places, spaces and institutions are named after him, and his currency as a symbol to various people and various purposes[6] – is credited with, and which others have found so compelling. Speaking at a memorial service organised in Soweto, Johannesburg on 10 December 2013 in honour of Nelson Mandela, US President Barack Obama noted that Mandela

> not only embodied Ubuntu; he taught millions to find that truth within themselves. It took a man like Madiba to free not just the prisoner, but the jailor as well; to show that you must trust others so that they may trust you; to teach that reconciliation is not a matter of ignoring a cruel past, but a means of confronting it with inclusion, generosity and truth. He changed laws, but also hearts[7].

Yet such Ubuntu and trust do not come easily for a deeply wounded deeply traumatised, who are still sharply divided post-apartheid South Africa where many are still at daggers drawn along racial lines (Lategan 2015). If media reports are anything to go by, it would appear Julius Sello Malema has, since his pre-Economic Freedom Fighters (EFF) days, best epitomised the growing trends in the politics of exclusionary citizenship and narrow nationalism among politicians in the new South Africa.[8] Until his expulsion from the ANC on 29 February 2012,[9] Malema provided another example of a public figure privileging the rhetoric of exclusion over actively exploring social cohesion among all and sundry in the

240

delicately poised rainbow nation. In 2010 Malema, then leader of the Youth League of the ANC (ANCYL), identified white South Africans – descendants of Cecil Rhodes and Paul Kruger as *amakwerekwere* of yesteryear – as the enemy within. He made nationalisation and land restitution as his favourite themes. While he invited his mostly unemployed supporters among black South Africans to aspire to be like the whites in comfort and consumption – to 'whiten up', as it were – he particularly targeted Afrikaners in his choice of public choral performance to drive his message home. On 3 March 2010, for example, at his birthday party in Pholokwane, Malema, sang *Ayesab' Amagwala* – a popular Zulu anti-apartheid, liberation struggle song that contains the words *'dubul'ibhunu'*, which translate into English as: 'Shoot the *boer*'[10] – a song that would have been music to Leander Starr Jameson's posthumous ears. As you would recall, Boer, 'farmer' in Dutch, refers to white South Africans from Dutch, German or Huguenot descent who speak Afrikaans, and are also known as Afrikaners. In Rhodes's day, the Boers were the *amakwerekwere* who felt sufficiently indigenised to refer to the more recent arrivals of British immigrants to the then South Africa in the making as *Uitlanders*. Malema, who in Rhodes's day would have been termed a Bantu tribal migrant (*makwerekwere* in other words) by Rhodes and his white peers, sang the song repeatedly and supposedly provocatively – including in April 2010 during a visit to Zimbabwe, where he openly supported Robert Mugabe's land restitution programme (the land Rhodes and Jameson had appropriated and assigned to white immigrants or *amakwerekwere* with impunity following his defeat of Lobengula) – causing much uproar in the media and the wider South African society. Anyone with a sense of history repeating itself may well have thought, as would Jacky Ndoumbe, a Cameroonian musician, *'les choses qui arrivent aux autres commencent déjà à m'arriver'* (the fate of others is catching up with me).

A debate – not dissimilar to subsequent debates on monuments, statues and other symbols of South Africa's colonial and apartheid heritages following the Rhodes Must Fall protests – ensued as politicians and others discussed whether the song should be allowed as part of South Africa's heritage and history, or prohibited as hate speech. The choice was between prioritising heritage to the detriment of harmony or harmony to the detriment of memory,[11] in a context where equality and redress were much more a constitutional provision than a real-life experience for the bulk of those dispossessed and dehumanised by apartheid and colonialism. The ANC's reaction was similar to Jacob Zuma's reaction to the controversy around his singing of *Umshini Wami* (Bring Me My Machine Gun). 'If you erase the songs, you erase the record of history', said Zuma of the anthem (Gunner 2009)[12], a reaction similar to his caution against a revisionist or selective reading of history following the RMF protests, when he said: 'When you read a history book and you come across a painful page, you do not just rip it out.'[13]

The controversies and tensions between heritage and harmony in the rainbow nation were only further enflamed by the death of Eugène Terre'Blanche – founder and leader of the Afrikaner Weerstandsbeweging (AWB, in English, Afrikaner Resistance Movement), an organisation formed in 1973 by right-wing extremist Afrikaners to resist what they saw as the weakening of apartheid regulations at the time – killed on 3 April 2010, allegedly by two of his black workers on his farm in Ventersdorp over unpaid wages. Tensions rose as some sought to link Malema's singing of 'Shoot the *boer*' and Terre'Blanche's murder. Right-wing extremist groups such as the AWB and the Suidlanders, for long quiescent, conducted protest marches in Ventersdorp and threatened to avenge the murder. Other groups became involved, including AfriForum and the Transvaal Agricultural Union (TAU SA), who lodged a complaint with the Equality Court against Malema, accusing him of hate speech. On 18 March, a 'Prosecute Malema' online campaign was launched to gather signatures for a letter directed to President Zuma; by 25 March, the South African Human Rights Commission had received 109 complaints against Malema for singing the song; and on 26 March and 1 April, the song had been ruled unlawful and unconstitutional by the North and South Gauteng High Courts, respectively, much to the dissatisfaction of many an ANC member (Rodrigues 2011: 1–4).

Malema, whom Xolela Mangcu qualifies as having come of age in the age of looting,[14] may live in Sandton, Johannesburg and cherish flashy designer clothes and shoes, big Breitling watches and gold, diamond-studded rings, the choicest wines and sushi off the belly buttons and nipples of naked beautiful girls (Forde 2011; Shapiro 2011)[15] – indeed, he may share the same appetites and material comforts of the richest of those who systematically and actively excluded him and those he claims to represent from the old South Africa – but somehow he feels more legitimately entitled to the new South Africa, and to a culture of victimhood, and of consumption with reckless abandon, even at the risk of consuming the dignity and humanity of fellow South Africans, something that someone who presents himself as a Robin Hood of sorts – stealing from the rich to give to the poor – may not perceive as being at their expense.

It is hardly surprising therefore, that regressive logics of belonging and citizenship remain active in South Africa despite the celebration of its cosmopolitanism and rainbow potentials. In early 2016, in his capacity as leader of the Economic Freedom Fighters, Malema took the fight for and against the ever-diminishing circles of inclusion to those with 'naturalised' citizenship who seem oblivious to playing according to the diktats of the dispossessed sons and daughters of the native soil. His target this time was what is popularly known in South African media as the Gupta family, declaring that Gupta media will not be allowed to attend EFF events any longer. 'We don't want to see The New Age and ANN7', Malema announced, adding that these were 'propaganda machinery' at the service of corruption, that must not be tolerated. He threatened the Gupta family, who incidentally have acquired South African citizenship, with practical action if they did not leave the country with immediate effect.[16] The Gupta family, who are 'said to have a close relationship with President Jacob Zuma and other highly placed ANC leaders'[17], sought and obtained a court interdict against the perceived threat of violence by Malema and the EFF. The court ruled in favour of the Gupta family, 'upholding their rights … as South African citizens to remain in South Africa and carry out business operations' without fear of intimidation and violence from the EFF.[18] Reacting to the ruling on behalf of the Gupta family, Atul Gupta said:

> The Guptas have been in South Africa since 1993 and are a proudly South African family. Some of the family's children were born and raised in South Africa. Oakbay Investments employs more than 4500 people in South Africa, and growing, and reinvests all profits in the country. The Gupta family will continue to invest in South Africa, promote South Africa and create jobs for South Africans. [19]

Speaking in his capacity as Editor-in-Chief of *The New Age* newspaper Moegsien Williams said:

> Our employees have the right to go to work and do their jobs without the threat of violence. We welcome today's ruling and hope that the EFF will cease its threats and intimidation of our staff immediately.[20]

Subsequently, Malema's discomfort with the Gupta family and their meddling was given added credence when Deputy Finance Minister Mcebisi Jonas alleged that Atul Gupta had offered him the position of Minister of Finance in 2015, in return for a commitment that he would prioritise and protect the huge business interests of the Gupta family in computers, air travel, energy, and technology. This claim suggested that the Guptas wield enormous power in South African government circles and especially over President Jacob Zuma, to the point of influencing appointments in the Zuma government. The Gupta family reportedly have such strong ties with the Zuma family, that Malema and his EFF have dubbed both families 'The Zuptas'[21]. According to the BBC, 'Bongi Ngema-Zuma, one of the president's wives, used to work for the Gupta-controlled JIC Mining Services as a communications officer. Duduzile Zuma, his daughter, was a director at Sahara Computers. Duduzane Zuma, a son, is a director in some Gupta-owned companies.' [22] The Gupta influence is apparently so profound[23], that senior ANC officials are worried about South Africa becoming a 'Mafia State'. Some point to an incident in 2013, when a private jet carrying guests to a Gupta family member wedding was allowed to land at a South African military air force base in Pretoria, and little became of the matter despite a national outcry.[24]

The allegations were widely debated across the country, not least in Parliament, where President Zuma was questioned on the matter by opposition politicians. When Democratic Alliance leader Mmusi Maimane, for example, asked President Zuma to comment on the allegation that the Guptas were in the habit of influencing the appointment of ministers in exchange for favourable business deals, Zuma said: 'I am in charge of the government. I appoint in terms of the constitution. There is no minister who is here who was appointed by the Guptas or by anybody else; ministers who are here were appointed by me.'[25] Not satisfied with President Zuma's response, three foundations representing ANC struggle stalwarts – Nelson Mandela, Oliver Tambo and Ahmed Kathrada, wrote a letter, jointly signed by Njabulo Ndebele, Frene Ginwala and Derek Hanekom, which they sent to the ANC secretary-general Gwede Mantashe, urging the ANC to 'remain true to our founders and to continue our life's work to champion the cause of freedom and democracy for our people. It is for these that they were "prepared to die"'.[26] The letter called for urgent 'corrective' action in the interest of all South Africans, in these word:

'We appeal to the NEC of the ANC as they meet at the weekend to take note of the mood of the people across the country, to reflect deeply on their solemn responsibilities, to make urgent choices, and to take urgent corrective actions in the best interest of South Africa and its peoples.'[27]

If by urgent corrective action the authors of the joint letter expect the national executive committee (NEC) of the ANC to recall President Zuma and sanction the Guptas, this did not happen. Gwede Mantashe declared after the meeting that 'despite intense speculation, the issue of Zuma's recall never arose'. Instead, NEC reportedly threw its weight behind the leadership of President Jacob Zuma, after 'frank and robust discussions on the serious allegations surrounding the Gupta family and its purported influence in the appointment of ministers, their deputies and other positions in key state-owned entities'.[28] Going by these allegations alone, the Guptas would qualify as a present-day Cecil Rhodes, who believed that everybody could be squared, bribed or corrupted, and insisted that

245

everyone had their price – from King Lobengula of Matabeleland to Queen Victoria of England, through politicians in South Africa and Britain – his imperial ambitions (Stent 1924; Baker 1934; Marlowe 1972; Flint 1974; Haresnape 1984; Thomas 1996; Brown 2015).

When debate and speculation on 'state capture' by the Guptas refused to die down, with intensifying calls for the Public Protector to investigate them[29], the Guptas issued a two-page advertisement headlined 'Gupta family: The Inconvenient Truth' in their newspaper, *The New Age*, refuting the allegations and asserting their ignorance.[30] They labelled the accusations xenophobic and said they felt scapegoated. Their statement read: 'As the global economic slowdown began to bite, the family became the scapegoat for every calamity and misfortune that South Africa has faced.' 'We have been quiet until now but given the recent xenophobic and hate speech against us, now is the time to set the record straight', they added, and proceeded to list all the unacknowledged benefits they had brought ungrateful South Africans. Responding, for example, to charges that they had colonised South Africa since 1993 when they first came to the country (an accusation reminiscent of RMF), the Guptas rejected the charges as 'a ridiculous suggestion', pointing to the 'more than 4500 jobs' they had created for South Africans and the R276 million in corporate taxes that they paid in 2015 alone. They acknowledged being friends with President Zuma since 2000, just as they were friends with President Mbeki, adding that 'Like many other South African businesses, we interact with the government.'[31]

In the world of domination and liberation, where things are always oscillating between contrived universalism and radical autochthony or alterity, belonging and citizenship are an unending cycle of ever-diminishing circles, just as the results of liberation struggles are not measured in material terms exclusively. In the topsy-turvydom of post-apartheid South African political economy, opportunity and opportunism are worryingly cosy bedfellows requiring closer public scrutiny in the interest of the impoverished and marginalised masses, for whom government and business would claim to work without relent.

Malema's shortcomings notwithstanding, it is difficult to ignore the weight of his pronouncements, some of which, nationalisation and land restitution for example, have followed him into his new role as leader of the EFF, where he has taken up other causes including decolonisation and the transformation of higher education. The Rhodes Must Fall and Fees Must Fall campaigns by students have found in Malema and his EFF party natural bedfellows in university campuses where student politics are still articulated along party-political lines, and accusations or insinuations of a third hand or force in student uprising and violence have tended to imply Malema and the EFF as that third force or not so hidden hand.[32] The resonance and solidarity they enjoy among students and support staff of various universities protesting outsourcing, among other things, is indicative of how much remains to be done to win the minds and hearts of South African youth and the working and under classes with the constitutional delights that are the sing song of those with racialized power and privilege in the not-so-new 'new' South Africa. Until genuine accommodation and solace are found for desperate voices such as human rights lawyer turned equitable education advocate Danai Nhando's, who believe that a clash along racial lines among students of the University of the Free State[33] was 'bound to happen sooner or later', Malema's and the EFF's rhetoric would continue to enjoy suffrage among black South Africans who feel sidestepped and underserved. Nhando notes (and this is a widely shared opinion by black students in campuses across the country, if social media are anything to go by):

> I remember writing an essay as a final year law student challenging the idea of institutionalised equality. The Constitution was still very new at the time and South Africa was being hailed globally as the epitome of democracy and reconciliation. I argued then, as I still argue now that the Constitution created an unrealistic ideal that equality now existed in South Africa merely because it was etched in the nation's Constitution. It is impossible to look at issues of racial inequality in South Africa without seeing the deep cuts imprinted across the hearts of the people. Somehow we thought that because our fathers said they had forgiven, we inherited their forgiveness. We believed that because declarations of equality were made from

247

podiums amidst handshakes and ululations we were now equal. It just isn't that simple![34]

Felicity Kunene who attended UFS in 2004, agrees. She writes:

> At the centre of grievances of the black students is the deeply rooted racism entrenched in the university system that robs them of their dignity. The conversation on race relations in post-apartheid South Africa can no longer evade the radar of our public discourse. By invading that rugby pitch and disrupting the game, the students placed South Africa's racial polecat into the national spotlight. One can only hope that its stench will awaken those lulled by a non-racialism that renders black people invisible and allows white privilege to exist without interruption.[35]

To like-minded students and many an unemployed or poorly remunerated black South African in or outside the academy, Malema speaks sense, as much as he speaks nonsense to many a powerful and privileged other, and is as much a champion as he is a politician. To undo the wrongs of the past, there needs to be a measure of effective restitution, greater inclusion or redistribution and division of wealth. However, what Malema has argued since his days as leader of the ANC youth league and today as leader of the EFF is not always acknowledged, because of his self-image and the way he is portrayed in the media, and also because of his combative attitude. Controversies and perceptions that his practices appear at variance with his preaching seem to sweep the substance of his argument under the carpet. Yet, the various and ongoing campaigns by students and disaffected and underpaid university workers would seem to suggest that, as far as what Robert Morrell has termed 'the burning issue of campus violence'[36] is concerned, there seems to be no professor in town at the moment that is more popular than Julius Malema, and no university of the future more promising than the Economic Freedom Fighters. But there is little sustained transformation to be gained from violence and intolerance, the very weapons of choice often used in the past to make life unbearable for the victims of colonialism and apartheid in general (Marks 2001) and in many historically disadvantaged mainly 'black' university campuses in particular (Ndebele 2007: 165-169).

248

As Adam Habib and Sizwe Mabizela, Vice Chancellors of University of the Witwatersrand and Rhodes University respectively, observe in a co-authored article published by the *Sunday Times*, with rising violence, destruction, loathing, intimidation and fear on university campuses, especially since the beginning of the 2016 academic year:

> universities are now forced to redirect valuable resources away from issues that really matter – scholarships, food and accommodation for needy students, and support for the academic project - to fund private security services in order to protect staff members, students and property.
>
> Universities are left with little choice – the costs of losing a life, of people being harmed, of malicious damage to property, and of losing the academic year are too ghastly to contemplate.
>
> However, this means that the poor are further impoverished by the actions of the very groups claiming to be fighting for their rights.
>
> If we allow this situation to continue without challenging it, the free and safe space of our universities will be compromised, and our institutions will be irreparably harmed.
>
> If our universities are indeed destroyed, it will not affect the wealthy, who can afford to send their offspring to universities abroad or fork out for private higher education that will no doubt fill the void.
>
> It is ultimately the poorest in our society and the middle classes who will miss out on obtaining a high-quality tertiary education. This will be truly tragic, for we will simply reinforce the very inequalities that we hope to challenge, address and eradicate.[37]

If violence and intolerance are what accounts for the surging popularity of 'professor' Malema and the EFF, it is unlikely that such an approach would be justified if South Africa were to demonstrate in no uncertain terms that it is determined to build a genuinely inclusive rainbow future.

Just as the zero-sum games of the nimble-footed *amakwerekwere* of both yesteryear and today must be substituted with a common morality which unequivocally champions human dignity and equality for all and sundry beyond tokenism or lip service, so too must all forms of autochthony and regressive nationalism. However, to simply denounce Julius Malema and his pronouncements without making a concerted and systematic effort at restitution, redistribution and inclusivity would be hypocritical – much like water off a duck's back for black South African masses who continue to feel dispossessed and to lament the advantages of citizens confined to the pages of their constitution. Pertaining to heritage, what creative and innovative ways are there to entertain conversations about the country's multiple heritages that are more conducive to nation-building than is currently the case? Again, it is hardly productive for the *amakwerekwere* of yesteryear to simply scream at daggers drawn that their symbols are sacred or for the ANC and other liberation movements or political parties to emphasise the unfinished business of liberation by bringing down oppressive statues and monuments, or in turn claiming that their liberation songs, however offensive by the standards of present-day political correctness sanctioned by the constitution, are sacrosanct. Nation-building requires more than talking at cross purposes and issuing ultimatums. It requires mutual accommodation, which comes from learning to talk and reason, even when one feels absolutely right about one's convictions, positions and the burning issues at hand.

Although a lot has been achieved materially for a small group of people, not enough has been done for the majority. Worse still, there is the stubborn feeling, even among economically empowered black people, that their collective memories of the struggle against apartheid are being muzzled by powerful minorities who are all too eager to consider apartheid and colonialism dead and buried and to divorce the probing tumultuous present from its turbulent violent history. This is done so easily in the name of being 'liberal', such as 'I don't see colour'. A failure to acknowledge injustice can be just as damaging as being responsible for causing the injustice.

The economy is still dominated by white South Africans and black empowerment has only meant the crystallisation of the black middle classes (Southall 2016) and a culture of tenderpreneurship. According to Terry MacKenzie-Hoy, a 'tenderpreneur' in South Africa is a person who has made an extraordinary sum of money from a contract (usually a national government, provincial government or municipal tender) that has been awarded for some sort of service. The reason why such a lot of cash flows from the contract is that the award value significantly exceeds the cost of the services, and the surplus goes into the pockets of the contractor and the officials who award the contract.[38]

According to the former general secretary of the Congress of South African Trade Unions (COSATU), Zwelinzima Vavi, a 'tenderpreneur' is one 'who through political connections wins tenders unfairly and provides shoddy services to communities while more genuine entrepreneurs are side lined as well as their skills and proper services'.[39] Tenderpreneurship is thought to have mostly benefited corrupt politicians and top civil servants seeking shortcuts to riches and to ostentatious consumption (Forde 2011; Posel 2010; Shapiro 2011).[40] Part of the wrangling around the renovations at President Jacob Zuma's Nkandla residence and insistence by the State Protector and opposition political parties that Zuma pay back some of the money, was not unconnected with tenderpreneurship. When on 31 March 2016 the Constitutional Court passed the judgement that by ignoring the 'remedial action' recommended by the Public Protector in her report on the development of his Nkandla homestead, President Zuma had failed in his duty to 'uphold, defend and respect' the constitution, and that the National Assembly had also failed in its duty to hold the executive branch to account[41], the decision was hailed by many as a great victory for accountability of public governance and democracy in South Africa.[42] In a nationwide televised reaction on 1 April 2016, President Zuma accepted the judgement and apologised to South Africans for ignoring the Public Protector's remedial action, citing poor legal advice, and promised to abide by the judgement.[43] President Zuma came short of yielding to widespread and growing calls for his resignation[44], not least from within the ANC, including an open letter to this effect from struggle veteran Ahmed Kathrada: 'I appeal to our President to submit to the will of the people and resign'[45], with some suggesting that things would fall apart for a divided ANC were Zuma to stepdown and step aside.[46] On Tuesday 5 April 2016, a parliamentary motion to impeach President Zuma, introduced by the Democratic Alliance and backed by the Economic Freedom Fighters and the majority of opposition parties, was defeated by 233 votes against and 143 votes in favour.[47]

251

It is in the perception of corruption with impunity and collusion between government and the business sector, if VS Naipaul (2010) is correct, that Winnie Madikizela-Mandela considers 'black economic empowerment ... a joke', describing it as 'a white confidence measure made up by local white capitalists' in collusion with their 'malleable black' partners, while 'those who had struggled and had given blood were left with nothing' and abandoned 'in shacks [with] no electricity, no sanitation and no sign of an education'.[48] According to Madikizela-Mandela, who was detained for 491 days and subjected to two trials by the apartheid regime on account of alleged terrorism (Mandela 2013; Ndebele 2006), while affluent blacks can now send their children to posh schools historically exclusive to white students, it is not clear the extent to which this is a justification of time spent on death row, long solidarity confinement and struggle heroes who died seeking a better future for all and sundry. Even Nelson Mandela, she continues, who went to jail a revolutionary, came out preaching peace and compromise, and all too ready to accept 'a freedom based on compromises and concessions'.[49]

With little consensus beyond a savage commitment to inflame tensions, while hoping for salvation from the constitution, South Africa appears to be a country of everyone-for-themselves-and-God-for-us-all. Little wonder that, for many, the God of all South Africans – *The State* – has become a scapegoat and a punch bag for its inability to do more than help those who help themselves. Abandoned and weakened by the competing and warring factions and interests called 'South Africa', *The State* finds itself unable to achieve little more than reproducing social geographies of apartheid.

Official and popular discourses are infused with a deep suspicion of those who move, particularly those moving to urban areas and between regions, countries and continents. To be visible for citizenship, nationality or belonging, bounded notions of geography and culture are deployed as currency. Claims of purity are more imagined and political than real in any socio-anthropological sense. The rhetoric is one of the necessity to avoid system crashes by avoiding overloading them, giving the impression

252

of a science of mobility where every country, region and community has a precise idea of its carrying capacity of human beings or human problems. Freedom of movement, especially by people deemed to be less endowed economically, is perceived by those who consider themselves more economically gifted, as a potential disaster, to be contained at all costs.

Far from this only being the plight or fate of obvious outsiders, such as foreigners and non-citizens (or *Uitlanders* and *amakwerekwere*), the controversy caused by a Tweet by Helen Zille, leader of the Democratic Alliance party in March 2012, referring to pupils from the Eastern Cape coming to the Western Cape province (where she is premier) as 'refugees', suggests that the problem of undesired mobility is not permanently resolved once the scapegoated outsider has been dispensed with.[50] It can also be argued that Zille is deliberately being misunderstood to fit the stereotypical view of the Democratic Alliance as a racially biased white party and that her intention was not aimed at 'undesired mobility' but a well-justified attack on the incompetence of the ANC run Eastern Cape education department to provide satisfactory education for pupils in that province, while at the same time bragging about the quality of education in her province. As a white woman and as a descendant of the *amakwerekwere* of yesteryear, and in view therefore of her in between status as an outsider within, could Zille ever become insider enough in the eyes of those claiming the status of bona fide sons and daughters of South Africa to remark on certain things?

If in the 19th century those who came closest to bona fide South Africans were already mixed, then what purity can one expect of those claiming the status of bona fide sons and daughters of the native soil in 21st century South Africa? According to Rotberg, the Griquas of the 19th century were:

> an ethnically-mixed people from much of the human material of early South Africa: Boer frontiersmen; remnants of Koisan hunters; gatherers and pastoralists; escaped slaves from the Cape; free blacks from the same domain; and Africans somehow detached from their own communities. They were in a generic sense the only true South Africans (cited in Brown 2015: 27).

There is need for greater tolerance and accommodation among the different communities that constitute the rainbow, a lesson that Njabulo Ndebele draws following the controversy ignited by Julius Malema's use of the term '*Makula*'[51], to refer to Indian South Africans. Recognising that South Africans under apartheid 'internalised the insensitivities and brutalities of colonialism and a formally racist society over time', until these became part of their reflex behaviour, Ndebele invites fellow South Africans, instead of rushing to court to complain against utterances by one another, to 'recognise the sources of potential hurt when we see them; register the outrage internally; smother the urge for instant reaction; run through the database of past experience; consider possible options of reaction; and then select an option'. He adds:

> New moral power will belong to those who do not spring to reflex self-defence and self-justification. Critical introspection will help them pry out new knowledge, redefine old notions, and clear the air for new relationships. Relationships between people are never defined or redefined instantly. They evolve from a constant effort of experience, education, and calibration.[52]

Such organic processes of reconciliation call for moral leadership across the social spectrum, leadership that is measured and unassuming, that is in touch in myriad ways with those on behalf of whom they make pronouncements and commitments. Above all, they call for leadership that distinguishes itself, not through flashy consumption and sterile accumulation, but by austere lives and commitment to principles. As former finance minister Trevor Manuel once put it, 'Fighting poverty doesn't mean making millions, but removing the yoke of poverty from millions'. This is imperative in a context where 'only 41% of adult South Africans work in either the formal or informal sector' – a situation compounded by a very poor quality of education structured, permeated and haunted by a logic of race (Soudien 2012), especially for the majority black population, among whom only 15 per cent of those who passed matric in 2010 received an aggregate mark above 40 per cent.[53] With the annual debacle around matric pass rates and how these are configured, South Africa could very well end up with youth that are functionally illiterate and innumerate. As it stands, one's education depends on whether one's parents have the financial and cultural capital to send one to a semi-private or private school, as government schools (depending on the province) are not always functional and, if they are functional, teachers are not necessarily equipped to teach the new curricula (Jansen 2011: 10–11). Beneath the rainbow façade of many a school in the post-apartheid, born-free context 'there exists an inward struggle with racial identity amongst both the staff and the student body' and transforming the classroom into a 'neutral place of discussion' remains to be achieved, as students and staff enter the classroom with 'inherited racial positioning' and lived realities that have little room for neutrality. Students and teachers continue to carry and are largely shaped in their perspectives and interactions by 'a distinct knowledge of the past framed in their own experiences and backgrounds' (Mazanderani 2011: 17–42; see also Bhana 2014).

States and policy makers inclined to police rather than facilitate mobility and a flexible disposition to citizenship stand to learn from the forging of everyday conviviality in urban Africa. Urban life in Africa depends on the extent to which Africans circulate or are circulated. The city, urban transport most especially, offers us a privileged site to observe how Africans in their flexible mobility negotiate their citizenship through relationships. Citizenship and belonging are negotiated in spaces of public transit, such as trains, taxis, and buses, and are dependent on a fine line of conviviality. As a multitude of travellers pass in and out of the city, each day, zones of mobility and public transport become places of intense negotiation and interaction. Conviviality emerges in the frequent interplay between dynamics of group autonomy on the one hand and interdependent communalism of groups on the other hand. Tensions are often put aside out of mutual necessity to make one's way throughout the city. Conviviality emerges out of the necessity to earn one's living, to surmount the tensions and divisions of inequality with attempts at flexibility propelled by the need to get by. In many ways, Conviviality results from compliance with cultural implications of power. Its intricacies in the lived everyday are, in fact, steeped in tensions (Nyamnjoh and Brudvig 2014a, 2014b).

Understanding the sense of belonging that citizens feel, display, mobilise, invest in, and invariably make ambiguous is essential to the challenge of exploring and theorising what Edgar Pieterse terms 'African cityness' (Pieterse 2010). An analytical focus on conviviality in the everyday narrative of 'insiders' and 'outsiders' and their relationships as 'intimate strangers' demonstrates the prickly paradoxes of intimacy and mutuality, representative of contestations with belonging taking place in urban African crucibles of becoming. Conviviality rests on the nuances inscribed and imbibed in everyday relations – the micro-trends of socialisation (Nyamnjoh and Brudvig 2014a, 2014b).

Conviviality makes possible interdependence among humans whose tendency is to seek autonomy even at the risk of dependencies. Urban conviviality has little room for neat dichotomies emphasising distinct places and spaces for different social categories and hierarchies, as urbanites, like porcupines compelled to huddle together to keep warm in winter, can ill afford to insist on rising above the messiness of everyday realities. The entangled, interconnected, and even mangled lives of urbanites suggest an approach towards understanding them that seeks to marry the emotional and the rational which they embody as social and relational beings.

How simple or complex, bounded or flexible – indeed, how convivial or not – we are in our articulation of what constitutes citizenship in Africa is informed by whom we are ready to include in our shopping basket as 'Africans', 'a fellow…', 'sisters', 'brothers', or 'one of us.' In his novel *Arrow of God*, Chinua Achebe uses a popular Igbo proverb – 'The world is like a Mask dancing. If you want to see it well you do not stand in one place' (Achebe 1964: 46) to remind us that change is a permanent feature of being human. In the course of our mobility and encounters as dynamic humans, new questions arise to which old answers are not quite suited. This might require making things up as one goes along, but an old broom, however experienced and thorough, cannot sweep with quite the same effectiveness as a new broom in a new context.

Far from being an invitation to abandon the past for the present, Achebe's is rather a call to creatively blend the past with the present in the interest of the future.

As a writer, Achebe invites us to contemplate the intricacies of being and belonging, through the characters he creates, for whom these are not matters with easy choices. If his public pronouncements on his own life are anything to go by, being and belonging to Achebe as an individual are no easy matters either. He recognises that his 'life has been full of changes' that have shaped the way he looks at the world, and that renders complex 'the meaning of existence and everything we value'.[54] The challenge of being and becoming African or anything else, is not so much identifying with people, places and spaces one is familiar with, but especially with spaces, places and people one is yet to encounter or to become familiar with. Hence Achebe's call for empathy and compassion, with the argument that:

> it's not difficult to identify with somebody like yourself, somebody next door who looks like you. What's more difficult is to identify with someone you don't see, who's very far away, who's a different colour, who eats a different kind of food. When you begin to do that then literature is really performing its wonders.[55]

Current critical interrogations involving South African universities and society, initiated by students and ordinary South Africans desperately struggling to make ends meet at the margins demonstrate the intricacies involved in situating the attributes of being and belonging as a citizen in South Africa, Africa and the world. These challenges require political vision, carefully articulated policies and astute leadership, tenacity, commitment, open-mindedness and humility at different instances of society. At universities specifically, there is need to draw on and enrich such efforts at understanding the possibilities and challenges of bringing about productive and inclusive leadership, documented in *Reflections of South African University Leaders 1981-2014*, edited by the Council on Higher Education (2016), which concluded its reflections just before the eruption of the monumental protests of 2015.

257

In what concerns the future of South Africa amid these pertinent – though unfortunately marred by the violent destruction of badly needed property, intimidation and intolerance in certain cases – interrogations by students and unemployed or underpaid workers, the Mandela-Rhodes Foundation offers a plausible model to work with, given the futility of zero sum games of struggles for dominance and liberation. There is need for pragmatic policies of reconciliation and justice, and of alleviating poverty through a carefully negotiated strategic programme of restitution, reparation and redistribution. The political and business elite need urgent sustained conversations with one another and with various civil society organisations – universities and student movements included – on and around taking the Mandela-Tutu Truth and Reconciliation initiative forward from a purely emotional cathartic exercise into one of economic and cultural development of a truly socially inclusive and cohesive nature. In this connection, the future of South Africa may well rest on how well the leadership harnesses the creative energies and resources of black and white *amakwerekwere* of yesteryear with those of today's *amakwerekwere*, in the interest of Nelson Mandela's cosmopolitan nation-building and Thabo Mbeki's African Renaissance aspirations.

Notes

[1] See Robert Morrell, http://www.dailymaverick.co.za/article/2015-11-11-op-ed-treasure-or-curse-south-africas-university-vice-chancellors/#.VtVX8ebCBV8, accessed 1 March 2016.

[2] As Luke Pearson indicates with reference to Australia, quoting former Australian Prime Minister Tony Abbott, this was the perfect justification for invasion and dispossession in the name of a mission to civilisation. See 'White Australia has a black history - and Indigenous Australians like me had our country invaded not "discovered"' http://www.independent.co.uk/voices/white-australia-has-a-black-history-indigenous-australians-like-me-had-our-country-invaded-not-a6959576.html, accessed 1 April 2016.

[3] For excerpts of the song and Mbongeni's reaction to its ban, see http://sbeta.iol.co.za/news/south-africa/ngema-regrets-public-ban-of-amandiya-88413, accessed 8 December 2015; see also Bronwyn Harris's detailed analysis of the song, New Song, Same Old Tune? http://www.csvr.org.za/index.php/media-articles/latest-csvr-in-the-media/2264-new-song-same-old-tune.html, accessed 8 December 2015.

[4] See https://www.youtube.com/watch?v=_R7vu9SuxaQ, accessed 8 December 2015.

[5] See 'Has Gupta family sealed Jacob Zuma's fate?' http://www.bbc.com/news/world-africa-35840900, accessed 18 March 2016; see also further discussion below.

[6] See Tinyiko Maluleke, 'Beyond a Giant, Saintly Mandela', *The Sunday Independent*, 5 July, 2015.

[7] See The White House Office of the Press Secretary, 'Remarks of President Barack Obama – As Prepared for Delivery Remembering Nelson Mandela, Johannesburg, South Africa December 10, 2013,' www.whitehouse.gov/the-press-office/2013/12/10/remarks-president-barack-obama-prepared-delivery, accessed 24 July 2015; see also www.youtube.com/watch?v=4vUB363cRqE&spfreload=10, accessed 24 July 2015.

[8] See, for example, Staff reporter, 'How Julius Malema pulls tender strings', *Mail & Guardian*, 5–11 August 2011; Forde F, 'How Malema amassed his millions', *Mail & Guardian*, 18–24 May 2012; Hofstatter S, Wa Afrika M & Rose R, 'Juju's jackpot', *Sunday Times,* 20 May 2012.

[9] Found 'guilty of portraying the ANC government and its leadership under president Jacob Zuma in a negative light, and for making statements on bringing about regime change in Botswana, at an ANCYL press conference on July 31, 2011', Malema was defiant and vowed to appeal: 'I will die with my boots on, and I will die for what I believe in…I have not done anything wrong…I am persecuted for speaking on behalf of (the) ANCYL…I've never been a sell-out and I'm not going to sell out today.' (Sapa, political bureau & own correspondent, Malema expelled, *Cape Times*, 1 March 2012). He eventually lost the appeal and the suspension was confirmed on 24 April 2012.

[10] In the 2013 Henk Pretorius film *Fanie Fourie's Lobola*, featuring Eduan van Jaarsveldt and Zethu Dlomo, the Boer is presented as more dangerous than the watch dog, on a sign that reads: 'Never mind the dog, beware of the Boer'.

[11] However, it should be noted that both memory and heritage are contentious and coloured by specific worldviews as post-apartheid nation-building is still in its infancy.

[12] See also Mangena I, Umshini Wami echoes through SA, *Mail & Guardian*, 23 December 2007.

http://mg.co.za/article/2007-12-23-umshini-wami-echoes-through-sa, accessed 30 May 2012.

[13] See http://www.news24.com/Archives/City-Press/Zuma-tackles-colonial-statues-xenophobic-attacks-20150429, accessed 6 October 2015. For the full video of the event, see https://www.youtube.com/watch?v=draGELk8grU, accessed 6 October 2015.

[14] See Xolela Mangcu, 'The Malema debate: Coming of age in the age of looting', *City Press*, 31 July 2011.

[15] See also Ritz C, 'The emperor has no clothes', *The New Age*, 1 March 2012.

[16] See Genevieve Quintal, 'Malema refuses "crook" Zuma's offer, calls for Guptas to leave SA', http://mg.co.za/article/2016-02-04-malema-refuses-to-settle-with-crook-zuma, accessed 5 March 2016.

[17] See Genevieve Quintal, 'Malema refuses "crook" Zuma's offer, calls for Guptas to leave SA', http://mg.co.za/article/2016-02-04-malema-refuses-to-settle-with-crook-zuma, accessed 5 March 2016.

[18] See http://www.timeslive.co.za/politics/2016/02/09/Gupta-family-win-court-interdict-against-EFF%E2%80%9A-Julius-Malema, accessed 5 March 2016.

[19] See http://www.timeslive.co.za/politics/2016/02/09/Gupta-family-win-court-interdict-against-EFF%E2%80%9A-Julius-Malema, accessed 5 March 2016.

[20] See http://www.timeslive.co.za/politics/2016/02/09/Gupta-family-win-court-interdict-against-EFF%E2%80%9A-Julius-Malema, accessed 5 March 2016.

[21] The EFF proceeded to release a music track entitled '#ZuptasMustFall'. To listen to it, see http://ewn.co.za/2016/03/18/ZuptaMustFall-track-Is-it-a-hit-or-a-miss, accessed 31 March 2016.

[22] See 'South Africa's Guptas hit back in Zuma finance minister row', http://www.bbc.com/news/world-africa-35846831, accessed 19 March 2016. Apparently, Zuma-facilitated access to business opportunities for the Guptas and members of his own family was not limited to South Africa, according to former COSATU General Secretary, Zwelinzima Vavi. He reports how President Zuma 'orchestrated a secret 'business meeting' between his son Duduzane, a Gupta brother and Teodoro Obiang Nguema, the president of Equatorial Guinea', http://www.timeslive.co.za/sundaytimes/stnews/investigations/2016/03/27/Vavi-blows-lid-on-aid-for-Gupta-audio, accessed 28 March 2016.

[23] See Sam Sole, Craig McKune and Stefaans Brümmer, 'The "Gupta owned" state enterprises', which 'reveals an extraordinary network of contacts close to the family that dominates the boards of SA's two largest parastatals, Eskom and Transnet', http://mg.co.za/article/2016-03-24-00-the-gupta-owned-state-enterprises, accessed 28 March 2016.

24 See 'South Africa's Guptas hit back in Zuma finance minister row', http://www.bbc.com/news/world-africa-35846831, accessed 19 March 2016.
25 See Craig Dodds, http://www.iol.co.za/news/politics/the-guptas-strike-back-1999542, accessed 18 March 2016. See also, Ranjeni Munusamy, http://www.dailymaverick.co.za/article/2013-02-01-the-guptas-the-new-age-and-government-an-inconvenient-truth/#.Vuv84HrCAdw, accessed 18 March 2016; Matuma Letsoalo, Jessica Bezuidenhout and Lisa Steyn, 'Gupta family "edged me out of Eskom"', says Tsotsi, http://mg.co.za/article/2016-03-17-gupta-family-edged-me-out-of-eskom-says-tsotsi, accessed 20 March 2016; Phillip de Wet and Carien du Plessis, 'More courted cadres to come clean', http://mg.co.za/article/2016-03-17-more-cadres-come-clean-about-being-courted-by-the-guptas, accessed 20 March 2016; Qaanitah Hunter and Sibongakonke Shoba, http://www.timeslive.co.za/sundaytimes/stnews/2016/03/20/Zuma-told-me-to-help-Guptas, accessed 20 March 2016; Jan-Jan Joubert, Vytjie 'Mentor tearfully opens up about Guptas', http://www.timeslive.co.za/sundaytimes/stnews/2016/03/20/Vytjie-Mentor-tearfully-opens-up-about-Guptas, accessed 20 March 2016.
26 See Mpho Raborife, 'Stalwarts' foundations call on ANC to take urgent "corrective action"', http://www.timeslive.co.za/politics/2016/03/20/Stalwarts-foundations-call-on-ANC-to-take-urgent-corrective-action, accessed 22 March 2016.
27 See Mpho Raborife, 'Stalwarts' foundations call on ANC to take urgent "corrective action"', http://www.timeslive.co.za/politics/2016/03/20/Stalwarts-foundations-call-on-ANC-to-take-urgent-corrective-action, accessed 22 March 2016.
28 See Peter Ramothwala, ANC NEC backs Zuma, http://www.thenewage.co.za/anc-nec-backs-zuma/, accessed 22 March 2016.
29 See http://www.timeslive.co.za/sundaytimes/stnews/2016/03/18/Public-Protector-will-investigate-Gupta-familys-state-capture, accessed 20 March 2016.
30 For a copy of the two page advert, see 'Has Gupta family sealed Jacob Zuma's fate?', http://www.bbc.com/news/world-africa-35840900, accessed 18 March 2016.
31 See Craig Dodds, http://www.iol.co.za/news/politics/the-guptas-strike-back-1999542, accessed 18 March 2016. See also, Ranjeni Munusamy, http://www.dailymaverick.co.za/article/2013-02-01-the-guptas-the-new-age-and-government-an-inconvenient-truth/#.Vuv84HrCAdw, accessed 18 March 2016.

³² See Munyaradzi Makoni and Karen MacGregor, 'University leaders seek help as protests turn violent', http://www.universityworldnews.com/article.php?story=2016022608152 1353, accessed 11 March 2016.
³³For details of what happened, see Naledi Shange, http://mg.co.za/article/2016-02-23-university-of-free-state-suspends-lectures-after-varsity-cup-violence, accessed 26 February 2016.
³⁴ See Dani Nhando, http://thoughtleader.co.za/readerblog/2016/02/23/ufs-clash-was-bound-to-happen-sooner-or-later/, accessed 26 February 2016.
See also Pontsho Pilane, a reporter for the *Mail & Guardian*, who argues that while campaigns for colour-blindness in universities currently in turmoil may be welcome at face value, they could in reality serve to turn a blind eye on excesses and injustices that continue to be perpetuated along racial lines to the detriment of black students who currently bear the brunt of a highly racialized higher education landscape in South Africa. As Pilane puts it:

> Preaching hope, unity and reconciliation while simultaneously ignoring justice and reparative actions from those in power is why this rainbow nation is a blatant lie and a slap in the face of South Africa's poorest and most vulnerable people. It is in the name of unity that many of those who supported apartheid and even committed heinous crimes (such as FW de Klerk and Adriaan Vlok) were granted immunity and redemption with very little repentance expected from them (see Pontsho Pilane, http://mg.co.za/article/2016-02-26-colourblind-campaign, accessed 26 February 2016).

³⁵ See Felicity Kunene, http://www.dailymaverick.co.za/opinionista/2016-02-26-ufs-same-racial-attacks-different-day/#.VtK-58eOITE, accessed 1 March 2016.
³⁶ As Robert Morell argues, and rightly so, it is counterproductive for those seeking a levelling of the playing field in an academic arena to substitute meaningful dialogue with violence and intimidation. Using the example of UCT, he writes:

> It has exhibited high levels of intolerance and used intimidation. It refuses to take any responsibility for actions committed in its name, claiming that it is a mass-based movement that has supporters, but no members and no leaders. In a recent interview in the Sunday Times (21 February 2016) a representative of RMF Simon Rakei clearly indicates an intransigent approach that opposes dialogue.

The result is that polarization and conflict are fueled. There is no commitment to working to build a better university that reflects a post-apartheid vision for a new South Africa.

Last week fears about RMF were confirmed when people acting in its name fire-bombed the Vice Chancellor's Office, a bus and a university vehicle, burnt artworks (including those by Keresemose Richard Baholo). These were unapologetic acts of violence.

[....]

This campus violence ... is an expression of a worrying close-mindedness, a myopia, which refuses to acknowledge any other point of view – not even that of the vast majority of students - and insists on being the only voice that should be heard and heeded. When it fails to persuade its audience, it uses violence (see, Robert Morrell, http://www.dailymaverick.co.za/article/2016-02-22-op-ed-the-burning-issue-of-campus-violence/#.VtACaObCBV-, accessed 26 February 2016).

[37] See Adam Habib and Sizwe Mabizela, http://www.timeslive.co.za/sundaytimes/opinion/2016/02/21/Student-protests-when-fear-and-loathing-trump-hope-and-unity, accessed 6 March 2016.

[38] See McKenzie-Hoy T, 'Tenderpreneurs frustrating legitimate contractors', *Engineering News*, 5 March 2010. http://www.engineeringnews.co.za/article/tenderpreneurs-frustrating-legitimate-contractors-2010-03-05, accessed 30 April 2012.

[39] See 'South African Press Association (Sapa), Cosatu warns against tenderpreneurs', *Business Report*, 4 March 2010. http://www.iol.co.za/business/business-news/cosatu-warns-against-tenderpreneurs-1.812852, accessed 30 April 2012.

[40] Corruption is supposedly so rife that Zwelinzima Vavi allegedly warned the ANC of the risk of South Africa becoming a 'banana republic' because of its 'predatory elite' (Ngalwa S & Majavu A, 'Vavi stuns ANC', *Sunday Times*, 12 June 2011). Vavi criticised the rise of 'a culture of impunity' and of 'me-first-and-to-hell-with-everybody-else' and called on South Africans to 'remain true to the fundamental principles and culture of...struggle – selflessness and sacrifice' (Vavi Z, The Malema debate: Let us get rid of the 'me-first' culture, *City Press*, 31 July 2011).

[41] For a full transcript the the judgement, see http://www.timeslive.co.za/politics/2016/03/31/TRANSCRIPT-Judgment-of-the-Constitutional-Court-on-Nkandla, accessed 1 April 2016.

[42] See Hugh Corder, Professor of Public Law at UCT, 'Zuma court ruling: South Africans witness a massive day for democracy',

https://theconversation.com/zuma-court-ruling-south-africans-witness-a-massive-day-for-democracy-57070?, accessed 1 April 2016.
[43] See the Daily Maverick for a full transcript of the president's televised reaction to the judgement, 'President Jacob Zuma: I respect the judgement and will abide by it', http://www.dailymaverick.co.za/article/2016-04-01-president-jacob-zuma-i-respect-the-judgement-and-will-abide-by-it/, accessed 1 April 2016.
[44] See Marianne Merten, 'Opposition reacts to Zuma's (non)apology: An obfuscation of the highest order', http://www.dailymaverick.co.za/article/2016-04-01-zuma-nonapology-reactions-an-obfuscation-of-the-highest-order/#.Vv-AlXrCAdw, accessed 2 April 2016.
[45] See Ahmed Kathrada's open letter to President Zuma, http://www.dailymaverick.co.za/article/2016-04-02-ahmed-kathrada-i-appeal-to-our-president-to-submit-to-the-will-of-the-people-and-resign/#.Vv9-4nrCAdw, accessed 2 April 2016;
see also 'Anti-apartheid veteran Kathrada calls for Zuma to resign', http://www.bbc.com/news/world-africa-35951006, accessed 2 April 2016.
Following the failed impeachment motion in parliament, many more ANC veterans, together with some influential members of civil society, marched to the Constitutional Court to intensify calls for President Zuma to resign. See, African News Agency, 'ANC veterans tell President Zuma to step down', http://mg.co.za/article/2016-04-06-anc-veterans-tell-president-zuma-to-step-down, accessed 6 April 2016.
[46] See Carien du Plessis, The ANC's centre cannot hold without Zuma', http://mg.co.za/article/2016-04-02-the-anc-centre-cannot-hold-without-zuma, accessed 3 April 2016.
[47] See African News Agency, 'Scandal-ridden Zuma survives impeachment motion', http://mg.co.za/article/2016-04-05-scandal-ridden-zuma-survives-impeachment-motion, accessed 6 April 2016.
[48] Wounds that will not heal, an excerpt from VS Naipaul's *The Masque of Africa: Glimpses of African Belief*, *Sunday Times Review*, 3 October 2010.
[49] Wounds that will not heal, an excerpt from VS Naipaul's *The Masque of Africa: Glimpses of African Belief*, *Sunday Times Review*, 3 October 2010.
[50] Fellow South Africans questioned how South African nationals and citizens moving from one part of the country to another could be considered refugees. See 'The Tweet that caused a storm', *Sunday Independent*, 25 March 2012.
[51] This translates either derogatorily as 'coolie' or simply as 'Indian', depending on context and intention.
[52] Ndebele N, 'Thinking of Malema on the Day of Reconciliation', *City Press*, 24 December 2011.

264

http://www.citypress.co.za/Columnists/Thinking-of-Malema-on-the-Day-of-Reconciliation-20111223 , accessed 30 April 2012.

[53] See Staff reporter, 'In search of win-win solutions', *Mail & Guardian*, 10–16 June 2011.

[54] www.goodreads.com/author/quotes/8051.Chinua_Achebe, accessed July 21 2013.

[55] www.nairaland.com/1233528/famous-quotes-prof-chinua-achebe, accessed July 23, 2013.

Epilogue 1

I, another Rhodesian Monster under Construction

Moshumee Teena Dewoo

*Indo-Mauritian,
Doctoral Student in African Studies,
University of Cape Town,
South Africa*

The human experience of the world is an incalculable sequence of unique and interminable private tales of 'Life as I, an insubstitutable being, know and suffer it', or tales which begin from the 'I' – isolated, unrepeated, unrepeatable centres of narrative gravity or vantage points. Our personal fields of reference develop and are moulded, in perpetuity, from these points, whose inconstant architectonics – i.e. our beliefs, baggage, encounters, emotions, values, subjective history, environments, modes of identification, and the forward progression of Life, History and Time as lived and seen from within these scopes – continually rewrite and reinforce our experience of life as incomparable, and absolutely functional and contextual. In this sense, while there unquestionably is such a thing as Reality (the unchanging, unchangeable and unchanged Truths about the world, such as, a moon remains a moon whether we choose to interpret or name it otherwise), there are, because of the billions of 'I' in the world and therefore billions of vantage points, just as many legitimate *umwelten* or realities. However, the closer our vantage points in relation to each other, and/or the larger our personal fields of reference, the higher the probability that our billions of realities at times connect and converge. Now then, this is but an account of our human experience of the world as 'I know it' (right now).

My 'I' began at my birth in Mauritius. As if it ever was the master of my beginning, perhaps to prove some sort of power over my 'I', the State of Mauritius threw onto my being, a birth certificate, claiming and cataloguing me not unlike those locally produced T-shirts, as 'Made in Mauritius'. You see, when it comes to claiming power over our existence, states are very much like those teammates with whom many of us have had to deal with at some point in our lives (if we were not those people ourselves), who never do their part in the projects which they are involved in, but are the loudest, most visible persons at the time of their delivery, commandeering and stealing from the not-so-lazy teammates, the end product as if it was theirs, of their doing. But how absolutely irrelevant to my (or in general, our) 'I' is this certificate, or any type of official documentation for that matter. We all are 'Made in somewhere', and states have no power over this. Official documentation is utterly useless in the 'I', which has intrinsic positional property unrelated to and independent of states.

We all begin at a particular (fixed) point of origin inside at least one absolute 'somewhere' where the 'I' also holds relational positionality, first to that 'somewhere' itself which is a pre-existing, prior 'event' (beginning X occurs relatively to event A, A being the pre-existing 'somewhere'), and also to all possible other, pre-existing, beginning or future events within that space (beginning X occurs relatively to events B, B1, B2, D, H, L, P, Q, etc.). For example, I began (event X, which is fixed) in Mauritius (event A, which occurred before I began), when 'The Final Countdown' was a number 1 hit and played on repeat worldwide (event D), 22 days after the opening of the Musée d'Orsay (event H), eleven days after the second arrest of Zwelakhe Sisulu (event L), decades after Laika was sent inside the Sputnik 2 into space by the USSR (event C), thousands of years before the birth of hundreds of stars (events B, B1, B2, B3, B101, B20880, and so on), and two seconds before a bird somewhere on Earth found a worm to eat (event Y1). I could have begun in a vacuum, which would still be 'somewhere' within which I would hold both an absolute and relational position. There is no escaping this. It is a Truth. Official documentation is inconsequential from our vantage points. States are lazy, kleptomaniacal, and delusion teammates, inutile and powerless over the 'I'.

268

Now, abhorring this song, I would certainly not have spoken about 'The Final Countdown' here:

1. If I had been in possession of a device which allowed me to go back in time, or if I could control (the progression of) life itself (as we conceive it), our universe, such that I could prevent the synchronicity of events which resulted in its making;

2. and/or if I had had the freedom of choice regarding my beginning, my birth, which would presuppose my existence 'elsewhere', (a preliminary) awareness of my own being prior to, as well as power over and knowledge of my (future) beginning on Earth. In such case, I would have chosen to begin such that 'The Final Countdown' was not an element of my 'I', my vantage point.

However, the fact of my current existence is that, much like the State of Mauritius, I have no power over my 'I'. I cannot go back in time to influence the repertoire of events surrounding my birth. And if I did (pre)exist elsewhere, it stands that I did not have the freedom of choice over my Earthly beginning, which would be why 'The Final Countdown' is included in my (current) reality, despite my disliking it. In this sense, I also cannot modify my physical being (Indo-Mauritian), my ancestry (my parents being Indo-Mauritian), and the History related to these. None of us have this type of power (at least not that I am aware of). But I do not really need to vagabond into the territory of obscure likelihoods and speculations about time travel and pre-Earthly existence to know that I could deny elements, or the entirety, of my 'I' as much as I want to, and it would still not affect the fact that it unfolded as it did, when and where it did, within an unmodifiable repertoire of events. I cannot outgrow or nullify the positionality of my 'I'. Therefore, independently of the State of Mauritius and of my own being, my 'I' began and is continuously being shaped from Mauritius. I suffer the world, life, from this site. My *umwelt*, my reality stems and grows from there.

I moved to South Africa about a decade ago, where I have been (and still am) a student of the University of Cape Town (UCT). I have been described one too many times as being more South African than Indo-Mauritian. In fact, I have often been mistaken (or should I say, stereotyped) for a Durbanite Indian (an Indian from 'Durbs', South Africa). And if I did in truth absorb, if I could use this term, some 'South Africanness', saying 'ja' instead of 'yes', for example, my 'I' exists independently of, and remains largely untouched, untainted by South Africa and the realities of its people. One such reality relates to the (mostly black) South African (never-ending) struggle against oppression, and for equality and justice, which took the form of the (again, mostly black) student (#RhodesMustFall) protests against the presence of (representations of) Cecil Rhodes at UCT in 2015. Even if topologically close to me, even as a student of UCT, the idea of Rhodes, his existence, his footprint in the world, is not a consequential part and direct element of my 'I'. Of course, I am well aware of the fact that he planned and financed UCT, and his vision for and of it. I also know about his legacy in South Africa and other African countries, his imaginary line ('from Cape to Cairo') along which wished to take over Africa, the putative good and the bad about him, the development and abuse, and his turning, as Professor Francis Nyamnjoh writes in this book, autochthons into *amakwerekwere* in their own land.

I must certainly have walked past the infamous bronze statue of him near the steps of Jameson Hall on UCT's Upper Campus a thousand times, a statue which Nyamnjoh reminds us here, was splattered with faeces during one of the #RhodesMustFall protests. Not once did I pause at the statue; not once did I think: 'What a monster Rhodes was! How dreadful must it be for my black South African friends that UCT, in post-independence, post-apartheid South Africa glorifies this monster.' I do stop and sit at the top of the stairs as often as I can, overlooking, ignoring as I do when I walk past his statue, both the good and the evil which Rhodes spurted onto South African soil, losing myself in the infinity of life and the seeming borderlessness of what lies beyond UCT. Most of my thoughts about this institution materialise on these steps, where

270

I more often than not, pride myself in being a student of UCT, not only for its high academic standards and its brilliant scholars, but also, for what it stands for, from my vantage point and in my Indo-Mauritian reality: Africa can give an education as good as the developed world, and I am receiving that education.

I see Rhodes at UCT. But he is not one of the monsters in my head, in my wardrobe or under my bed. I see his legacy at UCT, and the legacies of colonial monsters and colonialism in South Africa in general. But again, these are not the monsters in my head, in my wardrobe or under my bed. They are not part of my 'I', which began in another land, and continues in modern day South Africa as a series of experiences which are, in truth, mostly those of tourists who gaze quickly, from afar, unaffected, and through camera lenses into the filtered, embroidered realities of those whose soils they visit, with some sort of sickly curiosity coupled with detachment.

But however detached I am (or think that I am) with regard to the South African 'Rhodes issue', even if my vantage point is unique and (seemingly) unconnected to South Africa, Nyamnjoh's broad, fluid, and yet systematic and structured exposé on Rhodes as *amakwerekwere*, the #RhodesMustFall movement, and the shaping of identities in Africa is an ingenious reminder that our fields of reference are constantly rewriting themselves, expanding. Even if topologically distant from my 'I', Rhodes is not very different from the many monsters of my reality, including some Indian, Dutch, French and English men (colonial masters, kidnappers, and politicians, for example, who are part of my immediate History and field of reference). He transpires in this book much less as an evil, white man who used, abused and decided on the existence of autochthon Africans for self-aggrandisement projects, and more of a relatable archetype or symbol, a sketch of the many monsters inside and outside South Africa who, through power, money and privilege, are able to do as he did, determining, reducing, shaping and controlling the lives of others.

But the Rhodesian monster is not just a sketch of 'other' very bad persons. It is what we all are, having the privilege to exclude ourselves from and include ourselves in others' realities while analogously not having power over the 'I'. When I sit on the stairs

271

of the Jameson Hall, when I overlook Cecil Rhodes's statue and the plight of my (mostly black) South African peers begging and fighting that he no longer be glorified, and that true decolonisation must happen in South Africa, I do so because I can, but also, because I cannot do otherwise.

I do so because I have a choice, from a position of security, power and privilege, from a vantage point so far removed from Rhodes and his footprint that I am unworried, almost blasé, protected (perhaps) from that which my peers have been protesting against. I can see Rhodes but do not have to be bothered by him. I could also see him and decide to the contrary, transferring my own abhorring Rhodesian monsters onto him, and protesting against them all by symbolically protesting against his presence at UCT. I am not just an allochthon student in South Africa: I am an allochthon with more power than many autochthons here, with the freedom of excluding from my reality, elements of the realities of my protesting UCT peers, and the freedom of including myself in theirs, so long as I think of my own many Rhodes as fitting into the archetypal Rhodes. In this sense, I somehow have the power to shape my reality; I am the protagonist of and decision-maker in my own story.

But I also cannot and could not make Cecil Rhodes a part of my 'I' in the same manner in which white folk in South Africa, for example, cannot. I can never experience him (or his legacy) the way my (black) South African peers have suffered, and still suffer him. Even if I became an expert in all things Rhodes-related, even if I wanted to bring him down symbolically, and fight for justice and equality, Rhodes the man is not an element of my 'I', in the same manner as Mahé de Labourdonnais, Seewoosagur Ramgoolam, or Ameenah Gurib-Fakim are not a part of the 'I' of my (black, white, Coloured, or Indian) South African peers. My 'I' being disconnected from the Cecil Rhodes repertoire, I relate to him only from another space, from afar, capable of scanning him but only as an external observer, an intimate stranger.

Life is known and suffered through fixed vantage points, our 'I'. But because these points are in permanent relational position to others, running 'across cultures, languages, spaces and places in cities and national contexts', as says Nyamnjoh in this book, one's individual experience of the world is a messy and unbounded 'work in progress'. It is a tale, among billions of others, always in the process of 'becoming' through the exclusion and inclusion of and one's interrelation with others, Nyamnjoh is also clear on this; a tale in which we are both powerful and powerless – Rhodesian monsters.

Epilogue 2

The Image of Cecil John Rhodes

Sanya Osha

Nigerian,
Research Fellow at the Institute for Economic Research on Innovation, and
Centre for Excellence in Scientometrics and STI Policy,
Tshwane University of Technology,
South Africa

Against the background of the Rhodes Must Fall campaign, the University of Cape Town (UCT) must now contemplate the various meanings and shades of decolonization which has been unfolding all over Africa for several decades. Decolonization is a word the UCT establishment seems to fear or abhor beginning with the debates Mahmood Mamdani instigated concerning the Africanisation of the curricula in the institution during the 1990s when he was eventually compelled to leave.

Cecil Rhodes clearly does not fit above the crest of decolonization because he was an arch-colonizer. It would appear that there are subtle manoeuvres to gently place Rhodes amid a decolonising milieu as a fairly benign historical icon, one that could be readily visited with indifference but certainly not derision or even worse, violence. He therefore cannot be allowed to loom as a colonially sanctioned symbol of indifference as powerful political undercurrents bearing despair, disenchantment and disbelief sizzle beneath him. UCT prided itself for being the foremost tertiary institution on the continent until it experienced a rude awakening amidst an unavoidable political turmoil from which it had initially distanced itself.

The universe of images (*mundos imaginalis*) according to even its original Hermetic understanding, is directly linked to the mass production of desire. So what would be the meaning of Cecil Rhodes as unambiguous object of desire? This is the question to which the students of UCT proffered an answer; an offensive anachronism in the insatiable quest for acceptable and easily digestible symbols of democracy and liberation.

The students agitating for a new political and intellectual order are only the grandchildren of likes of Ngugi wa Thiong'o and other similar African intellectuals who have raised serious questions about the surviving colonial symbols of acculturation and mental subjugation. Words, images and pictures are not simply what they appear to be and are indeed very powerful in processes involving the formation and consolidation of subjectivity.

Just as language, images and symbols can be implements of unfathomable oppression and historical erasure and distortion. They linger in our ordinary lives, dreams and most especially, our nightmares. In ancient times, images, sculptures and statues were believed to give off emanations that existed beyond and independent of themselves. They weren't just regarded as simply images, sculptures and statues. As such, they were deemed to carry implications and causal effects that did not always directly emanate from themselves. It would be a most anti-intellectual as well as insidious stance to attempt to ignore the meaning of Cecil Rhodes the context of an unsurprisingly problematic decolonizing South Africa.

Giordano Bruno's work on image-magic is quite instructive here. Bruno had famously declared in his *De Magia* that it was easier to entrance a million people than it is to enrapture a single person. An image works on the subconscious in influencing the entirety of consciousness, leading to the powerful awakening of desire, not unusually, collective desire. Advertising practices work in a similar manner in informing the form and content of consciousness merely by the adept manipulation of images. The replication of such imagery of desire isn't often meant to satiate it but to promote a seemingly ceaseless suspension of its immediate gratification. It is an anti-climactic consumerist ploy that mirrors and reinforces the capitalist ethic of the spectral production of desire together with its endless deferral.

The statue of Rhodes stands for a certain (or perhaps uncertain) number of symbolic representations. A reactionary mind would choose to cloak Rhodes with apathy in order to mitigate what he represents in history. Such a mind would want to prevent a critical interrogation of what he stood for so as to ignore or becloud the history of violence that trails him. Invariably, such a stance would entail an enforcement of a disconnect with history, an inducement of amnesia, so as to mask a fundamental truth of history together with its enduring legacy of violence.

The image of Rhodes has evidently failed to enchant millions and is the cause of hate, disaffection and violence. It clearly does not possess theurgic attributes. In contemporary South Africa, Rhodes has not been able to produce desire or its subjects and so one is forced to ask what is his value in relation to the imperatives of capital? In both political and historical terms he has become more of an encumbrance than an asset which is why he is being banished to the lower strata of South African history.

At this juncture, Rhodes is only able to generate disaffection and intolerance and whatever value he possesses currently is ultimately tarnished by his rabid colonialist temperament and accomplishments that conflict with an age desirous of resonant heroes. To be sure, he was markedly a man of his age – and perhaps in some respects, he cannot be blamed for it – in ways that remain fundamental but he failed to transcend it in ways that this epoch considers crucial. The failure to transcend his age is what he must now suffer for. To be a true hero, an individual must possess the ability to find resonance beyond his or her times.

The previous silence around Rhodes constituted a refusal of history together with its dynamics and their power to reconfigure the present. The silence around the figure of Rhodes sought to enforce a disconnect between a newly decolonized people (in formal terms) and the multiple ramifications of their history as well as the possibilities for defining their identities within the present. Clearly, the silence built around Rhodes camouflaged the putrescence of a wound that has yet to heal; and so two issues remain unsolved; an uncomfortable metaphoric and literal silence and a severe collective injury.

The cosmetic appeal of the South African Truth and Reconciliation process isn't deep enough or appropriate for dealing with the festering and progressively worsening sores of history. A moral simplicism that avoids asking probing questions and seeking other radical methods of appeasement might be appropriate for superficial short term results but certainly isn't appropriate for the pursuit, scrutiny and assimilation of truth which ironically contradicts the actual outcome and impact of the South African Truth and Reconciliation Commission. Such often desperate political expediency never bodes well for long term gains.

The youth of UCT and other institutions plagued by the same problems are galvanized by a quest to unravel the realities of the truths regarding their past no matter how unpalatable and Rhodes was the most obvious point at which to begin. Their relatively privileged position in South Africa's supposedly best institution could not shield them from the discomforts of their present circumstances and the disconcerting silence they had been forced to endure. They posed the very questions that nagged mature adults but who lacked the gumption to interrogate and articulate them in a meaningful and radical manner.

Once again, the youth of nation have created a revolutionary moment beginning from below, away from the established sectors of the nation and state which are invariably too lackadaisical or too conservative to confront the imperatives and challenges of radical transformation. The youth have succeeded in shaking the nation, awakening it from its contented slumber; an undoubtedly laborious task requiring considerable resources of courage and drive. Indeed the nation should be grateful to them. It is now incumbent upon the nation to seize the momentum and re-define itself against its decaying and disagreeable parts.

Thando Mgqolozana, a young South African author recently decried the fact that South African literary festivals are largely white dominated thereby misrepresenting or ignoring the demographics of the country. But even more significantly, it should be pointed out that the South African literary scene is a barely visible appendage of contemporary Western literary culture. The scene also reflects the inheritance and retention of a lopsided apartheid era literary preoccupation and infrastructure. As Ben Williams, the former Books Editor of the *Sunday Times* points out, this literary infrastructure includes what he terms 'the white publishers, distributors, booksellers and editors'. It ought to be the case that a black literary infrastructure is emerging but it is not yet established enough to accommodate the huge black population.

The direction of Mgqolozana's anger and frustration is also noteworthy; the white South African literary establishment. Williams agrees that a transformation of the dominant literary infrastructure is necessary to support the project of decolonization but his position and Mgqolozana's demonstrate what has always been obvious and historically visible: decolonization has multiple angles and imperatives. It is possible that a black literary infrastructure can be developed independent of the existing structures not so much as to demolish them but to act as a contrast and reflect the diversity of the literary cultures within the country. As Williams suggests, the digital age makes the outcome of such a task a little less predictable but it does indicate a broader range of alternatives available for a decolonizing project. Mgqolozana's poses the kind of questions the students of UCT posed in a much more succinct and brusque manner.

In the case of UCT and other institutions in a similar position, the situation is slightly more complex as the institutions to be transformed are far more entrenched and perhaps also more intractable. It isn't merely about the materiality of the institutions themselves but also the hegemony of the ideologies that inform as well as underpin them. An onslaught against them is likely to elicit stubborn resistance, the violence of which can lead to an unrecognizable transformation of the institutions: an act that the entrenched orders of power will most probably consider a measure of random, anti-bureaucratic violence with the resultant backlash. This is a scenario that requires the most apposite template of reconciliation to tackle it.

It also requires the transcendence of the apparent either/or dichotomy – which is sadly a defining hallmark of contemporary racial relations – in order to embrace its latent heterogeneity. Undoubtedly, it would necessitate the casting off of old skin to don a new one; a process that is akin to bricolage, metissage and the most intriguing practices of creolization. It is difficult to think of a more elegant way to frame it. But a situation in which students of a particular institution feel racially and socially excluded not only in terms of institutional participation but also with regards to the kind of knowledge they are equipped with, is not tenable.

In addition, the disruptions at UCT have posed the stark question: what orders of knowledge are being produced at the institution and what are the supporting ideologies in which they are couched? Protestations attesting to the objectivity of science provide only cold comfort. There are always unresolved grey areas around constructs of knowledge and that is where the battles need to be waged. The relevance of the knowledge generating process would increase exponentially when the black South African subject becomes a participant in that process rather than merely its object.

Francis Nyamnjoh's book couldn't have come at a more appropriate time; it has the prerequisite levels of urgency, immediacy and directness. But it is also imbued with a deep knowledge of the histories of decolonization in Africa. Thus the Rhodes Must Fall campaign has something déjà vu about it and those at its vanguard would do well to avail themselves of the benefits accruing from the pre-existing vistas of conceptual and institutional decolonization in other parts of Africa.

It seems South African exceptionalism has been re-excavated amid the Rhodes Must Fall campaign. Within this context, complex aspects of decolonization were unveiled but there was a baffling lack of reference to other relevant theories of decolonization. It appears the wheel is being re-invented anew with an unnecessary expenditure of energy on debates which are already exhausted and most often passé. Nyamnjoh alludes to this point in his book; an unfortunate re-visitation of familiar turns of history without the accompanying lessons and critical awareness. This book also does much to draw attention to the unfortunate disregard for relevant African experiences that might prove profitable for South African historical and intellectual advancement.

References

Abu-Lughod, L., 1990, 'The Romance of Resistance: Tracing Transformations of Power through Bedouin Women', *American Ethnologist*, 17(1): 41-55.

Achebe, C., 1964, *Arrow of God*, Oxford: Heinemann.

Achebe, C., 2000, *Home and Exile*, New York: Anchor Books.

Adam, H. and Moodley, K., 2015, *Imagined Liberation: Xenophobia, Citizenship, and Identity in South Africa, Germany, and Canada*, Philadelphia, Pennsylvania: Temple University Press.

Adhikari, M., 2005, *Not White Enough, Not Black Enough*, Athens: Ohio University Press.

Acolff, L.M., 2015, *The Future of Whiteness*, Cambridge: Polity.

Akinyele, R. T., 2000, 'Power-sharing and Conflict Management in Africa: Nigeria, Sudan and Rwanda', *Africa Development*, 25(3&4): 209-233.

Alexander, P., Lekgowa, T., Mmope, B., Sinwell, L., Xezwi, B., 2012, *Marikana: A View from the Mountain and a Case to Answer*, Johannesburg: Jacana.

Alhaji, J. J., (As told to F.B. Nyamnjoh), 2015, *Sweet Footed African: James Jibraeel Alhaji*, Bamenda: Langaa.

Amony, E. and Baines, E., 2015, *I Am Evelyn Amony: Reclaiming My Life from the Lord's Resistance Army*, Madison: University of Wisconsin Press.

Asmal, K., Chidester, D., and James, W., 2004, *Nelson Mandela in His Own Words*, London: Abacus.

Bahi, A., 2013, *L'Ivoirité Mouvementée. Jeunes, Médias et Politique en Côte d'Ivoire*, Bamenda: Langaa.

Baker, H., 1934, *Cecil Rhodes*, London: Oxford University Press.

Bank, A., and Bank, L. J., (eds.), 2013, *Inside African Anthropology: Monica Wilson and Her Interpreters*, The International African Library Series, Cambridge: Cambridge University Press.

Beinart, W., 2001, *Twentieth-Century South Africa*, Oxford: Oxford University Press.

281

Beinart, W., 2003, *The Rise of Conservation in South Africa: Settler, Livestock and the Environment 1770-1950*, Oxford: Oxford University Press.

Beinart, W., and Hughes, L., 2009, *Environment and Empire*, Oxford: Oxford University Press.

Beinart, W., and Wotshela, L., 2012, *Prickly Pear: A Social History of a Plant in the Eastern Cape*, Johannesburg: Wits University Press.

Bhana, D., 2014, 'Race Matters and the Emergence of Class: Views from Selected South African University Students', *South African Journal of Higher Education*, 28(2): 355–367.

Biko, S., 2004 [1978], *I Write What I Like*, Johannesburg: Picador Africa.

Bosch, T., 2016, 'Twitter Activism and Youth in South Africa: the Case of #RhodesMustFall', *Information, Communication & Society*, DOI: 10.1080/1369118X.2016.1162829.

Bottomley, E.-J., 2012, *Poor White*, Cape Town: Tafelberg.

Bourdieu, P., 1984, *Distinction: A Social Critique of the Judgement of Taste*, Cambridge, Massachusetts: Harvard University Press.

Bourdieu, P., 1990, *The Logic of Practice*, Stanford: Stanford University Press.

Bourdieu, P., 1996, *The State Nobility*, Cambridge: Polity.

Branch, A., and Mampilly, Z., 2015, *Africa Uprising: Popular Protest and Political Change*, Cape Town: HSRC Press.

Brown, R., 2015, *The Secret Society: Cecil John Rhodes's Plan for a New World Order*, Cape Town: Books (Penguin Random House South Africa).

Busch, B. and Busch, L., 2014, *Interviews with Neville Alexander: The Power of Languages against the Language of Power*, Scottsville: University of KwaZulu-Natal Press.

Butler, J., 1990, *Gender Trouble: Feminism and the Subversion of Identity*, New York: Routledge.

Butler, J., 1993, *Bodies that Matter: On the Discursive Limits of 'Sex'*, New York: Routledge.

Carpenter, J.A., 1998, 'Review: Review Essay: Religion in American Academic Life', *Religion and American Culture: A Journal of Interpretation*, 8(2): 265-281.

Chidester, D., 1996, *Savage Systems: Colonialism and Comparative Religion in Southern Africa*, Charlottesville: University of Virginia Press.

Chinweizu, 1975, *The West and the Rest of Us: White Predators, Black Slavers and the African Elite*, New York: Random House.

Clarke, K. M. and Thomas, D. A., (eds), 2006, *Globalization and Race: Transformations in the Cultural Production of Blackness*, Durham: Duke University Press.

Coates, T.-N., 2015, *Between the World and Me*, New York: Spiegel & Grau.

Comaroff, J., and Comaroff, J. L., 1991, *Of Revelation and Revolution: Christianity, Colonialism, and Consciousness in South Africa*, Volume One, Chicago: Chicago University Press.

Comaroff, J., and Comaroff, J. L., 1997, *Of Revelation and Revolution: The Dialectics of Modernity on a South African Frontier*, Volume Two, Chicago: Chicago University Press.

Comaroff, J., and Comaroff, J. L., 2001, 'Naturing the Nation: Aliens, Apocalypse and the Postcolonial State', *Journal of Southern African Studies*, 27(3): 627-651.

Council on Higher Education, (ed), 2016, *Reflections of South African University Leaders 1981 to 2014*, Cape Town: African Minds Publishers.

Crapanzano, V., 1985, *Waiting: The Whites of South Africa*, New York: Random House.

Crush, J., Chikanda, A. and Skinner, C., (eds), 2015, *Mean Streets: Migration, Xenophobia and Informality in South Africa*, Cape Town: SAMP/ACC/IDRC.

Diop, C.A., 1996/1952, 'When Can We Talk of an African Renaissance? And Towards an African Political Ideology', in: *Towards the African Renaissance: Essays in African Culture and Development 1946–1960*, London: Karnak House & Estate of Cheikh Anta Diop.

Elias, N., 2000, *The Civilizing Process*, Oxford: Blackwell.

Englund, H., 2006, *Prisoners of Freedom: Human Rights and the African Poor*, Berkeley: University of California Press.

Erasmus, Z., 1997, "Oe! My hare gaan huistoe': Hair-styling as Black Cultural Practice', *Agenda*, 13(32): 11–16.

Fanon, F., 1967a, *The Wretched of the Earth*, Harmondsworth: Penguin.

Fanon F., 1986 [1967b], *Black Skin, White Masks*, London: Pluto Press.

Farmer, D. J., 1998, 'Schopenhauer's Porcupines: Hegemonic Change in Context', *Administrative Theory & Praxis*, 20(4): 422-433.

February, V., 1991, *Mind Your Colour: The Coloured Stereotype in South African Literature*, London: Kegan Paul.

Ferguson, N. 2011, *Civilization: The West and the Rest*, London: Penguin Books.

Fitzpatrick, J. P., 1924, 'Introduction', in: Stent, V., *A Person Record of some Incidents in the life of Cecil Rhodes*, Cape Town: Maskew Miller, pp. vii-xv.

Flint, J., 1974, *Cecil Rhodes*, Boston: Little, Brown and Company.

Fonlon, B., 1965, 'Idea of culture I', *ABBIA: Cameroon Cultural Review*, 11: 5–29.

Fonlon. B., 1967, 'Idea of culture II', *ABBIA: Cameroon Cultural Review*, 16: 5–24.

Fonlon, B. N., 2009 [1978], *Genuine Intellectuals. Academic and Social Responsibilities of Universities in Africa*, Bamenda: Langaa.

Fontein, J., 2015, *Remaking Mutirikwi: Landscape, Water & Belonging in Southern Zimbabwe*, Woodbridge, Suffolk: James Currey.

Forde, F., 2011, *An Inconvenient Youth: Julius Malema and the 'New' ANC*, Johannesburg: Picador Africa.

Foucault, M., 1988, 'Technologies of the Self', in: Martin, L.H., Gutman, H. and Hutton, P.H. (eds), *Technologies of the Self: A Seminar with Michel Foucault*, Amherst: University of Massachusetts Press, pp.16-49.

Foucault, M., 1995, *Discipline and Punish: The Birth of the Prison*, New York: Vintage Books.

Frankenberg, R., 1993, *The Social Construction of Whiteness: White Women, Race Matters*, London: Routledge.

Geschiere, P., 2009, *The Perils of Belonging: Autochthony, Citizenship, and Exclusion in Africa and Europe*, Chicago, IL: University of Chicago Press.

Geschiere, P., and Nyamnjoh, F. B., 2000, 'Capitalism and Autochthony: The Seesaw of Mobility and Belonging', *Public Culture*, 12(2): 423-452.

Gobodo-Madikizela, P., 2003, *A Human Being Died That Night: A Story of Forgiveness*, Cape Town: David Philip.

Gourevitch, P., 1998, *We Wish To Inform You That Tomorrow We Will Be Killed With Our Families*, New York: Farrar Straus and Giroux.

Gqola, P. D., 2016, *Rape: A South African Nightmare*, Johannesburg: Jacana Media.

Gumede, W. and Dikeni, L. (eds), 2009, *The Poverty of Idea: South African Democracy and the Retreat of Intellectuals*. Johannesburg: Jacana.

Gunner, L., 2009, 'Jacob Zuma, the Social Body and the Unruly Power of Song', *African Affairs*, 108(430): 27–48.

Haffajee, F., 2015, *What If There Were No Whites in South Africa?*, Johannesburg: Picador Africa.

Hall, M., 1998, "Bantu Education?' A Reply to Mahmood Mamdani', *Social Dynamics*, 24(2): 86-92.

Haresnape, G., 1984, 'Preface', in: Plomer, W., *Cecil Rhodes*, Cape Town: David Philip, pp. iii-xvii.

Harrison, F. V., 2008, *Outsider Within: Reworking Anthropology in the Global Age*, Urbana: University of Illinois Press.

Herzfeld, M., 1992, *The Social Production of Indifference: Exploring the Symbolic Roots of Western Bureaucracy*, Chicago: University of Chicago Press.

Higgins, J., 2013, *Academic Freedom in a Democratic South Africa: Essays and Interviews on Higher Education and the Humanities*, Johannesburg: Wits University Press.

Higgins, J., and Vale, P., 2016, 'Editorial: State of Urgency', *Arts & Humanities in Higher Education*, 15(1): 3-6.

Hochschild, A., 1999, *King Leopold's Ghost: A Story of Greed, Terror, and Heroism in Colonial Africa*, Boston: Houghton Mifflin.

Honwana, A. M., 2012, *The Time of Youth: Work, Social Change, and Politics in Africa*, Boulder: Kumarian Press.

Honwana, A., 2013, *Youth and Revolution in Tunisia*, London: Zed Books.

Hook, D., 2014, *Steve Biko: Voices of Liberation*, Cape Town: HSRC Press.

Hountondji, P. J., 2002, *The Struggle for Meaning: Reflections on Philosophy, Culture, and Democracy in Africa*, Athens: Ohio University Press.

Hunter, M., 1961, *Reaction to Conquest: Effects of Contact with Europeans on the Pondo of South Africa*, London: International African Institute/Oxford University Press.

Hunter, M. L., 2002, "'If You're Light You're Alright": Light Skin Color as Social Capital for Women of Color', *Gender and Society*, 16(2): 175-193.

Hyam, R., 1976, *Britain's Imperial Century 1815-1914: A Study of Empire and Expansion*, London: B.T. Batsford.

Imam, A., Mama, A., Sow, F., 1997, *Engendering African Social Sciences*, Dakar: CODESRIA.

Isin, E. F., 2012, *Citizens without Frontiers*, London: Continuum.

Jansen, J., 2011, *We Need to Talk*, Northlands: Bookstorm & Pan Macmillan.

Jansen, S., 2008, *Gangs, Politics & Dignity in Cape Town*, Oxford: James Currey.

Jourdan, P., 1910, *Cecil Rhodes: His Private Life by His Private Secretary*, London: John Lane the Bodley Head.

Kalula, E., 2013, *The Will to Live and Serve: Personal Reflections on Twenty Years of Continuity and Change in the Faculty of Law, 1992-2012*, Cape Town: University of Cape Town.

Klaaren, J., 2011, 'Citizenship, Xenophobic Violence, and Law's Dark Side', in: L.B. Landau, (ed.) *Exorcising the demons within: xenophobia, violence and statecraft in contemporary South Africa*, Johannesburg: Wits University Press, pp. 135–149.

Kopytoff, I., 1987, *The African Frontier: The Reproduction of Traditional African Societies,* Bloomington: Indiana University Press.

Landau, L. B., (ed.), 2011, *Exorcising the Demons Within: Xenophobia, Violence and Statecraft in Contemporary South Africa*, Johannesburg: Wits University Press.

Landau, P. S. and Kaspin, D. D., (eds), 2002, *Images & Empires: Visuality in Colonial and Postcolonial Africa*, Berkeley: University of California Press.

Lategan, B. C., 2015, '"Incompleteness" and the Quest for Multiple Identities in South Africa', *Africa Spectrum*, 50(3): 81-107.

Lipton, M., 1986, *Capitalism and Apartheid: South Africa, 1910-1986*, Aldershot: Wildwood House.

Lunderstedt, S., [Undated], *The King of Diamonds: Cecil John Rhodes, His Life in Kimberley*, Kimberley: Kimberley Marketing and Promotions.

MacDonald, M., 2006, *Why Race Matters in South Africa*, Pietermaritzburg: University of KwaZulu-Natal Press.

Magubane, B., 1971, 'A Critical Look at Indices Used in the Study of Social Change in Colonial Africa', *Current Anthropology*, 12(4/5): 419-445.

Magubane, Z., 2004, *Bringing the Empire Home: Race, Class, and Gender in Britain and Colonial South Africa*. Chicago, IL: University of Chicago Press.

Makgoba, M. W., (ed.), 1999, *African Renaissance: The New Struggle*, Cape Town: Mafube Publishing.

Maldonado-Torres, N., 2007, 'On the Coloniality of Being', *Cultural Studies*, 21(2-3): 240-270.

Malusi and Mpumlwana, T., (eds), 1996, *Steve Biko: I Write What I Like*. Randburg: Raven.

Mama, A., 2007, 'Is it ethical to study Africa? Preliminary thoughts on scholarship and freedom', *African Studies Review* 50(1): 1–26.

Mamdani, M., 1996, *Citizen and subject: Contemporary Africa and the legacy of late colonialism*, Cape Town: David Philip.

Mamdani, M., 1998a, 'Is African studies to be turned into a new home for Bantu education at UCT?', *Social Dynamics*, 24(2): 63-75. Also published in *CODESRIA Bulletin*, No. 2, pp.11-15.

Mamdani, M., 1998b, *When does a settler become a Native? Reflections of the colonial roots of citizenship in Equatorial and South Africa*, 208 (n.s.), Cape Town: University of Cape Town.

Mamdani, M., 2001, *When Victims Become Killers: Colonialism, Nativism, and the Genocide in Rwanda*. Princeton: Princeton University Press.

Mamdani, M., 2007, *Scholars in the Marketplace: The Dilemmas of Neo-Liberal Reform at Makerere University, 1989–2005*, Dakar: CODESRIA.

Mamdani, M., 2010, *Saviors and Survivors: Darfur, Politics, and the War on Terror*, Dakar: CODESRIA.

Mandaza, I., 1997, *Race, Colour and Class in Southern Africa: A Study of the Coloured Question in the Context of an Analysis of the Colonial and White Settler Racial Ideology, and African Nationalism in Twentieth Century Zimbabwe, Zambia and Malawi*, Harare: Sapes Books.

Mandela, N., 1995, *Long Walk to Freedom*, London: Abacus.

Mandela, N., 2010, *Conversations with Myself*, London: Macmillan.

Mandela, W. M., 2013, *491 Days: Prisoner Number 1323/69*, Athens: Ohio University Press.

Mangezvo, P. L., 2014, *Xenophobic Exclusion and Masculinities among Zimbabwean Male Migrants: The Case of Cape Town and Stellenbosch*, Thesis [PhD], Department of Sociology and Anthropology, Stellenbosch University, Stellenbosch, South Africa.

Mangcu, X., 2012, *Biko: A Biography*, Cape Town: Tafelberg.

Mangcu, X., (ed.), 2015, *The Colour of Our Future: Does Race Matter in Post-Apartheid South Africa?*, Johannesburg: Wits University Press.

Mano, W., (ed.), 2015, *Racism, Ethnicity and the Media in Africa: Mediating Conflict in the Twenty-First Century*, London: I.B. Tauris.

Maquet, J. J., 1961, *The Premise of Inequality in Ruanda*, London: Oxford University Press.

Marks, M., 2001, *Young Warriors: Youth Politics, Identity and Violence in South Africa*, Johannesburg: Witwatersrand University Press.

Marlowe, J., 1972, *Cecil Rhodes: The Anatomy of Empire*, London: Paul Elek.

Martin, L. H., Gutman, H. and Hutton, P. H., (eds), 1988, *Technologies of the Self: A Seminar with Michel Foucault*, Amherst: University of Massachusetts Press.

Maseko, P., and Vale, P., 2016, 'Struggle Over African Languages', *Arts & Humanities in Higher Education*, 15(1): 79–93.

Matlwa, K., 2007, *Coconut*, Johannesburg: Jacana

Maurois, A., 1953, *Cecil Rhodes*, London: Collins.

Mauss, M., 1973, 'Techniques of the Body', *Economy and Society*, 2(1): 70-88.

Mazanderani, F. H., 2011, *Cracked Heirlooms: Race, Identity and the Teaching of Apartheid in Four Classrooms in the 'New' South Africa*. Honours dissertation, University of Cape Town.

Mbeki, T., 1999, 'Prologue', Makgoba, M. W., (ed.), *African Renaissance: The New Struggle*, Cape Town: Mafube Publishing, pp. xiii-xxi.

Miller, D., 2004, 'South African Multinational Corporations, NEPAD and Competing Regional Claims on Post-apartheid Southern Africa', *African Sociological Review* 8(1): 176–202.

Mkhize, N., 2016, 'Away with Good Bantus: De-linking African Language Literature from Culture, 'Tribe' and Propriety', *Arts & Humanities in Higher Education*, 15(1): 79–93.

Mngxitama, A., Alexander, A., and Gibson, N. C., (eds), 2008a, *Biko Lives! Contesting the Legacies of Steve Biko*, New York: Palgrave MacMillan.

Mngxitama, A., Alexander, A., and Gibson, N. C., 2008b, 'Biko lives.' in: Mngxitama, A., Alexander, A., Gibson, N. C., (eds) *Biko Lives! Contesting the Legacies of Steve Biko*. New York: Palgrave MacMillan, 1–20.

Modisane, B., 1986 [1963], *Blame Me on History*, New York: Simon & Schuster Inc.

Morreira, S., 2015, 'Steps Towards Decolonial Higher Education in Southern Africa? Epistemic Disobedience in the Humanities', *Journal of Asian and African Studies*, DOI: 10.1177/0021909615577499, pp.1-15.

Morreira, S., 2016, *Transnational Rights and Local Knowledge in Zimbabwe*, Stanford: Stanford University Press.

Moyo, S., 2000, *Land Reform under Structural Adjustment in Zimbabwe: Land Use Change in the Mashonaland Provinces*, Uppsala: Nordic Africa Institute.

Moyo, S., 2008, *African Land Questions, Agrarian Transitions and the State: Contradictions of Neo-liberal Land Reforms*, Dakar: CODESRIA.

Moyo, S. and Chambati, W. (eds), 2013, *Land and Agrarian Reform in Zimbabwe. Beyond White-Settler Capitalism*, Dakar: CODESRIA.

Moyo, S., Tsikata, D., and Diop, Y. (eds), 2015, *Land in the Struggles for Citizenship in Africa*, Dakar: CODESRIA.

Moyo, S. and Yero, P., 2005, *Reclaiming the Land: The Resurgence of Rural Movements in Africa, Asia and Latin America*, London: Zed Books.

Mpe, P., 2001, *Welcome to Our Hillbrow*, Pietermaritzburg: University of Natal Press.

Naidu, S., 2004, 'South Africa and Africa: Mixed messages?' In E Sidiropoulos (Ed.), *South Africa's Foreign Policy 1994–2004: Apartheid Past, Renaissance Future*, Johannesburg: South African Institute of International Affairs.

Naipaul, V.S., 1969 [1961], *A House for Mr Biswas*, London: Penguin Books.

Naipaul, V.S., 1979, *A Bend in the River*, Harmondsworth: Penguin Books.

Naipaul, V.S., 2001, *Half a Life*, London: Picador.

Naipaul, V.S., 2010, *The masque of Africa: Glimpses of African Belief*, London: Picador.

Ndebele, N. S., 2006, *The Cry of Winnie Mandela*, Banbury: Ayebia Clarke Publishing.

Ndebele, N. S., 2007, *Fine Lines from the Box: Further Thoughts about our Country*, Roggebaai: Umuzi.

Neocosmos, M., 2010, *From 'Foreign Natives' to 'Native Foreigners': Explaining Xenophobia in Post-Apartheid South Africa: Citizenship and Nationalism, Identity and Politics*, Dakar: CODESRIA.

Newman, K.S. and De Lannoy, A., 2014, *After Freedom: The Rise of the Post-Apartheid Generation in Democratic South Africa*, Boston: Beacon Press.

Ngugi wa Thiong'o, 1986, *Decolonising the Mind: The Politics of Language in African Literature*, London: James Currey.

Ngugi wa Thiong'o, 2007, *Wizard of the Crow*, London: Vintage Books.

Nhlapo, T. and Garuba, H., (eds), 2012, *African Studies in the Post-colonial University*, Cape Town: University of Cape Town Press.

Nnoli, O., (ed.), 1998, *Ethnic Conflicts in Africa*, Dakar: CODESRIA.

Ntsebeza, L., 2012, 'African Studies at UCT: An Overview', in: Nhlapo, T. and Garuba, H., (eds), 2012, *African Studies in the Post-colonial University*, Cape Town: University of Cape Town Press, pp.1-22.

Ntsebeza, L., 2014, 'The Mafeje and the UCT Saga: Unfinished Business?', *Social Dynamics*, 40(2): 274-288.

Nuttall, S., (ed.), 2006, *Beautiful/Ugly: African and Diaspora Aesthetics*, Durham: Duke University Press.

Nyamnjoh, F. B., 2002, 'Local Attitudes towards Citizenship and Foreigners in Botswana: An Appraisal of Recent Press Stories', *Journal of Southern African Studies*, 28(4):751-771.

Nyamnjoh, F. B., 2006, *Insiders and Outsiders: Citizenship and Xenophobia in Contemporary Southern Africa*, London: CODESRIA–Zed Books.

Nyamnjoh, F. B., 2007a, *The Disillusioned African*, Bamenda: Langaa.

Nyamnjoh, F. B., 2007b, 'From Bounded to Flexible Citizenship: Lessons from Africa', *Citizenship Studies*, 11(1): 73-82.

Nyamnjoh, F. B., 2007c, '"Ever-Diminishing Circles": The Paradoxes of Belonging in Botswana', in: Marisol de la Cadena and Orin Starn, (eds.), *Indigenous Experience Today*, Oxford: Berg, pp. 305-332.

Nyamnjoh, F. B. 2010, *Intimate Strangers*, Bamenda: Langaa.

Nyamnjoh, F. B., 2012a, 'Potted Plants in Greenhouses: A Critical Reflection on the Resilience of Colonial Education in Africa', *Journal of Asian and African Studies*, 47(2):129-154.

Nyamnjoh, F. B., 2012b, 'Blinded by Sight: Diving the Future of Anthropology in Africa', *Africa Spectrum*, 47(2-3): 63-92.

Nyamnjoh, F. B., 2013a, 'Fiction and Reality of Mobility in Africa', *Citizenship Studies*, 17(6-7): 653-680.

Nyamnjoh, F. B., 2013b, 'From Quibbles to Substance: A Response to Responses', *Africa Spectrum*, 48(2): 127-139.

Nyamnjoh, F. B., 2015a, *'C'est l'homme qui fait l'homme': Cul-de-Sac Ubuntu-ism in Côte d'Ivoire*, Bamenda: Langaa.

Nyamnjoh, F. B., 2015b, 'Incompleteness: Frontier Africa and the Currency of Conviviality', in: *Journal of Asian and African Studies*, DOI: 10.1177/0021909615580867.

Nyamnjoh, F. B. and Brudvig, I., 2014a, 'Conviviality and Negotiations with Belonging in Urban Africa', in: Engin F. Isin and Peter Nyers, (eds), *The Routledge Handbook of Global Citizenship Studies*, New York: Routledge, pp. 217-229.

Nyamnjoh, F. B. and Brudvig, I., 2014b, 'Conviviality and the Boundaries of Citizenship in Urban Africa', in: Susan Parnell and Sophie Oldfield, (eds), *The Routledge Handbook on Cities of the Global South*, New York: Routledge, pp. 341-355.

Nyamnjoh, F. B. and Fuh, D., 2014, 'Africans Consuming Hair, Africans Consumed by Hair', *Africa Insight* 44(1):52-68.

Nyamnjoh, F. B. and Page, B., 2002, 'Whiteman Kontri and the Enduring Allure of Modernity among Cameroonian Youth', *African Affairs*, 101(405): 607-634.

Nyamnjoh, F. B. and Shoro, K., 2014, 'Testing the Waters of African Renaissance in Post-Apartheid South Africa', in: Thenjiwe Meyiwa, Muxe Nkondo, Margaret Chitiga-Mabugu, Moses Sithole and Francis Nyamnjoh, (eds), *State of the Nation 2014: South Africa 1994-2014: A Twenty-year Review*, Cape Town: HSRC, pp. 477-495.

Oguibe, L. 2004, *The Culture Game*, Minneapolis: University of Minnesota Press.

Olusoga, D. and Erichsen, C. W., 2011, *The Kaiser's Holocaust: Germany's Forgotten Genocide and the Colonial Roots of Nazism*, London: Faber & Faber.

Ong, A., 1999, *Flexible Citizenship: The Cultural Logics of Transnationality*, Durham: Duke University Press.

Owen, J. 2015, *Congolese Social Networks: Living on the Margins in Muizenberg, Cape Town*, Lanham: Lexington Books.

p'Bitek, O., 1989 [1966], *Song of Lawino*, Nairobi: East African Educational Publishers.

Peberdy, S., 2009, *Selecting Immigrants: National Identity and South Africa's Immigration Policies 1910–2008*, Johannesburg: Wits University Press.

Phillips, H., 1993, *The University of Cape Town 1918-1968: The Formative Years*, Cape Town: UCT in association with the UCT Press.

Pierre, J., 2013, *The Predicament of Blackness: Postcolonial Ghana and the Politics of Race*, Chicago: University of Chicago Press.

Pieterse, E., 2010, *Cityness and African Urban Development*, Working Paper No.2010/42. UNU-WIDER.

Pillay, U., Hagg, G., Nyamnjoh, F., with Jansen, J., (eds), 2013, *State of the Nation: South Africa 2012-2013: Addressing Inequality and Poverty*, Cape Town: HSRC.

Pityana, B. N., Ramphele, M., Mpumlwana, M. and Wilson, L. (eds), 1991, *Bounds of Possibility: The Legacy of Steve Biko & Black Consciousness*, Cape Town: David Philip.

Plomer, W., 1984 [1933], *Cecil Rhodes*, Cape Town: David Philip.

Pogrund, B., 2015 [1990], *Robert Sobukwe – How can Man Die Better*, Johannesburg: Jonathan Balls.

Posel, D., 2010, 'Races to consume: Revisiting South Africa's History of Race, Consumption and the Struggle for Freedom', *Ethnic and Racial Studies*, 33(2): 157–175.

Powell, C., 2014, *ICTs and the Reconfiguration of Marginality in Langa Township: A Study of Migration and Belonging*, Bamenda: Langaa.

Prinsloo, E. H., 2016, 'The role of the Humanities in Decolonising the Academy', *Arts & Humanities in Higher Education*, 15(1): 164–168.

Ramose, M. B., 2003, 'Transforming Education in South Africa: Paradigm Shift or Change?' *South African Journal of Higher Education*, 17(3): 137–143. Available at: www.ajol.info/index.php/sajhe/article/view/25413, accessed 5 April 2011.

Ramose, M. B., 2004, 'In Search of an African Philosophy of Education', *South African Journal of Higher Education*, 18(3): 138–160.

Ramose, M. B., 2010, 'Learning Inspired Education', *Caribbean Journal of Philosophy* 2(1). Available at: http://ojs.mona.uwi.edu/index.php/cjp/article/view/2507, accessed 5 April 2011.

Ramphele, M., 2013, *A Passion for Freedom*, Cape Town: Tafelberg.

Ranger, T., 1999, *Voices from the Rocks: Nature, Culture, and History in the Matopos Hills of Zimbabwe*, Bloomington: Indiana University Press

Roberts, B., 1987, *Cecil Rhodes: Flawed Colossus*, London: Hamish Hamilton.

Robins, S., 2014, 'Poo Wars as Matter Out of Place: "Toilets for Africa" in Cape Town', *Anthropology Today*, 30(1): 1-2.

Rodney, W. 2012 [1972], *How Europe Underdeveloped Africa*, Dakar: CODESRIA& Pambazuka Press.

Rodrigues, E., 2011, *(Un)papering the Cracks in South Africa: The Role of 'Traditional' and 'New' Media in Nation-Negotiation around Julius Malema on the Eve of the 2010 FIFA World Cup™*, MA Thesis, University of Cape Town.

Ross, F. C., 2010, *Raw Life, New Hope: Decency, Housing and Everyday Life in a Post-Apartheid community*, Cape Town: UCT Press.

Ross, F. C., 2013, 'Ethnographies of Poverty', in: Pillay, U., Hagg, G., Nyamnjoh, F., with Jansen, J., (eds), *State of the Nation: South Africa 2012-2013: Addressing Inequality and Poverty*, Cape Town: HSRC, pp. 446-465.

Salo, E., 2004, *Respectable Mothers, Tough Men and Good Daughters: Producing Persons in Mannenberg township*, Unpublished Doctoral dissertation, Emory University, USA.

Salpeteur, M. and Warnier, J-P., 2013, 'Looking for the Effects of Bodily Organs and Substances through Vernacular Public Autopsy in Cameroon', *Critical African Studies*, 5(3): 153–174.

Samkange, S., 1966, *On Trial for My Country*, London: Heinemann.

Sanders, T., 2008, *Beyond Bodies: Rainmaking and Sense Making in Tanzania*, Toronto: University of Toronto Press.

Saunders, C., 1979, *Black Leaders in Southern African History*, London: Heinemann.

Saccarelli, E. and Varadarajan, L., 2015, *Imperialism: Past and Present*, Oxford: Oxford University Press.

Shapiro, J., 2011, *Zapiro: The Last Sushi: Cartoons from Mail & Guardian, Sunday Times and The Times*, Johannesburg: Jacana.

Sharp, J., 2008, "Fortress SA': Xenophobic Violence in South Africa', *Anthropology Today*, 24 (4):1–3.

Schipper, W.J.J., 1990a, 'The White Man Is Nobody's Friend: European Characters in African Fiction', in: Schipper, W.J.J., Idema, W. L., Leyten, H. M., (eds) *White and Black: Imagination and Cultural Confrontation* (Bulletin 320), Amsterdam: Royal Tropical Institute, pp. 31–53.

Schipper, W.J.J., 1990b, 'Homo Caudatus: Imagination and power in the field of literature,' in: Schipper, W.J.J., Idema, W. L., Leyten, H. M., (eds) *White and Black: Imagination and Cultural*

Confrontation (Bulletin 320), Amsterdam: Royal Tropical Institute, pp. 11–30.

Sichone, O., 2008, 'Xenophobia and Xenophilia in South Africa: African Migrants in Cape Town', in: P. Werbner, ed. *Anthropology and the New Cosmopolitanism: Rooted, Feminist and Vernacular Perspectives*, Oxford: Berg, pp. 309–332.

Silvester, J. and Geweld, J.-B., 2003, *Words Cannot Be Found: German Colonial Rule in Namibia: An Annotated Reprint of the 1918 Blue Book (Sources on African History, 1)*, Leiden: Brill.

Soudien, C., 2010, 'Grasping the Nettle? South African Higher Education and its Transformative Imperatives', *South African Journal of Higher Education*, 24(5): 881–896.

Soudien C., 2012, *Realising the Dream: Unlearning the Logic of Race in the South African School*, Cape Town: HSRC Press.

Southall, R., 2016, *The New Black Middle Class in South Africa*, Oxford: James Currey.

Sparks, A. and Tutu, M.A., 2011, *Tutu: The Authorised Portrait*, Johannesburg: Pan Macmillan.

Stent, V., 1924, *A Person Record of Some Incidents in the Life of Cecil Rhodes*, Cape Town: Maskew Miller.

Steinberg, J., 2015, *A Man of Good Hope*, London: Jonathan Cape.

Steyn, M., 2001, *Whiteness Just Isn't What it Used to Be: White Identity in a Changing South Africa*, Albany, NY: State University of New York.

Steyn M., 2008, 'Repertoires for Talking White: Resistant whiteness in Post-apartheid South Africa', *Ethnic and Racial Studies*, 31(1): 25–51.

Teppo, A. B., 2004, *The Making of a Good White: A Historical Ethnography of the Rehabilitation of Poor Whites in a Suburb of Cape Town*, Research Series in Anthropology, Helsinki: University of Helsinki.

Terreblanche, S., 2002, *A History of Inequality in South Africa 1652-2002*, Scottsville: University of KwaZulu-Natal.

Thomas, A., 1996, *Rhodes*, London: BBC Books.

Thomas, W. H., (ed.), 1974, *Labour Perspectives on South Africa*, Cape Town: David Philip.

Tripp, A., Casimiro, I., Kwesiga, J., and Mungwa, A., 2008, *African Women's Movements: Transforming Political Landscapes*, Cambridge: Cambridge University Press.

Tutu, D., 1999, *No Future Without Forgiveness* Johannesburg: London: Random House.

Tutu, D., 2004, *God Has a Dream: A Vision of Hope for Our Times*, Cape Town: Double Day publishers.

Tutuola, A., 1952, *The Palm-Wine Drinkard*, London: Faber and Faber.

Tutuola, A., 1954, *My Life in the Bush of Ghosts*, London: Faber and Faber.

Vale, P. and Maseko S., 1998, 'South Africa and the African Renaissance', *International Affairs*, 74(2): 271–287.

Vambe, L., 1972, *An Ill-fated People: Zimbabwe Before and After Rhodes*, London: Heinemann.

Van der Waal, K.C.S., and Robins, S., 2011, "De la Rey' and the Revival of 'Boer Heritage': Nostalgia in the Post-apartheid Afrikaner Culture Industry', *Journal of Southern African Studies*, 37(4): 763-779.

Van der Westhuizen, C., 2007, *White Power & the Rise and Fall of the National Party*, Cape Town: Zebra Press.

Van Kessel I., 2001, 'In Search of an African Renaissance: An Agenda for Modernisation, Neotraditionalism, or Africanisation?', *Quest* 15(1/2): 43–52.

Van Wyk, J.S., 2014, *Buying into Kleinfontein: The Financial Implications of Afrikaner Self-Determination*, MA thesis, University of Pretoria.

Vigneswaran, D., 2011, 'Taking Out the Trash? A "garbage Can" Model of Immigration Policing', in: L.B. Landau, (ed.), *Exorcising the Demons Within: Xenophobia, Violence and Statecraft in Contemporary South Africa*, Johannesburg: Wits University Press, pp. 150–171.

Viswanathan, G., 1998, *Outside the Fold: Conversion, Modernity, and Belief*, Princeton: Princeton University Press.

Wade, P., 1993, *Blackness and Race Mixture: The Dynamics of Racial Identity in Colombia*, Baltimore: John Hopkins University Press.

Walker, F. D., 1911, *The Call of the Dark Continent: A Study in Missionary Progress, Opportunity and Urgency*, London: The Wesleyan Methodist Missionary Society.

Warnier, J-P., 2006, 'Inside and Outside, Surfaces and Containers', in: Tilley, C. et al. (eds) *Handbook of Material Culture*. London: Sage, pp.186–195.

Warnier, J-P., 2007, *The Pot-King: The Body and Technologies of Power*, Leiden: Brill.

Warnier, J-P., 2009, 'Technology as Efficacious Action on Objects... and Subjects', *Journal of Material Culture*, 14(4): 413–424.

Warnier, J.-P., 2013, 'Quelle Sociologie du Politique? À l'École de Weber et Foucault en Afrique', *Socio 01*, 95-108.

Webster, E., (ed), 1978, *Essays in Southern African Labour History*, Johannesburg: Ravan Press.

Weddady, N., and Ahmari, S., (eds.), 2012, *Arab Spring Dreams: The Next Generation Speaks Out for Freedom and Justice from North Africa to Iran*. New York: Palgrave Macmillan.

West, M., 2009, *White Women Writing White: Identity and Representation in (Post-) Apartheid Literatures of South Africa*, Cape Town: David Philip.

Williams, B., 1921, *Cecil Rhodes*, London: Constable and Company Ltd.

Wilson, F., 1972, *Migrant Labour in South Africa*, Johannesburg: The South African Council of Churches and SPRO-CAS.

Zeleza, P. T. and Olukoshi. A., (eds), 2004a, *African Universities in the Twenty-First Century: Volume I, Liberalisation and Internationalisation*, Dakar: CODESRIA.

Zeleza, P. T. and Olukoshi, A., (eds), 2004b, *African Universities in the Twenty-First Century: Volume II, Knowledge and Society*, Dakar: CODESRIA.

Zeilig, L., 2014, *Frantz Fanon: Voices of Liberation*, Cape Town: HSRC Press.

Zenker, O., 2015, 'South African Land Restitution, White Claimants and the Fateful Frontier of Former KwaNdebele', *Journal of Southern African Studies*, 41(5):1019-1034.